Time To Begin

Early Education for Children with
Down Syndrome

VALENTINE DMITRIEV, Ph.D.
Second Edition

All rights reserved. No part of the material protected by this copyright notice may be reproduced or used in any form or by any means, electronic or mechanical, including photocopying, recording, or by any information storage and retrieval system, without prior written permission of the copyright owner.

NOTICE: Author grants permission to the user of this book to make copies of Appendixes A and B for school or clinical purposes. Duplication of this material for commercial use is prohibited.

Library of Congress Cataloging-in-Publication Data Dmitriev, Valentine.

Time to Begin: Early education for children with Down Syndrome: / Valentine Dmitriev.-2nd ed.

Rev. ed. of: Time to begin. c1982.

Includes bibliographical references. ISBN 0-89079-860-5 (alk. paper)

1. Mentally handicapped children-Education-United States.

2. Developmentally disabled children-Education-United States.

3. Down syndrome-Patients-Education-United States. I. Dmitriev, Valentine. Time to begin. II. Title.

Time to Begin - Early Education for Children with Down Syndrome is lovingly and gratefully dedicated to a unique group of children and their unique parents. These are the children with Down syndrome, children with other special needs, and their wonderful parents.

This book is an outgrowth of my work with such families. Through our shared experiences, these remarkable people have given me a great gift. They have enriched my life beyond measure, taught me humility, and challenged my professional skills.

Valentine Dmitriev, Ph.D.

Photo Credits: Center on Human Development and Disability, Media Services, University of Washington, Seattle, Washington, Randy Warren and W. Stewart Pope. Other photographs, supplied by parents, are gratefully acknowledged.

Figures 1, 2 and 3, and Table 4 are reprinted with permission of Andrews and McMeel, Inc.

Contents

Acknowledgments vi
How To Use This Book vii

PART I: A PROGRAM FOR CHILDREN WITH DOWN SYNDROME 1
Introduction...2
The Origin...4
The School 10

1. How a Child Grows: The First Two Years 13
The Four Main Areas of Development 15
Assessment Tools..16
Developmental Milestones...17
Parent-Infant Interaction 21
Individual Personalities of Babies 22
A Baby's Interaction 23

2. The Infant and Child with Down Syndrome 25
Typical Versus Delayed Development 26
What Is Early Intervention? 28
Strengths of Children with Down Syndrome..29
Problems and Concerns..31
Health-Related Problems 33
Preventive Medical Care 34

3. Mental, Language, and Social Development.............................37
Mental Ability...37
Language and Communication 41
Cognitive and Academic Skills..41
Social and Self-Care Skills 42
Weaknesses and Special Needs 43

4. Emotional Impact...46
Fight Behaviors...46
Flight Behaviors 52
Fathers Hurt Too 63

PART II: INTRODUCTION TO EARLY INTERVENTION 66

5. Exercises and Goals: The First 2 Years 67
Down Syndrome: Physical Types 68
How Behavior Is Learned 74

6. Gross Motor Development: Birth to 3 Months.........................76
Lying-on-the-Back Exercises...77

Simultaneous Arm and Hand Exercises 80
Exercises Lying Face Down 82

7. **Gross Motor Development: 3 to 6 Months** **85**
   Learning To Sit 86
   Rolling Over from Back to Stomach 87
   Bearing Weight 88
   Scooting 90
   Propped Sitting 92
   Therapy-Ball Exercises 92

8. **Gross Motor Development: 6 to 12 Months** **94**
   Self-Supported Sitting 94
   Protective Extensions and Righting Reactions 96
   Trunk Rotation 100
   Independent Sitting 101
   Crawl Position 102
   Prone to Sit 104
   Pull to Stand 105

9. **Gross Motor Development: 12 to 24 Months** **107**
   Kneeling 108
   Kneel to Stand 108
   Standing 109
   Cruising 110
   Walking with Support 111
   Independent Walking 111
   Board Walking 112
   Advanced Exercises 112
   Exercises with Equipment Walkers 112

10. **Fine Motor/Cognitive Social Development: Birth to 6 Months** **114**
    Exercises for Visual Responsiveness 114
    Exercises for Auditory Acuity 116

11. **Fine Motor/Cognitive Social Development: 5 to 12 Months** **119**
    Learning Principles and Techniques 119
    Beginning Eye-Hand Coordination Exercises 123
    Independent Look, Reach, and Grasp 124
    Toy Manipulation 125

12. **Fine Motor/Cognitive Social Development: 12 to 24 Months** **129**
    Preparation 129
    Intermediate Eye-Hand Coordination Exercises 133
    Future Exercises and Activities 138

13. **Cognitive Development and Discrimination Learning** **140**
    Early Discrimination Learning 141

Materials 145
Matching and Selecting: Level 1 146
Introduction to Color Discrimination: 20 to 24 Months 147
Matching and Selecting: Level 2 Introduction to Object Discrimination: 24 to 36 Months 149

14. Early Intervention for Language Development 154
Mother-Child Verbal Interaction 156
Babbling as a Prerequisite Skill 158
Visual Reinforcement of Babbling 160
Total Communication 164

15. The Importance of Imitation 166
Imitation-Level 1: 8 to 18 Months 168
Imitation-Level 2: 18 to 36 Months 169
Imitation-Level 3: 24 to 48 Months 170
A Sequence of Imitation Skills 175

16. The Development of Eating Skills 177
Feeding Problems 177
Spoon-Feeding 178
Finger-Feeding 179
Solid Food and Chewing 181
Tongue Protrusion 182

PART III: TODDLERHOOD AND BEYOND: SOCIAL AND BEHAVIORAL COMPETENCE 189

17. The Process of Socialization 190
Appearance and Good Manners 192
Achievements in Academics, Art, Music, and Sports 193
Problems 194

18. The Toddler and Social Development: 18 to 36 Months 197
Toilet Training 200
Play Skills and Social Development 200

19. Playmates and Social Development 208
Teaching Social Interaction Between Young Children 210
Planning for Playtime with a Playmate 210

20. Understanding and Managing Problem Behaviors 216
Understanding Behavior 216
The ABC of Behavior 218
Universal Needs and Goals 220
Modifying Undesirable Behaviors 222

21.	**Common Behavior Problems: Birth to 6 Years**	224
	Poor Health	224
	Other Common Problems-Their Possible Causes and Solutions: 18 Months to 5 Years	226
22.	**Inclusion in Early Childhood Education**	233
	Inclusion: Goals and Philosophy	233
	Parent Involvement	235
	Administration and Teacher Involvement	236
	Problems in School: Age 5 and Beyond	237
	Parental Advocacy and Achievement	239
23.	**Appendix A: Records of Development**	242
24.	**Appendix B What Should a Parent Look for in a Classroom?**	247
25.	**Appendix C National Resources List for Down Syndrome**	249
26.	**Glossary**	250
27.	**References**	253
28.	**About The Author**	257

Acknowledgments

I wish to acknowledge my indebtedness and express a sincere thank-you to Sharon Shimizu, founder of Caring, and past editor of *Sharing Our Caring*, for her continued interest, support, and invaluable help; to Tina Tossey, former editor of *Sharing Our Caring*. I also wish to include a special word of thanks and appreciation to Cynthia C. Tierney for her technical assistance, dedication, patience, and cooperation.

How To Use This Book

Early Education for Children with Down Syndrome is intended as a reference, as a textbook, and as a manual for parents, teachers, and other professionals who wish to accelerate the development of children with Down syndrome or with other developmental delays.

This updated version is the outgrowth of my 32 years involvement as a teacher of infants and young children with Down syndrome, and my personal experience as the developer and coordinator of the Model Program for Children with Down Syndrome at the Experimental Education Unit, Center on Human Development and Disability, University of Washington, in Seattle, Washington.

The manual gives the reader practical and specific techniques to use in a program of early intervention. The exercises and activities are based upon what is currently known about child development. Moreover, these procedures were the backbone of the model program that has been so successful in accelerating the mental, physical, social, and language performance of children with Down syndrome.

In addition to the practical aspects of the book, I have tried to convey my philosophy about early intervention in general and children and parents in particular. I strongly believe that to be satisfying and successful a program must have a "soul."

A program of early intervention, or any educational program for that matter, must be more than a mechanical adherence to a prescribed set of procedures. It must have the human element of warmth and gentleness, and a deep and tender caring for each child's uniqueness and human potential. Such a loving approach enables the parent or teacher to view a child's developmental deficits realistically but without frustration, and to recognize each gain in development, however small, with satisfaction and delight.

For this reason the readers are advised to read the first five chapters of the book before reviewing the section on the instructional aspects of the program. The introductory chapters contain important basic information and set the stage for the material that follows.

Once the manual is put to use as a guide for a child's program, the instructional chapters will, of course, have to be studied very carefully. The first reading, however, should be a mere skimming to get a general idea of the content. At this time pages that may be of special interest to the reader can be noted. The program is designed for children from birth to approximately years of age. Key developmental ages are identified and specific exercises are prescribed for each age group. For each set of exercises, refer to the appropriate checklist of prerequisite gross motor, fine motor, and other developmentally important skills in Appendix A.1.

Using the checklists as a guide, the parent or teacher can assess the child's current level of functioning and indicate on a chart which skills have already been attained, which are emerging, and which should become part of the child's program objective. This information will help determine each child's developmental level and individual instructional needs. It is also suggested that the initial assessments begin at the earliest stage of development, birth to 3 months of age, and proceed from there, regardless of the child's chronological age. Such a policy will ensure that no developmentally significant milestone has been overlooked.

The final chapters in Part III are not age specific. The focus is on general topics such as behavior management, inclusion in public schools, and the effects, positive and negative, of teaching techniques on classroom performance.

PART I:
A Program for Children with Down Syndrome

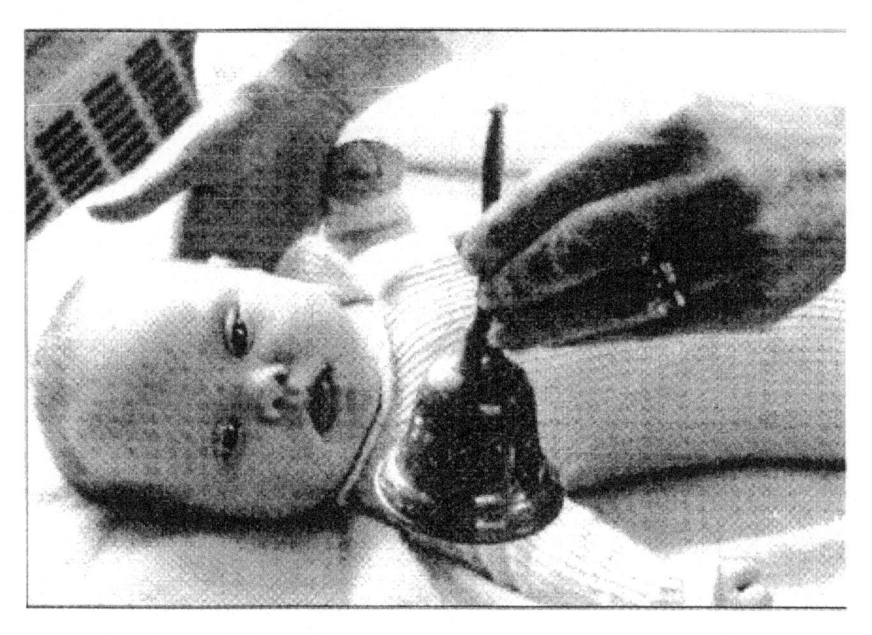

Photo I.1. Baby's head is turned, prompting a visual response to the sound of a bell.

Introduction

Photo I.2. Two-year-old Brian shows good eye–hand coordination.

Two-year-old Brian attended an early preschool program 4 afternoons a week. His teachers focused on improving his independent walking, his beginning speech, and a variety of other developmentally appropriate social, cognitive, and fine motor skills.

Photo I.3. Three-and-a-half-year-old Jennifer improves her fine motor skills by stringing small blocks and beads.

Jennifer, at 3½ years of age, was a busy, active child. She attended an intermediate preschool for children with Down syndrome. She mastered a series of pre-academic skills involving shape, color, and picture recognition. She played cooperatively with the other children in her group and learned to ride a tricycle.

Shortly after her fourth birthday, and at the beginning of a new school term, Jennifer entered the advanced preschool. In this class, she acquired a basic sight vocabulary. She read simple words and sentences such as, "I see Mommy," "I see Daddy," "red apple," "big bus." Photographs and pictures illustrated the text that she read.

Photo I.4. Alison sight-reads and matches words during a reading lesson.

Alison was enrolled in a kindergarten for children with Down syndrome. She learned about the days of the week, seasons, and holidays. As her spontaneous speech and sight-reading vocabulary expanded, she began learning how to read phonetically. After her sixth birthday, she entered a primary class in a public school.

Brian, Jennifer, and Alison are members of a group who have two important things in common. First, they were born with the chromosomal anomaly known as Down syndrome (DS), a condition that results in mental and developmental delays. Second, they participated in an innovative model program specifically designed for children with Down syndrome, located at the University of Washington from 1971 to 1982. The idea for the program occurred in the summer of 1967.

The Origin

Donald, a 14-year-old boy with Down syndrome, was one of the "difficult" residents of a back ward at a state institution for individuals with disabilities.

Donald had no speech, only a few sounds. He was big, heavy, and prone to outbursts of rage. When crossed in any way, Donald threw himself down kicking and screaming, or in some cases, physically attacked a person, usually by throwing a chair. Because of his unmanageability and seemingly low potential, Donald was not enrolled in a school program. Nevertheless, I was able to work with him on an individual basis for 30 minutes a day for 3 weeks.

From the moment that Donald first sat across the desk from me and I held up a red poker chip {as the first exercise to elicit eye contact), Donald became an attentive, responsive, and eager pupil. He loved these sessions. In 3 weeks, he learned how to put puzzles together and how to match and sort colors and pictures. We were beginning to work on matching number sets to three when the program ended. The only time I had trouble with Donald was when it was time to leave. Then we had to coax him out of the room with a glass of fruit juice.

Donald was one of 40 children participating in the pilot-school program at Fircrest, a residential state school for the severely and profoundly retarded in Seattle, Washington. I had been invited to assist in the development of the school, and in the summer of 1967, I worked with Donald and 39 other children ranging in age from 6 to 19.

These children had many problems and many different disabling conditions. There were children who were brain damaged, hearing impaired, and emotionally disturbed. There were some who were hyperactive, destructive, and aggressive. There were others who were silent, lethargic, and with- drawn. A number of them had been born with Down syndrome.

Although the children differed in age, appearance, behavior, and degree and manifestation of their disabilities, one problem common to all was the lack of learning readiness. Less than one fourth of the total number of children were able to perform even the most elementary pre-academic skills such as eye contact and hand coordination, or had the ability to discriminate in a meaningful way. They were not able to understand objects, sounds, and occurrences encountered in their minute-to-minute, day-to-day existence.

As a result, the main thrust of the educational program was geared toward teaching these basic skills because, in order to learn, a child or adult must be aware of his or her environment. The child must be able to focus on tasks, use toys and materials appropriately, and be able to follow directions. The children were taught to remain seated at their desks, to look at the teacher or materials that were placed before them, and to reach for, grasp, hold, and release objects when directed. In order to develop their eye-hand coordination, they were taught many preschool activities such as stacking blocks, putting rings on a stick, inserting pegs into a peg board, and placing puzzle pieces into a form board. After these basic skills were mastered, the children learned how to discriminate and identify geometric shapes {squares, circles, triangles), colors, objects, and pictures. The underlying purpose of these activities was to help the pupils interact more intelligently with the environment and to pave the way for further learning.

Susie was a success story. Born with Down syndrome, she was 11 years old, and had lived at Fircrest since early infancy. She was a pleasing, responsive girl who could say a few words and who was generally attentive to adult demands. Yet Susie had never been in any kind of a school program. With Susie, as with the other children, I had to begin by teaching her how to work with puzzles and pegs and how to match and recognize colors, shapes, and pictures.

Susie learned very quickly, progressing rapidly from color and picture recognition to words and letters. By the end of 8weeks, Susie was reading the pre-primer book, Dick and Jane-the only book that was available to me at that time. After my departure, the teachers who trained in the pilot program remained to carry on a regular school program. Susie continued her attendance for 3 more years. At the end of this period, Susie left Fircrest to live in a foster home and to continue her schooling. By the time she reached her 20s, Susie was living in a group home and working in a sheltered workshop.

In spite of the extreme delays that were first observed among our pupils, I was able to complete the 8-week assignment at Fircrest with a sense of satisfaction. All of the children made significant progress; and my goal to demonstrate that learning and improvement were always possible had been realized. Moreover, in the following months, a permanent preschool and academic program was established at the institution.

My sense of achievement, however, was tinged with the feeling of dismay. Dominant in my mind was the realization that the very same skills that were taught at Fircrest to 6, 10, and 15-year-olds are acquired by typically developing youngsters within the first 2 years of life.

The questions that followed seemed logical and inevitable. "What would happen," I asked myself, "if we began teaching these basic developmental skills to infants with special needs at the very time that these skills emerged in the normal baby? Would not this early training enable at-risk children to profit from the experience and to accelerate their development?"

Today, fortunately, infant programs and infant learning are recognized as necessary and crucial to a successful program in special education, but in 1967, infant learning was virtually unknown. In my decision to seek out developmentally disabled babies and to begin a program of developmental acceleration, I was embarking upon uncharted seas.

I could foresee that my undertaking and any claims that might be made by success would be viewed with skepticism. In those years the belief that maturation would take care of all developmental delays was very strong. I feared (and rightly so, I'm sure) that any progress made by infants who had obvious delays, but no definite medical diagnosis of the problem, could be credited totally to maturation and not necessarily to the effectiveness of the program.

Thus, I realized almost immediately that I would have to begin my work with a group that could be unequivocally diagnosed as having an identifiable and identically documented problem. I decided to focus my initial efforts on infants with Down syndrome (DS) for the above reasons and for the following considerations. The incidence is high. One baby out of every 800 to 1000 live births has DS. It is recognizable at birth. In addition to several physical symptoms that are characteristic of this disorder, a medical diagnosis is possible. Individuals with DS are known to have extra chromosomal material. An analysis of a sample of blood taken from a child or adult suspected of having DS can usually prove or disprove a diagnosis. In 1967, the general prognosis for the development of these children was still extremely pessimistic; they certainly were not considered educable. And, at an early age the majority were placed in institutions for the severely retarded. The limited amount of material that had been published on DS by 1967 was repetitious and stereotyped (I was curious to find out whether material that seemed like myth and misconception was indeed accurate information).

Finally, a last consideration was my own experience at Fircrest with children with DS. It had raised doubts in my mind as to the validity of the low expectancy for the mental development of this population.

Nevertheless, in that fall of 1967 when I returned to my regular duties at the Developmental Psychology Laboratory Preschool (an experimental pro- gram for normal children) at the University of Washington, the questions that had been raised by my Fircrest experience were just beginning to develop in the back of my mind.

I was taking my time, allowing these ideas to germinate, not really planning to undertake any immediate action, when the whole matter was taken completely out of my hands. Suddenly I was plunged into a current of events that was to carry me faster and farther than I had ever dreamed, and which is still shaping my life, bearing me and my associates with overwhelming speed to ever-widening horizons.

One morning, just a few days into fall quarter, I met Dennis. This boy became the catalyst that changed the whole course of my life and the lives of all the children with DS and their parents, whom I was, and still am, destined to meet.

Dennis was 7 months old. He had been born with DS and also club feet. He appeared on the scene, his legs encased in plaster casts, riding on his mother's back in a backpack. His older brother was attending the Developmental Psychology Laboratory Preschool, and Dennis just happened to be accompanying his mother when she came to take Eric home from school. I saw Dennis, and suddenly everything that I had experienced and thought about during my Fircrest stay exploded in my mind with unbearable urgency. I stopped Dennis's mother in the hall and, without even considering the pros or cons, quickly outlined the kind of infant learning program that I would like to try. I explained that I had never worked with developmentally delayed babies before, and that although what I was proposing was some- thing unknown and untried, I did know children and child development, and that I would try to help her son attain developmental landmarks at a rate as close to normal as possible. She agreed, and we decided that I would work with Dennis for 20 minutes, 4 days a week.

That day and for the next few days, I carefully prepared for my first session with Dennis. I reviewed my books on child development and decided to use *Developmental Diagnosis* by Gesell and Amatruda (1969) as my main curriculum guide. This book is based on 20 years of careful observation of typical growth patterns of infants and preschool children. It proved invaluable in setting developmental objectives for Dennis and for devising exercises and teaching procedures for attaining these goals.

From my first brief interview with Dennis, I could see that he was already exhibiting some developmental delays. Hampered by the heavy casts on his legs, Dennis spent a major portion of his waking hours reclining in an infant seat. As a result he did not make good eye contact. Accustomed to leaning back in his seat, his vision focused on some point near the ceiling. He did not look at things directly in front of his eyes, even when they were offered to him. He did not reach for nor grasp toys in the usual manner of a 7-month-old child. He was not able to sit upright by himself, another skill that most children attain between 6 and 8 months of age.

I began working with Dennis. Within 8 months Dennis's pediatrician, encouraged by Dennis's progress, had referred to me five new babies with DS. As I worked with Dennis and the other infants, I began developing a set of procedures for attaining specific results. I discovered, for example, that several easily performed pull-to-sit exercises proved to be very helpful in increasing head, neck, and trunk control (it is necessary, of course, for a child to acquire these skills before he can sit, stand, and walk). Other exercises that focused on developing eye-hand coordination, language, mental, and self-help skills were similarity created.

Since traditionally at that time, children with DS were not expected to attain head, neck, or trunk control, or sitting and walking skills until their 2nd, 3rd, or even 4th year of life, the rapid improvement shown by the infants under this regime of exercises was encouraging and exciting.

The School

From this conception, the program for children with DS was formally established in 1971. The program was part of the Model Preschool Center for Handicapped Children and the College of Education at the Experimental Education Unit (EEU). The EEU is a component unit of the Center on Human Development and Disability at the University of Washington in Seattle.

There were several reasons for establishing a program exclusively for children with DS. First, we (the members of the EEU and College of Education at the University) wanted to learn more about this population. We wanted to find out how much and how well these children would learn and develop in a program that focused specifically on their individual and group needs.

When the first informal class was organized in 1967, children with DS were generally placed in programs for the "trainable." However, it had been my observation that in such an environment, children with DS were not challenged to develop their full potential. It was the goal of our program to prove that, given the opportunity and the right instruction, these children could learn and could function at a much higher level than previously thought possible.

We also wanted to develop a curriculum and method of instruction that could be used by other programs in other settings with equal success. The University program provided four classes specifically designed for children with DS: Infant Learning, Early Preschool, Preschool, and Kindergarten.

The children in the classes came from urban, suburban, and rural areas. Some traveled distances of 50 to 100 miles to attend class, with transportation provided by their families. Although most were Caucasian, there were also African American, Hispanic American, and Asian American children in the program.

Referrals to the program were made by pediatricians, public health officials, and clinics. Additional referrals came from staff members of the Clinical Training Unit (another component of the Center on Human Development and Disabilities at the University of Washington). Frequently parents enrolled their child after having heard or read something about the program.

There were three stipulations for participation.

The child must have DS (although developmentally delayed non-DS babies have been accepted into the Infant Learning Program until other appropriate placement could be found).

The child must not be older than 5 years of age.

A parent or close family member must be able to participate in the program (it has been necessary to make two exceptions, both for single parents).

Within these guidelines, all children with DS were accepted into the pro- gram regardless of their development or ability at the time of entry. A child was eligible for admission as soon as his or her application form had been completed by the family and their physician. There was no charge for tuition because the cost of the program was funded by federal and state agencies for the purpose of providing service, training, and research.

The range of class levels allowed considerable flexibility in placement. It was never necessary to place a child on a waiting list. Each class was staffed by a head teacher and an assistant. As coordinator of the program, I was responsible for developing curriculum objectives, classroom supervision, staff and university student training.

In addition to accelerating the development of children with DS, the purpose of the program was to give help and training to their parents and to university students. Parents participated once a week as teacher aides to learn the prescribed teaching procedures so that they could maintain their child's gains at home. University students worked in the classrooms daily.

In 1975, the DS program was validated by the Joint Review and Dissemination Panel of the Bureau of Education for Handicapped Children, U.S. Department of Health, Education, and Welfare, as an exemplary program, worthy of replication and adoption by schools and centers throughout the nation.

A partial list of the most successful replications includes the following programs and sites: PRIDE, Clark College, Vancouver, Washington; Child Development Center, Sumner, Washington; Preschool for Handicapped Children, Astor Elementary School, Astoria, Oregon; Up With Downs, Brighton School, San Antonio, Texas; Columbus Public Schools, Columbus, Georgia; Providence

Child Development Center, Calgary, Alberta, Canada; Comunidad de Downs, Mexico City, Mexico; MacQuarie University, North Ryde, New South Wales, Australia; and Espanias, Barcelona, Spain.

The original program was disbanded in 1980 due to a lack of federal funding, and the children moved on to various public school settings. Between 1974 and 1980, the EEU program graduates attended a model pro- gram for DS children at the Green Lake Elementary School, Seattle, Washington. The program was a research project entitled, *"The Acceleration and Maintenance of Developmental Gains in School Age Children with Down Syndrome and Other Developmental Delays"* (Dmitriev, 1988). The progress of EEU graduates who had participated in the early intervention classes was compared to that of other children with DS and children with other disabilities. At the end of 6 years, it was found that, as a group, the children at the EEU continued to achieve higher scores than their peers who had not had the benefits of the same early learning program, both on the Peabody Picture Vocabulary Test (Dunn, 1959), which measures mental maturity on the basis of verbal comprehension, and on the Vineland Social Maturity Test (Doll, 1953).

It was also found that the DS model—its curriculum and teaching procedures—is equally appropriate for use with other children with disabilities. Best of all, as the capabilities of children with DS became recognized, more of these children were placed in classes that served children with only slight disabilities, such as children with some speech problems or only slight learning difficulties, until the day inclusive education was mandated by law.

Future chapters will describe in detail techniques used in teaching developmental and cognitive skills to the children in this program.

1. How a Child Grows: The First Two Years

The first 24 months of a child's life are indeed crucial. This is a period of dramatic and rapid growth. Within this relatively short time, the child progresses from being a helpless "horizontal" infant to an upright, independent toddler. Equally important, the brain and nervous sys- tem continue to develop and mature.

This growth occurs according to a fairly predictable timetable related to internal forces of maturation, but the developing child's environment plays a significant part in determining when, and to what extent, these changes take place. For example, the healthiest of children, seemingly endowed with excel- lent potential, will fail to thrive and will show marked mental and physical delays if he or she is placed in a deprived environment.

A deprived environment can mean many things including a lack of proper nutrition, inadequate contact with a mother or mother substitute, a lack of sensory stimulation (things to see, hear, or touch), a lack of opportunity for movement and muscle development, or a combination of any of these factors. The more factors that are absent in the environment, the poorer the chances are for total development.

A study by Wayne Dennis (1960) emphatically illustrates this point. He reported on the gross motor delays found in a group of normal, institutionalized orphans in Iran. Although this may be considered an old study, it is significant because it is among the earliest works to challenge the then prevalent belief that physical development is largely the result of maturation, and that development is little affected by learning or experience. For these reasons, this study is described as a forerunner of the early intervention programs of today.

Normal children from three orphanages in Teheran, Iran, were studied. Two of the institutions were public and the third was private. The children in the study ranged in age from 1 year to 3 years, 9 months. The number of children tested from the public orphanages was 123, and the number from the private orphanage was 51.

In order to provide a sample of approximately similar ages, children were randomly selected from each of several rooms in the orphanages. There were no observable differences between the rooms. Any child with a physical or sensory deficit or with an illness, either current or recent, was excluded.

The children were tested on their performance of five major gross motor skills:

- Sitting alone
- Creeping or scooting
- Standing while holding on
- Walking with help
- Walking alone

The results showed extreme delays in all areas in the group from the public orphanages. Compared to typical home-reared children, the group from the private orphanage also showed some delays, but they were not as severe. By the age of 33 months, 94% of this population was walking alone. By contrast only 8% of the public orphanage group in that age range could walk independently. (It must be remembered that a typical infant usually begins walking between 12 and 18 months of age. In fact, the majority of the children with DS in the Down syndrome program began walking independently between 15 and 24 months of age.)

What Dennis found was that inherently normal children who were reared in a deprived environment became as, or even more, developmentally delayed than genetically impaired children. He concluded that the lack of opportunity for exercise and lack of handling by attendants—the children were never propped up to sit, never placed in a prone position—accounted for their physical delays. Moreover, the cribs were narrow and restrictive with very soft mattresses that further hampered movement and exercise.

Dennis did not report on the children's intellectual development, but on the basis of what was known from other studies about the negative effects of lack of interaction and stimulation on mental growth, we can suspect that the Teheran orphans were also delayed cognitively.

This, however, is but one side of a coin. If a "bad" environment can have such a profound effect on the development of a normal infant, what about the effects of a "good" environment on the development of a child who was born with an anomaly such as DS? Does it help? Of course it does. This is what early intervention is all about. External forces can be structured in such a way as to maximize a child's potential in spite of inherent deficits.

Before we can talk about how to provide a program of intervention, we must know more about how a child develops. We must consider, for example, the schedule of sequential development so that intervention efforts can be timed to coincide with specific developmental milestones.

The Four Main Areas of Development

Basically there are four main areas of development: gross motor, fine motor/cognitive (mental), communication, and personal-social.

- **Gross Motor Behavior** refers to large body movements involving head control, sitting, standing, creeping, crawling, walking, running, jumping, and so on.

- **Fine Motor/Cognitive (Mental) Behavior** refers to eye-hand coordination, reaching, grasping, object manipulation, and problem solving. Some- times it is referred to as adaptive behavior.

- **Communication** refers to the whole spectrum of visual and auditory communication including facial expressions, gestures, sounds, words, phrases, and sentences.

- **Personal-Social Behavior** refers to a child's reaction to his or her socio- cultural environment. Under this category the levels of self-management and maturity such as bladder and bowel control, self-feeding abilities, independence in play, and responsiveness to training and social conventions are examined. Even these behaviors, which may show many individual variations, are expected to occur within specific time (age) frames.

Assessment Tools

A number of developmental psychologists and other professionals have observed hundreds of normal young children. According to the child's age in terms of days, weeks, or months, they have identified when certain skills are generally acquired in each of these four main areas. Based on these observations, developmental tests have been created.

The *Developmental Sequence Performance Inventory*[1] (Model Preschool Down Syndrome Program, 1974), the Gesell Developmental Schedule (Gesell & Amatruda, 1969), the *Bayley Scales of Infant Development-Second Edition* (Bayley, 1993), the *Denver II* (Frankenburg, Dodds, Archer, Shapiro, & Bresnick, 1989), the *Vineland Social Maturity Scale* (Doll, 1965), and the *Vineland Social-Emotional Early Childhood Scales* (Sparrow, Balla, & Cicchetti, 1998), the new version of the 1953 *Vineland*, were among the tests used in the DS program at the University of Washington, and are still commonly used by pediatricians, nurses, therapists, and teachers for assessing a child's development and progress.

In addition to these long-established assessment tools, there are now a number of equally useful, widely employed new or revised instruments which are also designed to give general or specific information depending on what kind of data are needed. There are basically three categories of assessment measures: screening tools, norm-referenced instruments, and criterion- referenced instruments (Allen & Martotz, 1994).

A screening test can be administered very quickly and does not require extensive training on the part of the examiners. The purpose of the *Denver II* (Frankenburg et al., 1989), or the newer *AGS Early Screening Profiles* (Harrison et al., 1990) and similar instruments, is to identify possible developmental deficits in order to refer a child for further diagnosis. Screening tests do not result in a specific score or rating.

Assessments based on norm-referenced or criterion-referenced instruments are much more detailed and must be administered by a

---

[1] The Developmental Sequence Performance Inventory was developed for the DS program at the University of Washington to meet its specific needs.

trained therapist, teacher, or psychologist, and the results can be interpreted in terms of mental age of developmental maturity. The purpose of a norm-referenced test is to determine how a child's level of performance—in the main areas of development—compares to the performance of other children of the same age. The obtained information is useful in identifying a child's strengths and weaknesses and possible eligibility for special education placement.

In addition to evaluating the level of a child's development, criterion- referenced assessments such as the *Brigance Diagnostic Inventory of Early Development-Revised* (Brigance, 1991) and the *Hawaii Early Learning Profile* (Furuno et al., 1988), for example, are designed to assist teachers in curriculum decisions, program planning, and progress evaluation.

Developmental Milestones

In order to accurately assess a young child's development, it is important to identify the characteristic behaviors that can be expected to occur at more or less specific times (key ages) during infancy and toddlerhood. On the basis of what a child is doing at the onset of, or within a key age, a parent can judge whether the observed behavior is developmentally advanced, normal, or delayed.

Specialists in early child development recognize three major key ages designated by the kind of body control that a baby exhibits.

- **Key Age 1: 0 to 16 weeks.** During this period total body movements occur in a horizontal position. The child moves his or her legs, head, and arms while lying on his or her back (supine) or stomach (prone).

- **Key Age 2: 28 to 40 weeks.** During this period, control of the head, trunk, and arms occurs. The child is in a sitting position.

- **Key Age 3: 12 to 18 months.** During the third period, control of the torso and legs occurs. The child is in an upright position; standing and independent walking may occur.

Tables 1.1, 1.2, and 1.3 list the major developmental skills that children in these three key ages can be expected to acquire in gross motor, communication, fine motor/cognitive (mental), and personal-social development.

After looking at the following tables, it can be seen that a child has to acquire some very definite skills according to a fairly precise schedule in order to make systematic progress.

Under normal circumstances, given a favorable environment, a child can be expected to acquire many or all of these skills with little conscious effort on the part of his or her parents. A great deal of learning occurs as a result of the child's interaction with the environment.

Table 1.1
Key Age: 0–16 Weeks
Maturity Zone: Lying

Gross Motor	Communication	Fine Motor/ Cognitive (mental)	Personal-Social
1. Lifts head prone position	Responds to bell	Follows objects with eyes, from side to front (mid-line, turns head 90 degrees)	Regards face
2. Holds head up, prone position	Vocalizes not crying	Moves arms and legs symmetrically (equal movements)	Smiles responsively
3. Holds chest up with arm support, prone position	Laughs	Follows object with eyes past mid-line (turns head more than 90 degrees)	
4. Sits with support, head steady		Holds hands together	
5. Rolls to side		Holds, reaches for objects	

Table 1.2

Key Age: 28–40 Weeks
Maturity Zone: Sitting

Gross Motor	Fine Motor/ Communication	Personal-Cognitive (mental)	Social
(all motor skills with adult assistance)			
1. Bears weight on legs when supported	Squeals	Reaches for objects	Is initially shy
2. Pulls to sitting, no head lag	Turns to voice	Takes two cubes, one in each hand while sitting	Feeds self
3. Sits without support	Vocalizes *ma-ma da-da*	Passes cube from hand to hand	Resists releasing toy when someone pulls on it
4. Stands, holding on		Grasps small objects using pincer grasp	Works for toy out of reach

Table 1.3

Key Age: 12–18 Months
Maturity Zone: Locomotor

Gross Motor	Communication	Fine Motor/ Cognitive (mental)	Personal-Social
1. Gets self up to sitting position	Imitates speech sounds	Uses pincer grasp (thumb and index finger)	Plays ball
2. Pulls self to stand	Vocalizes specific *ma-ma, da-da* words		Indicates wants without crying
3. Walks holding on to furniture			Drinks from a cup
4. Stands alone			
5. Walks well			
6. Walks backward			

Most babies are born with the ability to see, hear, taste, smell, and feel. They are also equipped with what have been termed the "14 survival reflexes," such as the rooting and sucking reflexes. A touch to the cheek near the baby's mouth will cause the baby to turn his or her head in search of the nipple of a breast or bottle. The baby will also make sucking and swallowing motions when the nipple is placed in his or her mouth. As the baby outgrows the need for these primitive survival reflexes, they disappear and are replaced with other responses.

The baby can also grasp and hold objects that are placed in the palm of his or her hand. At birth, this is a reflex. As the baby grows older and the nervous system matures, the grasp becomes deliberate. It becomes, in fact, a link in a chain of behaviors which consist of looking at an object, reaching for it, grasping, holding, and, later, voluntarily releasing it. In many instances, intervention efforts for babies with DS and other developmental delays are focused on helping these children abandon reflex behaviors when they are no longer appropriate in favor of more advanced skills.

One of the principles of behavior is the following: If a child's action results in a pleasing or rewarding consequence, there is a high probability that this action will be repeated. Thus, many skills the baby learns are a result of pleasing rewards, which happen as a consequence of the baby's actions.

Picture this: A mobile is hanging over a crib. For a period of time, the baby may watch it, making no effort to reach for it or touch it. One day, while exercising, the baby kicks his or her legs and accidentally hits the mobile. Suddenly, the mobile moves, sparkles, and makes a pleasant sound. This excites and pleases the baby who, in his or her excitement, moves his or her arms and kicks again, striking the mobile. The baby may continue to activate the mobile by chance a few more times, but before long the baby will learn what has to be done to set the mobile in motion. The baby's deliberate kicking demonstrates the baby's acquired control over his or her environment. The baby has achieved success. This is only one example of how a child learns a new skill through successful interaction with his or her surroundings.

Parent-Infant Interaction

Before we consider the special needs of the child with a disability, it is essential to focus briefly on the area of parent-infant interaction and its effect on a child's development.

Although father-infant interaction is gaining recognition as a powerful force in the child's emotional development, and more fathers are assuming active parenting roles beginning with expectant parent classes, it is still the mother who is generally responsible for the hour-to-hour, daily care of the infant. Obviously, this contact between mother and baby becomes even more intense and personal with breast-feeding. Therefore, in considering the bonding process between infant and parents, additional emphasis must be placed on the role of the mother, especially during the first few weeks of life.

Obstetricians are now discovering that babies delivered by natural child-birth, or with minimum sedation, are quite different from the sluggish babies born to heavily drugged women. The naturally born neonate (newborn) is alert and ready to meet the world minutes after his or her appearance. Almost immediately the newborn is fixating his or her gaze, regarding objects, and responding to sound. It was previously believed that newly delivered babies went to sleep right away, but now it has been noted that, contrary to this belief, the newborn remains alert for about an hour. If the newborn is placed in the circle of the mother's arms, the newborn will stay awake, looking intently into her eyes, as if fascinated by her presence. We may not yet fully understand the significance of this alert gazing, but I suspect this may be nature's way of sealing a permanent bond between mother and child.

Dr. T. Berry Brazelton, a well-known pediatrician at the Harvard Medical Center, has conducted extensive research on newborns' interactions with their mothers. He has found, for example, that by 3 weeks of age, a baby is already discriminating between objects and his or her mother. Moreover, in the presence of his or her mother, the baby acts in very specific ways.

Most important, it appears that the expression of the mother's face has a powerful influence on how the infant responds. Presented with a smiling, expressive face, the infant becomes active, gurgles, and kicks happily, inviting a social interchange with his mother. On the other hand, an infant that is consistently approached by a mother with a frozen, expressionless face-a mother who never warms up to the infant-may become a passive, depressed child (Brazelton, 1973, 1978).

Individual Personalities of Babies

Babies have individual personalities that are evident at birth and that remain, more or less, characteristic traits for life (Bee, 1975; Chess & Thomas, 1973; Komer, 1971). Babies can be grouped into three categories: the "easy" baby, the "slow-to-warm-up" baby, and the "difficult" baby. More specifically, there are six basic ways in which babies differ.

Vigor of responding. Some babies react very strongly and quickly to noise, touching, and other general stimuli. They become active, show delight, or cry. Other babies are slower to respond; a stronger or more prolonged stimulus is necessary to get them to react.

General activity rate. Some babies are more active than others. They are constantly moving their arms, legs, and bodies. In fact, it is hard to keep these babies still even at times when it would help to have them quiet, such as during diapering or bathing. Other babies lie more quietly and may spend much more time looking passively at things around them.

Restlessness during sleep. Just as adults vary in their sleep patterns—some tossing and turning and others "sleeping like a log"—babies show differing sleep habits. Some are restless sleepers, and others sleep soundly.

Irritability. Some babies appear fussy from birth. They cry a great deal and are difficult to comfort. Others seem more content, and rarely cry for no reason at all.

Rate of habituation (how quickly a baby becomes accustomed to a new stimulus). The first few times that a baby hears a sound (a ringing bell, for example), he or she may startle, or turn attention to it. If the sound persists, the baby will soon stop reacting-the baby has grown accustomed to the stimulus. Habituation is, in a sense, learning, and it is closely related to how children will develop in their cognitive and perceptual abilities. The capacity to habituate enables the child to block out disturbing background noises and non-relevant visual stimuli and to focus on something specific. It is possible that hyperactive, fidgety, and non-attending children may not have learned to habituate. As a result, they are perpetually and indiscriminately distracted by everything that they see and hear. This ability to habituate has a direct bearing on how a child will learn, and we will return to this concept when cognitive instruction for children with DS is discussed.

Cuddliness. There are individual differences in how babies react to being picked up and held. Some babies automatically relax and adjust their bodies to adults' bodies and seem willing to snuggle up and be cuddled. Other babies do not .fuse their bodies in this way. They appear aloof and resistant, even when they are tired or unhappy.

A Baby's Interaction

Just as the mother's personality can influence a baby's behavior, the baby's personality can, in turn, influence the way the mother responds to the baby. Most of us would agree that it is much easier to care for and enjoy a con- tented, cuddly baby who sleeps through the night without fussing, and who responds vigorously with obvious delight when approached by his or her parents.

We can sympathize with the mother who has a crying, irritable baby who does not like to be held, who does not relax while in a crib, and who is generally hard to please and hard to understand. It should be easy to comprehend how such a baby might "turn the mother off "until there is little spontaneity and reciprocal enjoyment between them. Research has shown that mothers of such difficult babies often end up feeling like incompetent failures, which further compounds a difficult relationship (Smart & Smart, 1973).

It should be evident that babies who are quick to respond might also develop faster, since their appealing temperaments invite more positive feed- back from their parents. Parents of responsive babies are more readily tuned in to their children's growth, and are more likely to respond in a way that encourages further learning.

Contrast this positive, reinforcing relationship with that of a difficult baby who, through the sheer accident of being born with an irritable, restless temperament, alienates his or her parents. Unfortunately, in such instances, parents may become so negative in their attitude toward their baby that they are no longer aware of positive behaviors, even when they occur. Consequently, the baby may not be as motivated to progress. Thus, a negative cycle of failures and rejection may be set in motion.

A baby born with developmental delays, which may hamper his or her responsiveness, is more vulnerable to failure. Thus, it is even more important for parents to understand how their actions can influence development.

2. The Infant and Child with Down Syndrome

The first questions new parents of a baby with DS frequently ask are "What can we expect?" "How will our baby develop?" "Will our baby be very different?"

If so, in what way?" "Will our baby be able to respond to us?" "What is early intervention?" These questions reflect parental anxiety and fear of the unknown.

The preceding chapter was devoted to typical development in order to answer some of these questions. It was pointed out, for example, that from the moment of conception, a child is locked into a predetermined timetable of development, a path which a normally developing child will follow from birth to adulthood. We already know that among the many stages through which the growing child will pass, the most rapid and developmentally significant changes occur during the first 3 years of life. It is during this transitional period between infancy and early childhood that, under typical circumstances, children achieve all of their basic physical, cognitive, language, social, and self-help skills. Furthermore, it is expected that these skills will be attained in accordance with predictable developmental patterns, thus laying the foundation for future progress as preschoolers, school-age children, and beyond. As a rule, these developmental goals are reached in an orderly manner, seemingly spontaneously, with more success than failure.

Children with Down syndrome, however, may not be as fortunate. Due to inherent weaknesses, they are unable to keep pace with developmental timetables. Development is uneven and unpredictable. Without early intervention, serious delays are likely to occur.

Typical Versus Delayed Development

Table 2.1, prepared by Canning, Pueschel, Murphy, and Zausmer (1978), compares the ages at which normal children and children with OS attain specific developmental milestones. Milestones refer to a series of skills in the four areas of development which a child is expected to achieve at a designated time, signified by a key-age, which may be calculated in terms of weeks, months, or years. Each milestone represents a skill, which is prerequisite to the next step in development. By comparing a child's chronological age to the milestone that he or she has attained, it is possible to ascertain the level of maturity and rate of progress.

It can be seen from Table 2.1 that although the child with DS follows the usual sequence of growth, milestones are generally attained at a slower pace. On the average, some skills, such as walking, may be delayed by as much as 11 months.

However, it should also be noted that in both sets of children, individual differences occur. Some children develop faster than the average, and some develop considerably slower. When serious delays occur, the range between "on target" and belated timelines can extend over many months, even years. Fortunately, such extreme retardation does not happen very often.

Early intervention programs and physical therapy can greatly facilitate the normalization of developmental patterns, and most infants and toddlers with OS can be expected to follow the average or the earlier schedule for attaining milestones.

Table 2.1
Developmental Milestones

	Down Syndrome Children		"Normal" Children	
	average in months	range in months	average in months	range in months
smiling	2	1½ to 4	1	½ to 3
rolling over	8	4 to 22	5	2 to 10
sitting alone	10	6 to 28	7	5 to 9
crawling	12	7 to 21	8	6 to 11
creeping	15	9 to 27	10	7 to 13
standing	20	11 to 42	11	8 to 16
walking	24	12 to 65	13	8 to 18
talking, words	16	9 to 31	10	6 to 14
talking, sentences	28	18 to 96	21	14 to 32

Note. Reprinted from *Down Syndrome: Growing and Learning* (p. 70), by S. M. Pueschel, C. D. Canning, A. Murphy, and E. Zausmer, 1978, Franklin, WI: Sheed & Ward. Copyright 1978 by Sheed & Ward, an Apostate of the Priests of the Sacred Heart. Reprinted with permission.

Table 2.1 suggests that typically, in accordance with standardized assessment tools, a child's chronological age matches his or her mental and physical maturity. In the case of a child with a disability, the mental, physical, and emotional growth does not always keep pace with the chronological age. For example, a child's mentality and other skills may be developing at half the rate of what is expected.

Thus at age 2 the child's maturity might be equal to that of a 1-year-old. Two years later, at the chronological age of 4, the child may have achieved the functioning level of a 2-year-old. If this pattern of development is allowed to continue and no educational efforts are made to help the child catch up, each passing year will bring a widening discrepancy between the child's chronological and mental ages. This increasing gap between a child's age and how he or she functions is referred to as a decline, deceleration, or deterioration in development and performance. Fortunately, in most instances, such extreme deceleration can be prevented through early intervention.

What Is Early Intervention?

Based on the timetables and patterns of development, early intervention is a systematic program of physical therapy, exercise, and activity designed to forestall and remedy developmental delays inherent in children with disabilities, including those with DS. In many instances the program is individualized to meet the specific needs of a child, which helps infants and children reach growth milestones in the four main areas of development.

In addition to benefiting children with disabilities, programs of early intervention have a great deal to offer parents in terms of support, encouragement, and information. The programs teach parents how to interact with their infant or toddler, how to meet specific needs, and how to enhance development. Furthermore, early intervention centers give parents the opportunity of finding solace through sharing their concerns and bonding with other parents during a time when many mothers and fathers feel isolated, helpless, and bewildered.

Early intervention research and case histories have shown that children with Down syndrome have a far greater potential for learning and for functioning as contributing members of society than believed possible 25 years ago (Dmitriev, 1981, 1988, 1997). At the same time, it is important to remember that each child, whether the child has Down Syndrome or not, is a unique individual with his or her own strengths and weaknesses, abilities and deficits, and rate of development. Individual variances exist even when mile- stones are reached on schedule. Expectations must be balanced. A defeatist attitude, or an attitude of low expectations, sets limits on what a child can achieve. At the same time, unrealistically high expectations place undue burdens on a child, which can only lead to failure. Acceptance of the child, of who and what the child is, is the best approach. An optimistic attitude, with realistic expectations and the ability to recognize and reinforce the smallest increments of progress, is the attitude that is most likely to have a positive, encouraging effect on development. In this way, early intervention programs succeed in maximizing achievement. (For more information on early intervention programs, please refer to Appendix B.)

Finally, and most importantly, parents must remember that a child with DS is first a child. The fact that the child was born with extra chromosomal material which results in physical and developmental deficits is secondary. At birth, the baby with DS has the same basic abilities of most newborns to see, hear, taste, feel, and smell. The baby with DS needs love, comfort, human close-ness, and opportunities to learn and to succeed. With this introduction, we can turn our attention to the uniqueness of children with DS: their strengths, weaknesses, special needs, and possible solutions to their problems.

Strengths of Children with Down Syndrome

Contrary to what people may have been led to believe, the child with DS has many strengths.

Rapid Learning

The child with DS learns skills very rapidly, especially skills involving fine motor (except writing) and cognitive activities. The obvious enjoyment and satisfaction of these children as they work with puzzles, colors, shapes, letters, and words are a delight to behold. Paper and pencil work is harder and requires more effort on the part of the teacher and the child.

Responsive to Shaping

The child with DS is also exceedingly responsive to shaping procedures, which greatly simplify the task of teaching a new skill. The word shaping, as it is used here, means physically assisting or guiding a part of the child's body (arm, leg, head, hand) to make the desired response. Shaping is a way of physically showing a child what it is that we want him or her to do, until the child learns to make the response independently.

For example, in teaching a 2-year-old the parts of the body, the teacher wants the child to touch his or her head when the teacher says, "Show me your head." Even if the child knows the word *show* and the word *head*, the child may not know how to put the two together to make the correct response. So the teacher shapes the child. The teacher takes the child's hand and touches it to his or her head, thus teaching the child the correct response to the direction, "Show me your head."

Visual Acuity

The child with DS usually has excellent visual acuity. This means that these children are able to discriminate between shapes, pictures, letters, numbers, and words with remarkable accuracy at a very early age. Despite the common vision problems of strabismus (cross-eyedness) and nearsightedness, we have been able to capitalize on visual acuity to teach many pre-academic and academic tasks.

Responsive Social Being

Even as an infant, the child with DS has the potential to be a very responsive, social being. Kenny, a 3-month-old baby who was in the Infant Learning class, was born with a cleft palate. (He is, in fact, only one of the estimated 200 children that I have known to have this additional problem.) AP, a result of this defect, Kenny was unable to eat well and was still very tiny and frail. Yet, despite his physical weakness, Kenny's dark brown eyes were bright and alert. When his mother looked at him and talked to him, he tried to "talk" back. He moved his lips (now surgically repaired) in imitation of her lip movements and looked at her intently, communicating with his shining eyes and soft cooing noises.

Receptive Language

Children with DS have excellent receptive language. Generally they know and are able to understand far more than they may be able to express. Parents, teachers, and professionals must focus their efforts on helping these children to develop verbal expressive language abilities that will reflect, more accurately, their inherent potential.

Little Developmental Lag

Research has shown that during the first 3 months of life, the majority of babies with DS show very little developmental lag in any area of growth including motor, social, cognitive, or communicative. By age 6 months, however, without intervention, some delays, usually gross motor, can begin to appear. The extent of some of these delays is shown in Table 2.1.

On a positive note, the fact that these babies start out on an almost equal basis with other babies better enables them to keep pace with typical growth expectations as they enter a program of intervention.

Problems and Concerns

Despite the many strengths of children with DS and the higher expectations that we may now have for them, it would be unrealistic to deny the existence of a number of health, mental, and physical problems associated with this condition. Hypotonia (poor muscle tone), small stature, and a characteristic facial appearance are among the major physical symptoms of this disorder.

Hypotonia

Poor muscle tone causes delays in physical development. As a result, the achievement of such necessary skills as head, neck, and trunk control, and independent sitting, standing, and walking may occur later than they do among children without disabilities (see Table 2.1). However, data have shown that physical therapy and early intervention aimed at developing muscle control can greatly accelerate the acquisition of these skills.

Small Stature

Generally children with DS are not as tall as their nondisabled peers. The average height for normal 3-year-olds is about 38 inches, and for children with DS, approximately 34 to 36 inches. By age 12, there may be a difference in height between the two groups of about 10 inches. Currently there is a strong, as well as controversial, interest in human growth (hGH) therapy. Preliminary results indicate a significant increase in height among young children who received hGH replacement treatments after they were medically diagnosed of having an hGH deficiency. These treatments, however, did not cause children with Down syndrome to become taller adults. Human growth hormones may also have a negative effect on patients prone to leukemia. Obviously more research and follow-up data are needed before the pros and cons of hGH treatments can be resolved (Foley, 1995).

It also should be noted that in height and build, children with DS resemble their parents. It can be expected that those born to tall, slender parents will have a similar physical appearance. They will be taller, and perhaps more wiry, than the children born to shorter couples.

Facial Characteristics

A great deal has been written about the symptomatic appearance of individuals with DS. Many authors have dwelled on this aspect of the disorder more than anything else. Personally, I find these stereotypic descriptions of the nose (small) and eyes (with oriental-like epicanthal folds) tiresome and unnecessary. First, these descriptions tend to distract attention from viewing each child as a unique individual; second, such descriptions tend to make some parents unduly sensitive about their child's appearance.

In the past, individuals with DS may have been seen as unattractive because they appeared sluggish, with unanimated, dull expressions. These people, in fact, were reflecting the dullness and hopelessness of their uninspired, institutional lives. It is very likely that other residents without DS appeared equally unappealing.

On the other hand, children who have the benefit of early education, and who face the world with animation and sparkling eyes, are invariably appealing.

As the child with DS grows older, and if his or her social awareness merits the trouble and expense, it is possible to further normalize the appearance through plastic surgery. During the late 1970s, these operations were frequently performed in the United States as well as in other advanced countries. In some cases an enlarged tongue was also surgically reduced. It appears, however, that surgery has become less popular as society learns to tolerate differences and to recognize the potential and value of individuals with DS. As attitudes change and become more positive, the perceived need for plastic surgery is proportionately lessened. Parents, teachers, physicians, and people with DS are now questioning the efficacy of such procedures. In the end, we must consider to what extent plastic surgery can actually improve the quality of life for this special population.

Eliminating the problem of tongue protrusion, as well as other ways that a child's appearance can be enhanced, will be discussed in greater detail in a subsequent chapter.

Health-Related Problems

The health of children with DS may range from relatively good to poor, with frequent upper respiratory infections, hearing impairment, congenital heart defects, and other organic problems.

Congenital Defects

Congenital heart defects (defects existing at birth) of varying degrees are found in about 35% of the babies who are born with DS. These defects may range from slight heart murmurs to more serious cardiac malformations. Fortunately, the present outlook for children with heart defects is much brighter than it has been in the past. Not only has the technology for open- heart surgery been improved to the point that it is no longer considered a final recourse, but doctors are also more willing to intervene surgically to repair damage before it becomes life-threatening.

Another less frequent congenital malformation, duodenal stenosis or atresia, results in an obstruction in the upper portions of the small intestine. This problem must be remedied by surgery as soon as it is discovered. Usually the problem is diagnosed shortly after birth. In some cases, however, it does not become apparent until the baby is several months old. Failure to gain weight and persistent regurgitation of food shortly after eating should be viewed with suspicion.

A young woman and her newly adopted baby with DS came to see me when the baby was 7 months old. Marie was a beautiful child, with wavy black hair and large, violet-blue eyes, but she was exceedingly pale, almost translucently white, with dark circles under her eyes. Marie's mother was concerned about her development. Although the baby seemed bright and alert, her muscle tone was poor. Moreover, Marie was not gaining weight and she was constantly spitting up her formula. In my presence Marie hungrily took 5 ounces of milk, but within minutes the food was regurgitated all over her bib. This was the usual pattern, her mother explained. The mother told me she had taken Marie to a pediatrician many times. The doctor claimed that there was nothing seriously wrong, and that Marie would get over it.

Upon my advice and the advice of other parents of children with DS, Marie's mother took her to the University of Oregon Hospital for an examination. A duodenal obstruction was diagnosed. By this time, Marie was so dehydrated and undernourished that a few more days' delay would have been fatal.

Marie and her parents lived in a small town. Very likely the physician who had been seeing Marie had never treated a child or infant with DS before. Once again, I urge parents not to accept glib answers to their expressed concerns about their children's health and well-being.

Other Health Problems

Like all mothers and fathers, the parents of children with DS have to cope with colds, upper respiratory and ear infections, allergies, and other child- hood diseases.

The child with DS may be particularly susceptible to upper respiratory infections. In addition to making the child miserable with congestion and possible bronchitis and pneumonia, these infections frequently result in middle ear inflammations called otitis media (middle ear infection). Recurring bouts of otitis media can lead to permanent hearing loss. In the past, the high incidence of hearing impairment among individuals with DS was not recognized. It is now estimated that some type of hearing loss occurs in about 60 to 70% of the DS population (Kavanagh, 1995). The importance of early diagnosis, prevention, and proper management by parents and those in the medical profession must not be underestimated.

Preventive Medical Care

Just as early intervention programs aim at preventing developmental delays, it is now recognized that preventive medicine is equally important in maintaining good health and avoiding future medical problems. The following checklist, adapted from a list prepared by the Children's Brain Research Clinic in Washington, D.C., gives parents and their child's physician a comprehensive timetable for monitoring the physical well-being of an individual with DS from birth through adulthood.

Down Syndrome Preventative Medicine Checklist
Adapted from Children's Brain Research Clinic, Washington, D.C.

Neonatal Period

History: Excessive vomiting—check for blockage of gastrointestinal system

Examination: Check for cardiac murmur. Check hips for displacement. Check for neonatal otitis media. Check for intact hearing.

Laboratory: Chromosomal karyotype, thyroid screen, vitamin A, and carotene

Recommendations: Refer neonate to infant learning program and parents to Down Syndrome parent group

Formula: If not breastfeeding, formula should have adequate fat—at least 30% of calories

2- to 12-month Examination

History: Check infectious history, especially ear infections

Examination: General pediatric and neurological exam. If nystagmus or strabismus present, early ophthalmological evaluation is indicated

Laboratory: Serum vitamin A, carotene and zinc.

Recommendations: Baseline auditory evaluation, including impedance testing. Ophthalmologic antibiotic if conjunctivitis is present. Routinely have pediatrician remove wax from external auditory canal every 6 months until puberty.

1 Year to Puberty—Annual Examination

History: Monitor educational techniques. Inquire for evidence of myopia. Record history of ear and other infections.

Examination: General pediatric and neurological.

Laboratory: Serum thyroid, vitamin A, and zinc

Recommendation: Auditory evaluation, including impedance test after every ear infection. Ophthalmological appointment annually for first 6 years of life.

Adolescence and Adulthood—Biannual Examination

History: Check educational and vocational level. Check for symptoms of hypothyroidism, seizures, vision loss, and constipation.

Examination: General physical and neurological.

Laboratory: Thyroid testing including thyroid antiglobin factor, vitamin A, and zinc.

Recommendation: Active life in a vocational program after academic education is completed. Immediate remediation of any medical problems

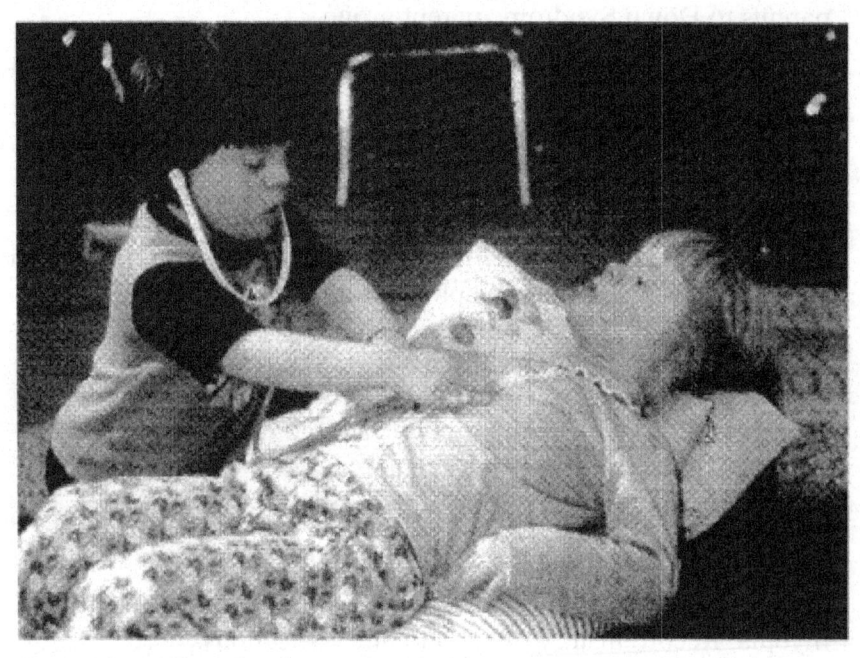

Photo 2.1. Playing doctor.

3. Mental, Language, and Social Development

Mental Ability

Although we already know that individuals with Down syndrome can read, write, and compute, and lead productive lives, the final word on the mental capabilities of this population is yet to be written. Until the mid-1970s, how- ever, literature described children with DS as being severely retarded. In those days, physicians and other professionals usually advised that these children be institutionalized early in life. For those who remained at home, there were few educational opportunities. In areas where public school special education classes were available, children with DS were usually placed in programs for very low-functioning, severely disabled children. Expectations for progress were low, and studies showed that the intellectual and social growth of a baby born with DS dropped rapidly after the first few months of life and continued to decelerate, so that by 8 years of age, the child was functioning at only about 30% of normal expectations.

In the last 25 years, however, there has been a growing recognition that appropriate early and public school education can prevent this decline, and that the majority of children with DS are able to function in the mild to moderate range of mental deficiency. These findings have been reported by such investigators as Rynders, Spiker, and Horrobin (1978), Canning and Pueschel (1978), and Dmitriev (1988, 1997).

Figure 3.1, adapted from Canning and Pueschel (1978), illustrates the previously reported deceleration in performance. Figure 3.2, also from Canning and Pueschel, shows the results of their long-term study of more than 100 children. It shows the majority of children with DS functioning within the mild to moderate range of mental delay.

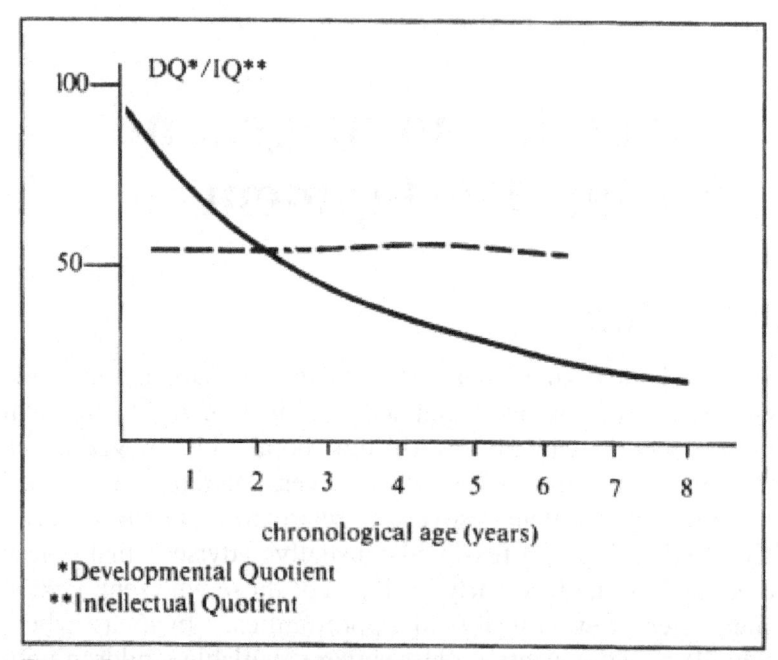

```
100 ─┤  DQ*/IQ**


 50 ─┤        ─────────────────────


      ├───┬───┬───┬───┬───┬───┬───┤
      1   2   3   4   5   6   7   8
          chronological age (years)
*Developmental Quotient
**Intellectual Quotient
```

Figure 3.1. "The downward sloping curve represents the decreasing intellectual abilities previously reported by many observers. The interrupted line shows the results of our studies indicating that early intervention, appropriate special education, and home rearing of children with Down syndrome have a positive effect upon their mental function." *Note.* From "An Overview of Developmental Expectations," by C. D. Canning and S. M. Pueschel, in *Down Syndrome: Growing and Learning* (p. 74), S. M. Pueschel, C. D. Canning, A. Murphy, and E. Zausmer (Eds.), 1978, Franklin, WI: Sheed & Ward. Copyright 1978 by Sheed & Ward, an Apostate of the Priests of the Sacred Heart. Reprinted with permission.

Figure 3.3 compares the performance of the experimental education unit's[2] DS graduates to the deteriorating performance previously observed among children with DS as shown in Figure 3.2. It can be seen that the EEU graduates have maintained their level of functioning through the years.

---

[2] Down's Syndrome Program, Experimental Program, University of Washington

By the end of 1980, 3 years after we started administering the Vineland Social Maturity Scale (Doll, 1965) on a regular basis, 79% of these children were still testing out between 70 and 90 on the

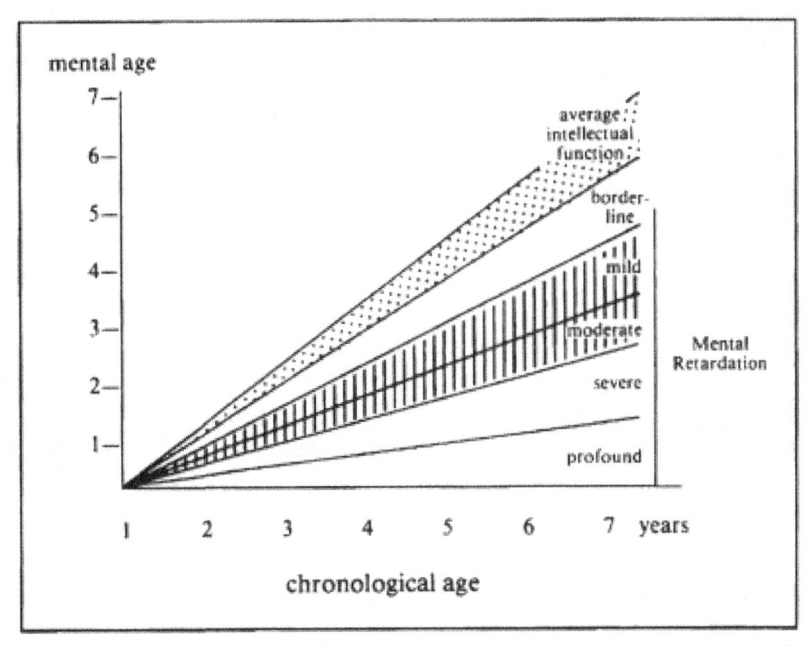

Figure 3.2. "The top shaded area represents children with average intellectual abilities. When children function below 'borderline' they are said to be mentally retarded. The majority of children with Down syndrome function in the mild to moderate range of mental retardation as indicated by the vertical bars in this figure." *Note.* From "An Overview of Developmental Expectations," by C. D. Canning and S. M. Pueschel, in *Down Syndrome: Growing and Learning* (p. 73), S. M. Pueschel, C. D. Canning, A. Murphy, and E. Zausmer (Eds.), 1978, Franklin, WI: Sheed & Ward. Copyright 1978 by Sheed & Ward, an Apostate of the Priests of the Sacred Heart. Reprinted with permission.

scale, and none received scores below 50. A comparably aged, nondisabled child would be expected to score between 90 and 100 on the same test. These former pupils, now in their 20s and early 30s, continue to meet our highest expectations as productive members of society. All are gainfully employed and live semi-independently with minor support from parents or other responsible individuals.

According to Mary Coleman (1988), MD, of the Children's Brain Research Clinic in Washington, D.C., severe retardation in children with DS is rare. When it occurs, it is usually the result of an additional anomaly such as brain damage or some other undetermined genetic,[3] two physical, or environmental problem. For example, investigators have found that children with DS who suffer from epileptic seizures may show greater developmental delays than their non-affected peers (Dmitriev, 1997). Since epilepsy is related to brain abnormalities, Dr. Coleman's observations may be correct. It should be remembered that although convulsive disorders are not considered to be inherent to DS, they do occur. The incidence has been reported to be as low as 1%, or as high as 12%, depending on how the various studies were conducted.

In order to avoid the damaging effects of repeated seizures, parents should seek the advice of a doctor if they note any unusual behaviors. Epileptic seizures manifest themselves in many different ways, from a momentary fixed staring, a slight tremor, or a sudden brief limpness, to the severe convulsions known as grand mal seizures. One is not likely to overlook a grand mal attack, but fleeting petit mal seizures, although they may occur 100 times a day or more, often go unnoticed. When these small seizures continue undetected, their effects can be more damaging than the more severe convulsions. It stands to reason that repeated neurological disruptions can seriously interfere with a child's attentiveness and learning. Unchecked, they can also lead to greater brain damage. So if a child with DS shows extreme delays in his or her development, or a sudden unforeseen regression, it may be wise to seek causes other than DS.

Finally, the reason I said that the last word on the mental development of individuals with DS is yet to be written is because the present generation of high-functioning children are only now reaching maturity, and also because we have yet to examine the long-term effects of inclusion in school placement and instruction. Perhaps we will also be able to isolate more specifically the factors that impede development, and thus be able to help even the rare child that is not keeping up with his or her peers with DS.

Mental development is related to language and communication skills, cognitive and academic skills, and social and self-care skills.

---

[3] Sometimes, in addition to the usual trisomy 21 that results in DS, an individual with DS may have other chromosomal abnormalities.

Each of these areas is interdependent and must receive equal consideration.

Language and Communication

Language is defined as a code or set of symbols by which we convey ideas and information about the world. Words, written or spoken, are the symbols that we use in language. Language is used for communication. We communicate in order to obtain or give information, or to ask for what we require.

There are two aspects of language: receptive and expressive. Developmentally, receptive language comes first. This is the ability to understand speech, to be able to follow directions, and to respond appropriately with words, gestures, or behavior. We already know that children with DS show an aptitude for receptive language. Frequently, however, visual cues paired with verbal directions may be necessary, especially if the child is very young or has a hearing loss.

Expressive language is the ability to communicate in written form or verbally with speech. Speech, the verbal form of expressive language, is delayed in children with DS. Spoken language is, in fact, the one area in which these children experience the greatest developmental difficulties, characterized by slower acquisition of new words, lack of fluency or spontaneity in speech, and poor articulation. To a degree, some of these problems are compounded by such factors as the structure and hypotonia of the vocal apparatus, delayed speech training, and hearing impairment. Nevertheless, verbal output and articulation can be enhanced if parents and teachers begin focusing on communicating with and eliciting communication from babies with DS from the very beginning of their lives. How this can be accomplished will be described in subsequent chapters.

Cognitive and Academic Skills

Early experiences with colors, shapes, pictures, in fact with everything that children typically enjoy, lay the groundwork for future school progress and are of utmost importance. Children who have mastered reading readiness skills in preschool or kindergarten readily learn how to read, first by sight and later phonetically.

Reading appears to be an activity at which many children with DS excel. However, reading should not be taught at the expense of other academic subjects such as math, writing, and spelling, although progress may be slower in these areas for some children.

Social and Self-Care Skills

Children with DS usually function very well in areas of social and self-care skills. The level of a person's functioning in these areas is measured by the degree of independence and appropriate social behavior he or she is able to exhibit in accordance with chronological age expectations.

As pointed out earlier (Figure 3.1), however, former studies have shown that children with DS show a consistent decrease in the level of their social development over time. Based on these observations, many professionals believe that deterioration in the level of performance is inevitable. In the past, the same reasoning prompted educators to question the effectiveness of early intervention programs.

Figure 3.3 shows, however, that children with DS who have remained in the University of Washington program from birth through the first 8 years of their lives continued to function socially, achieving an average of 80% of nor- mal expectations.

Nevertheless, recent research suggests that the social development of these children and adults has not kept pace with their cognitive achievements (Guralnick, 1989, 1990). The fault lies not with the individual but with professionals and parents who, relying on the old myth that this population is inherently socially unskilled, have not paid as much attention to social competence as they have to other aspects of development.

This does not mean that preschoolers with DS are not sociable youngsters. They smile at their teachers and respond in one or two words to simple questions. They participate happily in all supervised activities from snack time and music to active outdoor play. They show adequate self-management in toileting, hand-washing, dressing, and eating. Yet, closer observation of their behaviors in integrated or inclusive classrooms reveals that children with DS often lack the social competence of their nondisabled peers.

During free play, for example, when typically developing classmates select companions and initiate their own activities, the child with DS is often left on the sidelines.

At this point it becomes evident that the child with DS is deficient in some of the more complex social skills necessary for acceptance and successful participation within his or her peer group. Specifically, the child with DS does not always know how to initiate an activity, how to form friendships, or how to settle disputes through negotiation and compromise.

Early intervention begins at birth. As parents and therapists focus on the infant's physical, mental, and language development, they must pay equal attention to social development, despite the fact that there may be no evidence of delay during the first 3 or 4 months of life. Chapters in Part III will describe how parents and teachers can help young children with DS acquire greater social competence.

Weaknesses and Special Needs

In order to deal with a problem, we must first know what it is. This section will discuss some of the difficulties that parents and teachers of children with DS may encounter. It will also discuss ways in which these problems can be met and overcome.

The greatest and most obvious problem is that the child has DS. Although this statement may appear self-evident and hardly worth mentioning, one must look beyond the obvious in order to comprehend the full implications of this fact.

From the moment that a diagnosis of DS is confirmed, the baby and the family are thrown into an inexorable course of events. How well parents are able to deal with this trauma, to what extent husband and wife are able to provide mutual emotional support, how much support they are able to receive from family, friends, and professionals are factors that have great bearing on how the baby will develop.

We know that a newborn is not just so many ounces of a human who cries, nurses, and wets a diaper. From the moment of birth, the newborn is ready to interact and learn from his or her environment. We do not yet know to what extent future development depends on a child's initial introduction to life on the "outside," but we do know that the right kind of experiences are important.

In Chapter 1, I talked about attachment and interplay between mother and infant and described the effect of an unresponsive and depressed mother on the baby. I further described how the temperament of a baby might, in turn, influence maternal behaviors.

So the first difficulty that the newborn with DS and his or her parents must overcome is the possible disruption of the normal patterns of early mother-infant interaction. It is inevitable, to some degree at least, that the birth of a developmentally delayed baby will result in this disruption. We must accept the fact that disruption will occur; then we can deal with it.

Even under the best of circumstances, in terms of support and the emotional strengths of the mother and father, a period of adjustment and grieving for the expected child that was not born must be lived through. During this time of "mourning," the baby with DS may not receive the eye contact, the handling, the outpouring of love that helps babies thrive. This is another difficulty the baby with DS may encounter—his or her first few weeks of life may not be emotionally rewarding.

Another problem is that the baby's temperament may not elicit the most loving and spontaneously happy interaction from his or her parents. Babies who are fussy or lethargic, babies who have trouble feeding or other problems associated with DS (heart defects, obstructed bowel), compound the burden and despair of the new parents.

In addition to the basic problem of being born with DS, the foregoing are what I see to be the greatest difficulties facing the child with DS and his or her parents. In the following chapters I will attempt to address these difficulties in more detail. Procedures for dealing with poor muscle tone and for developing physical, mental, social, and cognitive skills will be outlined.

But first we must consider the emotional impact and the problems that may disrupt typical parent-infant interaction. The emotional stress must be resolved before real progress for the child with DS can begin. Each parent is an individual and unique. Each spouse brings to the family unit his and her own life experiences, expectations, and strategies for dealing with stress. As parents, we are responsible for our children's well-being, but first we must fulfill our responsibilities to ourselves. We can fulfill these responsibilities by identifying our inner turmoil and by seeking solutions. The next chapter discusses ways in which some of these negative feelings can be resolved and describes how other parents have fulfilled these responsibilities to them- selves and their child. Effective parenting begins with inner peace and self-esteem.

4. Emotional Impact

It is a physiological and psychological fact that in times of great emotional stress our bodies are thrown into a state of readiness for fight or flight.

Our instincts tell us to strike out in self-defense or to escape the danger by running away. New parents faced with the irrevocable fact that their baby has been born with DS may feel trapped. There is no one to fight and nowhere to run. This can create a terrible inner turmoil. Unless this turmoil can be resolved, the inner frustration builds up pressure like the racing motor of a mired vehicle. The wheels are spinning at a terrific speed and going nowhere. Without proper action the motor will eventually burn out, and the car will cease to function. In human terms this can mean physical and emotional illness. This tremendous source of energy that our bodies mobilize to meet stress must find an outlet. How this energy is expended and what form it takes, whether productive or unproductive, is crucial in determining the future mental health of the family and the general development of their special needs baby. Moreover, although a person cannot always literally fight or run, both productive and unproductive behaviors that parents of a child with DS exhibit can be classified under these two categories: fight or flight.

Fight Behaviors

Unproductive Fight Behaviors

Productive expenditure of this stress-created energy results in actions that release pent-up forces by directing them toward some positive activity outside of oneself. Unproductive expenditure of stress-created energy concentrates on repressing this energy within oneself. This happens when individuals see themselves as the enemy and turn their anger (aggression) on themselves. Such emotions create a wheel-spinning situation, they lead to nowhere, and generally result in a state of deep depression and a feeling of utter helplessness and futility. Another exceedingly unproductive, yet common, emotional response of parents to the birth of a baby with a physical or genetic problem is the feeling of extreme guilt and self-chastisement.

Coping with Unproductive Emotions

In seeking more productive ways of handling the emotional impact of the birth of a child with DS or any other disabling condition, one must first realize and firmly believe and know, that the birth of such a baby is an accident of nature, no more, no less. There is no need to compound the problem with feelings of guilt, shame, self-blame, or similar destructive emotions. People suffer heart attacks, brain hemorrhages; they are injured and sometimes permanently crippled in mind and body in automobile mishaps and other accidents. None of these, except if one is directly responsible for causing injury to another, evoke the tortured, unfounded self-hate that I have frequently encountered in parents of children with DS.

One distraught father wrote to me: "I cannot understand how such a thing could happen to us. No one in my family ever had any kind of disease . . . ." The correspondent appeared to be linking the event with something dis- graceful lurking in the family background.

In another instance a young woman with a 2-week-old baby girl came to me for consultation. At that time the final diagnosis had not been made, but the delivering physician indicated the baby might be "mongoloid." Frightened, the mother sought reassurance from me that the baby was "all right." What could I say? I made arrangements to have chromosome testing (karyotyping) done for a clinical diagnosis. Then I gave the baby a developmental evaluation. Physically she was a strong, beautiful infant, and I could point out to my visitor that her little daughter was developing extremely well and would probably continue to do so.

As we talked, the mother relaxed visibly and finally blurted out:

> It's not for myself. My husband and I . . . It doesn't matter . . . If . . if Katie is not all right . . . if she has DS. We love her already. I'm thrilled to have her. But how can I tell my mother? We're going home for Christmas next week. How can I face her?

How can she face her *mother*? As if she were a child who had misbehaved. Strangely and tragically, I have met other women who expressed the same fears in facing their families. Some have actually felt rejected by their mothers for giving birth to a less than perfect baby.

Sometimes there is a feeling of guilt toward one's spouse. I'm sure this is felt by husbands as well as by wives, but since my daily work with children brings me into more frequent contact with the mothers, I am more familiar with cases of guilt on the part of the woman. Sometimes, as in the following case, circumstances add a particular poignancy to the story.

After being alone for a number of years, Mrs. Davis, a mother of a teenage daughter, married for the second time. She and her new husband were very much in love and looked forward to starting a family. Her pregnancy was a period of joyful expectation. Mr. Davis had not been married before, and dreamed of becoming a father. His much desired little son was born prematurely and he had DS.

Mr. Davis appeared to adjust quickly, and as George Jr. gained in strength, a good father-son relationship was established. But it was well over a year before Mrs. Davis began showing signs that she might be able to forgive herself for failing her husband. There was, however, a positive side even to Mrs. Davis' self-blame. In her intense desire to make it up to her husband for failing to give him the perfect son, she sought the next-best solution. She became determined to make little George that "perfect" child. As one of the parents enrolled with her baby in our Infant Learning class at the university, she followed our suggested program with utmost fidelity and dedication. Sometimes she worked too zealously and at such length on his gross motor and cognitive program that we considered urging her to relax a little in her approach to his development. But we were also extremely pleased that Mrs. Davis was finding a productive way of handling her feelings. Meanwhile, little George was turning out to be a super-kid. At age 2 and a half, he approximated normalcy in all areas. Physically and verbally, he surpassed even our generally high expectations.

This little story illustrates how initial unproductive behaviors can be transformed into more positive responses. This in fact is the role of the professional: to help parents make this conversion.

Another type of self-blame is expressed in a damaged self-image. Parents of developmentally delayed children sometimes appear to lose their sense of self-worth. They begin seeing themselves as unattractive and undesirable socially, and perhaps even sexually to their marriage partner. In other words, they suddenly see themselves demoted to the rank of second-class citizen. One mother, referring to another mother of a child with DS, expressed it very succinctly: "Mrs. Martin is such a lovely person, so bright and attractive, it makes me feel a lot better. If someone like her can have a child with DS, then maybe I'm not so bad myself."

To a man, the fathering of a child with a genetic defect can be a serious threat to his masculinity. One man, a doctor whom I knew as a friend, was unable to accept that he had produced a child with DS, although the baby was a Trisomy 21 and, therefore, not the result of any hereditary factor. Nevertheless, this man felt driven to erase this "mistake." He had to prove that he was still able to father a normal child, and although the family already had four typically developing children, he forced his wife into another pregnancy within weeks after the birth of their boy with DS. One would expect that a medically trained, professional man would be able to face this problem more rationally, but strong emotions, especially emotions related to our feelings about ourselves, are not controlled by position or educational background. As one might suspect, the birth of the second child, a perfectly healthy little girl, did not resolve the problem nor the conflict in the home, and the marriage ended in a divorce. So the man's final response to the stress of having a child with DS was that of flight. And, although he continued to support his wife and family, and maintained contact with the older children, he completely dis- owned the one that had been born with DS. An endless litany of grief and self-abuse whispered inwardly like a confession.

> How could I do this to my wife? What will people say? Will I ever be able to take my baby out in public? I must have done something awful to deserve this! Why? Why? Why?

And I ask, why must parents of a special needs child be subjected to such inhuman suffering? Clearly the responsibility lies with society, a society that only recently has begun to discard old prejudices and intolerance of differences. Ancient myths and misconceptions are slow to be discarded. For too long, persons who should know better, such as professionals in the fields of medicine and education, have been guilty of perpetuating damaging stereotypes. As another step toward a more enlightened society, I would urge that we eradicate the words *mongol*, *mongoloid*, and *mongolism* in reference to Down syndrome. These are inappropriate, ugly words, and utterly false in the images that they evoke. Their usage is less prevalent now, especially in the United States, where parents and concerned professionals have conscientiously removed these terms from their vocabulary. Nevertheless, the words are still used in England, for example, and occasionally by "old-fashioned" physicians in the United States and other countries at the very time when parents are most vulnerable to the added pain that such thoughtlessness can inflict. I'm referring, of course, to the time when the doctor first confronts the parents, or in many instances the mother alone, to report that the baby she has just given birth to is not the one she expected, normal and perfect, but one with a genetic abnormality called mongolism. I urge all professionals to be extremely sensitive to the cruel impact of these words when they make their diagnoses.

Productive Fight Behaviors

In the preceding section, the emphasis was on manifestations of negative fight behaviors, defined by actions and emotions that are turned inward, resulting in attacks on one's inner-self. Now we will turn to the more positive aspects of the fight response. Basically, productive fight behaviors have two stages. Stage one is the release, the stage of catharsis, an opening of flood- gates to release the churning emotions within. The second stage is a more controlled, deliberate expenditure of that energy. Stage two could be called the "activity" stage.

> **Stage 1: The release stage**

Open anger, even rage, expressed in the initial moments of stress can be a positive reaction. Such an outpouring releases the immediate surge of energy and leaves room for more creative behaviors later on. Tears, and a frank verbal statement of one's feelings, "I'm hurt. I'm angry. It's not fair!" can have a healing effect. This is, in fact, a positive fight reaction to stress. The reaction strikes outward, away from the inner person, and is far more psychologically healthy than striking at oneself with thoughts of self-blame and worthlessness. The reaction is something to be lived through, shared, and then set aside in preparation for the second stage.

> **Stage 2: Activity**

Productive fight behaviors take many forms, and I am always amazed and humbled by the inner strength, courage, dedication, and resourcefulness of parents as they meet the challenge presented to them. Some of the most frequent productive behaviors exhibited by parents result in the following:

1. Closer bonding and support between husband and wife and among members of the immediate family

2. Spiritual growth and greater and deeper expression of one's faith and belief in God

3. Active and immediate involvement in the baby's development including recognition of the importance of early intervention, a burning desire to read and learn more about the problem of DS, and a desire to do everything possible to maximize the child's potential

4. Extremely tender and devoted attention to the baby's physical and emotional needs

5. A growing love for the child with DS that appears to surpass the love that parents generally have for their other children

6. An increasing involvement in activities outside the home that are aimed at benefiting their child and other children with disabilities

Examples relating to the last category include parents who become leaders in parent groups and other organizations that serve children with special needs and their families. Several couples that I know have been instrumental in starting programs for children with DS, which are based on the University of Washington program and serve areas where previously there had been no appropriate program for their children. Other parents have been active in establishing much needed liaisons among parents, pediatricians, and other professionals.

Less than 30 years ago, public schools were not required to provide education for so-called trainable children. In fact, the issue of the day was whether or not it was the responsibility of the schools to offer programs to a population that was considered incapable of learning. Severely and profoundly retarded children were not even considered for public school programs. Today, however, in addition to the Education for All Handicapped Children Act of 1975, which entitles every developmentally delayed child in the nation to a "free, appropriate education and related services designed to meet unique needs," there are a number of new laws mandating early intervention programs for infants and toddlers, and inclusion in public school classes at 3 years of age.

The important thing to remember is that parents are the force behind every law, every change in educational opportunities, and every improvement in attitude and service to the disabled. These parents are able to mobilize the energy created by emotional stress into productive fight behaviors that benefit humankind.

In short, productive fight activity has the power to bring out and augment the very best of all human qualities: love for spouse and family; spiritual growth; unselfishness and devotion to one's children; personal intellectual growth; and service to society.

Flight Behaviors

Unproductive Flight Behaviors

Fight or flight reactions are normal responses to stress or danger. Fight reactions can be unproductive or productive. The same is true of flight behaviors. Productive flight behaviors can be positive ways of coping with a difficult emotional situation. It is important to recognize the less desirable, unproductive flight behaviors before more positive responses can be developed.

One type of reaction to the birth of a baby with DS, which I classify as unproductive flight, is not readily recognized. Certainly parents rarely realize that their behaviors are unproductive and, if left unchecked, damaging to themselves and their child. Most frequently, these unproductive flight reactions are expressed in some form of denial.

> **Denial 1: "There is nothing wrong with my baby" syndrome**

This belief, conscious or unconscious, may result in a very passive attitude on the part of the parents. No attempts are made to encourage the baby to develop faster. Even when the baby should be chronologically ready to sit or take solids, the parents continue to treat the baby as a newborn. The parents seem to be saying to themselves, "Since there is nothing wrong, I don't have to interfere. Everything will be all right." Unfortunately, this attitude can lead to such complete passivity on the part of the parents that the child's developmental problems become a way of life, and little is done to remedy them.

Jeffry was a 9-year-old boy with DS, who would not walk without help, was not toilet trained, did not speak, and was still spoon-fed strained baby foods. By now Jeffry's parents' earlier belief that Jeffry might be a little slow but that he would learn to walk, talk, and eat properly when he was "ready" had shifted to one of resignation. At this point it seemed simpler to continue "walking," feeding, and diapering Jeffry rather than to try to teach him any of these skills.

Jeffry was enrolled in a public school special education class where the same passive attitude on the part of the teachers perpetuated his problems. Again he was walked, diapered, and spoon-fed. The teacher grumbled because it took her aide a full hour every day to feed Jeffry his three jars of baby food at lunchtime, but nothing was done to change the situation.

This story would not be worth telling if there had been substantiated evidence that because of some additional problem, such as brain damage, Jeffry was indeed functioning at the very best of his ability. This, fortunately, was not the case as we soon discovered when Jeffry became a student in our research program for school-age children with DS. Our first goal was to teach Jeffry to feed himself. Since he had the ability to grasp objects, it was not too difficult to teach Jeff to grasp the handle of his spoon after it had been filled with food and placed in his dish. The next step was to guide Jeffry's hand to his mouth. For the first few mouthfuls the spoon was guided all the way to his lips. After that had been accomplished successfully, assistance was given only as far as the chin. In order to obtain the food, Jeffry had to complete the spoon-to-mouth movement independently.

By the end of 3 weeks, Jeffry was feeding himself with complete independence, scooping the food and bringing the spoon to his mouth without fail. A toileting program and a walking program—teaching Jeffry to walk without adult support by holding on to the back of a chair and pushing it ahead of himself—were also started. Greatly encouraged by Jeffry's progress, we began planning a program to teach Jeffry to eat solid foods when, much to our disappointment, Jeffry's parents moved, and he was transferred to another school. I have no way of knowing what happened to Jeffry after that. His mother had been kept informed of our feeding, toileting, and walking programs, and she had agreed to continue our efforts at home. But old habits are hard to overcome, and unless Jeffry's new teachers maintained their sup- port, it is quite possible that Jeffry was allowed to revert to his previous dependent behaviors.

Sometimes Denial 1can result in conflict within the family. This happens when one member realistically tries to seek help for the developmental problems of the child, while other members, refusing or emotionally unable to see the need for intervention, argue against it.

In all fairness, however, I must point out that, in the past, such passive attitudes have been reinforced by well-meaning, but misguided professionals who have perpetuated the myths that "nothing can be done anyway, so why try," and "left alone, a child will outgrow his or her problem."

> **Denial 2: "There is a cure" syndrome**

Another type of flight is exemplified by the "shopping" parent. These parents run away from the problem by seeking the one doctor or the one magic pill or treatment that will cure their child.

I have great sympathy for these loving, despairing parents. In their frantic search, they readily fall prey to all sorts of quack schemes and unscrupulous individuals. Very often large sums of money are spent on this quest at great sacrifice to the family.

At this point, and regretfully, I must say bluntly and categorically: There is no known cure for DS. A great deal can be done, medically and education- ally. Every parent should have access to information on where to find these kinds of help. Moreover, it is the responsibility of doctors and educators to teach parents how to evaluate the merits of a proposed program or treatment realistically. Every treatment and every program that parents consider for their child must be evaluated on the bases of group and individual data.

In other words, parents have the right to demand to see documented records of the number of children treated and their progress. Parents must be able to distinguish between valid and reliable figures, and so-called claims. A parent should also be able to .distinguish between short-term and long- term, or permanent, progress. All of this is difficult to do, especially since an intense desire for a cure tends to increase one's gullibility. I urge parents to view all claims for miraculous treatments with a great deal of cautious skepticism.

If, nevertheless, some parents elect to place their child with DS in a particular suspect program, or subject their child to a course of some new and unusual treatment involving drugs or physiological manipulations, it is their responsibility to keep an impartial record of the child's day-to-day progress in terms that can be seen and measured. I would also urge parents to seek help from someone trained in behavioral sciences, such as an educational psychologist, in setting up such an observational record. Such assistance is usually available through university departments of medicine, psychology, or education. It is essential to do this to protect oneself and one's child from malpractice and quackery.

I mention this because I receive many letters from parents asking my opinion about various cures for DS. Some of these schemes make my blood run cold. Frequently, these so-called treatments are offered in foreign countries, but there are quack schemes in this country as well. The majority of these treatments are simply practices of physical torture.

In a certain Latin American school for children with disabilities, it was a standard practice to hang children upside down for designated periods of time. This was reported to me by the mother of one of the children enrolled in our DS program at the university who happened to visit the school during a trip to South America. She also showed me photographs of these unfortunate children, dangling, head down, suspended by straps around their ankles. The theory behind this barbarism is that the blood rushing to the child's head will increase head size, resulting in increased intelligence. An increased head size does not result in increased intelligence. Individuals with unarrested hydrocephalis have enormous heads. They are also, in many cases, severely retarded.

A few years ago, a particularly barbaric practice was occurring in the United States. A number of practitioners advocated a procedure for children with DS called "cranial or cranium adjustment." This treatment involved inflating a balloon that had been inserted into an infant's or small child's nose. This procedure supposedly enlarged the sinus cavities and the skull. According to reputable medical doctors, there was no physiological or scientific basis for these claims, yet this torturous operation was carried out on a weekly basis, or sometimes more often, over long periods of time.

Anyone who has experienced having a device or some foreign material pushed into the nostrils knows how excruciatingly painful such an operation can be. To submit an infant to such pain seems utterly irresponsible and inhumane. It can also be extremely dangerous, for it can result in damaged tis- sues and ruptured blood vessels. Significantly, I could find no medical reports, no serious documentation, of the so-called benefits from these practices.

For a time, a chiropractor in California who practiced cranial adjustment enjoyed considerable popularity among parents of children with DS. He spoke to parent groups and distributed pamphlets on cranium adjustment. As a concerned professional, I wrote to the man requesting materials on his methods and the rationale behind them. He never replied.

One courageous father elected to try out cranium adjustment himself, before submitting his child to the procedure. He found it so agonizing that he swore never to inflict such pain on his infant.

Another questionable course of treatment, called "cell therapy," came to the United States from Germany. The developer of this procedure was Dr. F. Schmid (1982). The treatment involved injections or implantations of lyophilized (dissolved) fetal cells taken from unborn sheep or cattle. Schmid appeared to be very sincere in his belief that these injections would stimulate brain growth, and he reported significant differences between so-called treated and untreated patients with DS. However, in conjunction with the cell therapy, Dr. Schmid prescribed intensive early intervention centered on gross motor, language, and cognitive development, and parent training. We have no data on how cell therapy affects the development of children without the added influence of early intervention. Once again, we are faced with claims that have not been based upon carefully controlled scientific study.

In 1981, Dr. Ruth Harrell and her colleagues reported IQ increases among children with DS and children with mental retardation who had participated in a diet therapy called "orthomolecular hypothesis." The children were treated with vitamin and mineral supplements. Although the study was not well controlled, and there were a number of flaws in how the research had been conducted, the study was sufficiently documented to serve as a springboard for further, more carefully regulated research. Dr. Forrest Bennett and his colleagues (1983) at the Center on Human Development and Disability at the University of Washington replicated the Harrell study under more precise conditions. The results of Bennett's study with two groups of young children with DS, carefully matched for age and ability and randomly assigned, showed no significant gains among the subjects who received the diet therapy compared to those in the control group who were given placebos.

The following is a partial list of other unconventional therapies that research has shown to be of no benefit to children with Down syndrome in terms of language or intellectual development (see the glossary at the back of the book for definitions of the following terms).
1. Pituitary extract
2. Glumatic acid
3. 5-hydroxytryptophan
4. Dimethyl sulfoxide (DMSO)
5. Siccacell/cell therapy
6. Megavitamins/minerals
7. Patterning

8. Facilitated communication

To reiterate, I would never accept any claim for increased intelligence or performance at face value. Before giving any credence to such a claim, I would want to see a record of the child's academic, social, and verbal performance, before and after treatment. I would have to be convinced that the scores did indeed reflect the effects of the treatment and not some other variables such as a child's increased age or other factors in the child's environment. In other words, the figures must be statistically significant. This means that the treatment was conducted in such a way that any difference in the performance before and after treatment can indeed be attributed to the actual treatment and not any other cause. For anyone who is not specifically trained in statistics, this can be a very difficult judgment to make. Last, but certainly not least, I would want to know how a given treatment is physically and emotionally affecting the child.

> **Denial 3: Blind spots**

Persons exhibiting a Denial 3 pattern of flight show a borderline response. Basically, these parents have a positive attitude toward their child and are involved in a great deal of productive activity. These parents are interested in the child's educational program, and they work hard at maintaining and reinforcing progress at home.

Occasionally, however, these parents have a "blind spot" and are not always able to view their child's progress realistically. They tend to push their child toward more and more complex tasks before he or she has mastered prerequisite skills. This can result in gaps in the child's learning, misunderstanding between parents and teachers, and eventual failure on the part of the child.

One mother, for example, brought me an impressive list of some sixty words that she attested her newly enrolled 3-year-old son with DS could say perfectly. After observing Dickie in the classroom and listening to his utterances, the teacher and I found that his talking consisted of frequently repeated vowel sounds and little else. Yet his mother was interpreting his babbling as fully comprehensible speech.

It was difficult to convince Dickie's mother that he did not yet have a vocabulary of articulate words. In fact, further evaluation showed us that Dickie needed to develop his receptive skills before we could begin working on his verbal language. This was obvious because when asked to point to or select an object that corresponded to the nouns on his mother's list, Dickie rarely made a correct response. This indicated that Dickie did not understand what the words meant, nor did he understand the fact that there was a relationship between these sounds and objects in his environment.

On the whole, however, this type of flight behavior does not seriously hamper a child's development and rarely causes any big problems. In fact, I suspect that all parents of typically developing children, as well as those of children with developmental delays, are guilty of this little failing at one time or another. A good understanding of normal developmental sequences and clearly defined performance objectives can help all of us to view our children's progress more realistically and productively.

> **Denials 4 and 5: Rejection and abuse**

A far more grave symptom of unproductive flight behavior is open or hidden rejection of the child with a disability. Sometimes, in the presence of others, these feelings are masked with a cloak of overprotectiveness or a state of forced euphoria, in which the parent appears unnaturally animated and elated. At other times, an observer simply sees evidence of neglect. The child may not be clean, the hair may be matted, the child may be thin or pale, or the child may be lethargic and not progressing. Failure to thrive in infancy can be a sign of rejection, often resulting from maternal depression. In almost all instances, these types of rejection are not recognized for what they are: manifestations of unhealthy ways of dealing with emotional stress.

Sometimes this stress becomes so great and the pattern of flight behavior is so inappropriate that rejection is transformed into actual physical abuse. For example, the child may suddenly develop a series of unexplained bruises and injuries. One tiny baby suffered a broken rib and a broken arm both within the first few weeks of life. In another extreme case, a divorced mother neglected to call a doctor when her 2-year-old daughter with DS became seriously ill. When the child was finally hospitalized with pneumonia, it was too late and she died.

Drinking alcohol is a common escape route for many people who find themselves in a seemingly unbearable situation. Unfortunately, parents of children with, DS are no exception.

Anyone who is so overwhelmed by the impact of having a child with disabilities that he or she resorts to such unproductive and destructive behaviors as child neglect, rejection and abuse, or drinking must seek professional help. Mental health and crisis clinics can give short-term help and make recommendations for long-term counseling. There are alternatives and better ways of behaving, even while in a flight response.

Productive Flight Behaviors

Earlier in this chapter, I wrote that new parents of a disabled child may feel locked into an insolvable situation. Compounded with the natural impact of grief and disappointment is an intense feeling of being trapped. All the behaviors that have been described so far occur as a result of this emotional stress. In some instances, this can become an almost claustrophobic reaction. To those who are experiencing this suffocating sense of imprisonment, I must say, there is a way out! There are options. There are other alternatives to choose. Under these circumstances of extreme stress, parents would be wise to consider these options. The obvious option, of course, is the temporary or permanent removal of the baby from the home.

Fortunately there is excellent, temporary foster care available. There are also many wonderful people who are lovingly eager to adopt a baby with DS.

From my acquaintance with children who have been placed in foster care or adopted, and with the families of these children, I know that such arrangements can benefit both the child and the natural parents.

Earlier, I described the importance of positive interactions between mother and infant during the first few weeks of life. I also pointed out that a mother's depression, if it occurs for long periods of time, can harm the baby's development. In such cases, I usually recommend temporary foster care. Such a move is advisable for two reasons. First, it places the baby in a welcoming environment, which usually has an immediate positive effect on the baby's development. Second, it gives the biological family a chance to come to terms with the problem, to evaluate their strengths, and to come to some decisions about their baby and all the challenges that lie ahead, without the pressure of having the baby in the home. This is especially true if the new-born has additional health problems that require care that the emotionally and physically burdened mother is unable to provide.

In two recent instances when I made such a recommendation, the babies were in foster care for about 3 months. The following is the story of the Reynolds family.

Physically, Jamie Reynolds was a perfectly healthy, good-looking little boy. His parents, however, found it impossible to accept the fact that he had been born with DS. Both the mother and the father showed signs of deepening depression and an almost overwhelming sense of shame. The whole family was suffering: the parents, Jamie, and his 3-year-old sister.

As I made my suggestion, I could almost see a ray of hope breaking through the gloom that surrounded them. Then, just as quickly, this glimmer of hope was suppressed. It is not easy to come to such a decision, even on a temporary basis. Parents are torn between the promised relief and feelings of guilt for abandoning their baby.

Within a few days, however, the family acted on my recommendation. Jamie was placed in temporary foster care. For the first few days, Mrs. Reynolds related to me later, she reveled in her newfound freedom. The birth of Jamie and the subsequent trauma began to fade away like a bad dream. Her good spirits resurfaced, she felt reborn, and her natural vitality returned. At the same time, she found herself thinking about Jamie and wanting to see him. Tentatively, she expressed some of these feelings to her husband. It turned out that he was having similar thoughts.

They arranged to visit Jamie. Several more visits followed. Finally, Jamie was brought home for a weekend. As Sunday night approached they found themselves reluctant to return Jamie to his foster mother. They did, but with each subsequent visit the bond tightened among them.

They were now viewing Jamie in an entirely different light. He had become their son, a person, very unique and precious. They wanted him. For better or worse, he was theirs, and they were ready to accept and love him as their child. Three months following his placement in the foster home, Jamie returned home and has been there ever since. The outcome of this story is fairly typical, and for this reason I view temporary placement as a form of practical and productive flight behavior.

If, however, the bonding between the parents and the baby does not occur, and the parents keep postponing the time for the baby's return to the family, I seriously urge the parents to release the baby for adoption. A failure to do this places the baby in an untenable position.

Legally the baby is in limbo. Children who are wards of the state, but not released for adoption, end up being shuffled from one foster home to another. Adoptive parents usually seek a baby or a very young child. Each passing year decreases a child's chances of finding a permanent family. As a result of being moved among different foster homes and forced to break what could be deep attachments and make new ones, many foster children become emotion- ally disturbed, which further hampers their chances of adjustment and future adoption. Therefore, in fairness to the child and the future adoptive family, parents must recognize this as their final responsibility to the child they produced.

One young woman, facing the prospect of placing her baby for adoption, asked with amazement in her voice, "But who would want to adopt a child with DS?" I almost smiled at her naiveté, because parents who are able to keep and raise their children with DS know the answer. She had asked me this question while overlooking the fact that three families had already applied to the adoption agency in hopes of becoming her baby's new parents. I reminded her of this and then told her about some of the wonderful adoptive parents that I have come to know over the years.

One such family is Mrs. Hooper and Emily. Emily is now 8 years old, and she has lived in Mrs. Hooper's foster care since birth. Last year, just before Christmas, Mrs. Hooper happened to meet me on one of my visits to Emily's classroom. She caught my hand impulsively.

"Do you know," she exclaimed, "that Emily is mine at last, really mine. They finally signed the adoption papers! No one can take her away from me now." She smiled radiantly through the sudden tears that misted her eyes. Emily was fortunate that she was able to remain with the same foster mother for the 8long years it took her natural parents to decide to release her. Difficult as that decision may be, it must be recognized that if adoption appears inevitable, it should be done as early in the child's life as possible. Another family recently adopted an infant boy with DS. In addition to their own nondisabled son, the family now consists of the new baby and two other adopted children with DS: an 8-year-old boy and a 10-year-old girl. Once the mother of this family made a very revealing statement: "Some women," she told me, "have careers outside the home in many different fields.

My career is loving and raising children with Down syndrome."

A third family adopted their preschool son's classmate, a 4-year-old little girl who, like their son, was born with DS.

A natural mother of a toddler with DS was pregnant. When I asked if she was planning to have amniocentesis, a procedure for determining if the new baby would be genetically sound, she shook her head. "Why should I? It makes no difference to us. We want another baby. If it should have DS, we would still love and enjoy it as much as we love and enjoy Tommy."

These examples illustrate that the presence of a child with DS should not be the end of all hope and happiness in the home. It can be the beginning of an experience that can bring its own rewards and fulfillment.

Fathers Hurt Too

A section on the emotional impact of having a handicapped child would not be complete without a special word about the plight of fathers. Society does not always recognize that fathers hurt too, and that the birth of a baby with DS or some other anomaly can affect them as deeply as it does the mother. True, the mother is generally the one to bear the immediate burden of care, and she does not always have the outlets offered by a job or career, especially during the crucial first few months of the new baby's life. On the other hand, however, the mother can become involved in an infant learning program and have the opportunity of meeting other women with whom she can share problems and concerns. She can also, when pressures become too great, find relief in tears without social censure.

Fathers, however, are expected to go on about their business of earning a living with others giving little thought to the emotional pain they may be suffering. Men, generally, do not feel that it is permissible to weep in public or private, nor are they able to talk freely about self-doubts or feelings of helplessness, frustration, shame, or any emotion that might imply weakness or lack of masculinity. Also, the opportunity of meeting and talking with fathers facing similar problems may not be readily available.

The problems and the hurt, however, are real. The earlier story about the doctor who could not accept the birth of a son with DS suggests some of the conflicts a man may experience. The fact that a number of other men have also terminated their marriages under similar circumstances seems to indicate unresolved emotional distress. Professionals and wives of these men should, therefore, be aware of the emotional needs of the fathers, and the fathers themselves should be willing to examine and express their inner feelings.

Programs that provide early intervention for babies and their mothers should also attempt to provide a special time for the infants and their fathers. Such a program, initiated as part of the Infant Learning class at the University of Washington, proved highly successful. Fathers and their children were invited to come to a Saturday morning class twice a month. The program focused on father-child interaction. Fathers were taught how to relate to their babies through songs, games, and basic gross motor exercises. In addition to the father-child aspects of the program, the men had an opportunity to listen to a speaker, usually a pediatrician, dentist, educator, or lawyer, speak on a topic of general interest. The morning ended with refreshments for babies and adults, and an informal discussion (Meyer, 1995).

It was significant, I thought, that men with younger babies seemed to seek advice and information from the fathers of older children, much in the same way that the mothers sought help and counsel from each other. Increased sharing between husband and wife and general family involvement in the baby's development were other positive results of these sessions.

Photo 4.1. Tina learns to sit by placing her hands on her thighs for support.

PART II:
Introduction to Early Intervention

5. Exercises and Goals: The First 2 Years

To plan an effective program of early intervention, it is necessary to con- sider the emotional disruption that can occur after the birth of a baby with DS. It is my hope that the preceding pages have helped to clear the psychological debris of unresolved conflicts and prepared a path for parents to follow in order to deal successfully with the more concrete develop- mental problems associated with DS. I will address the problems of poor muscle tone and mental and language delays, not only in terms of how to deal with these specific concerns, but also in terms of how these problems are interdependent.

I have already discussed the basic developmental tasks that the growing baby must be able to do in order to keep pace with normal maturational goals. I pointed out that development in one area may foster or hinder progress in another. For example, if a baby is slow in developing back and neck control, it can be anticipated that he or she will show comparable delays in learning how to sit or walk independently. Similarly, if a baby does not learn how to fixate or follow a moving object with his or her eyes, this deficit will be reflected later on in activities that require eye-hand coordination. All aspects of early physical development, from the first movements after birth to the time when a baby is able to walk unaided, are crucial. In fact, I believe that the closer a delayed child's physical developmental time schedule is to that of typical development, the better the child's chances are for functioning at a level approaching normalcy. This, in essence, is the philosophy underlying the Infant Learning class.

The chapters that follow will describe exercises that can be effective in helping infants and children with DS to accelerate their development, and how some of the problems commonly associated with this condition can be prevented. Before we begin, however, we must look at the four physical types of children with DS and explore the "laws" that govern their behavior.

Down Syndrome: Physical Types

Table 1 in Chapter 2 gave the ages at which children with DS can be expected to attain: a number of developmental landmarks. It was stressed that these norms may vary according to the type of physical development a baby exhibits at birth. Babies with DS can vary greatly in muscle tone and inherent physical abilities. Through experience I have identified four distinct physical types common to these babies.

Type 1

The first type occurs in about 15% to 25% of the babies that I see. This is the baby that has good muscle tone, whose arms and legs feel firm. Developmental milestones such as head control, bearing weight on the feet (with support), lifting the torso on extended arms and rolling over are usually attained before the baby is 4 months old. As time goes on, these children continue to show good physical development.

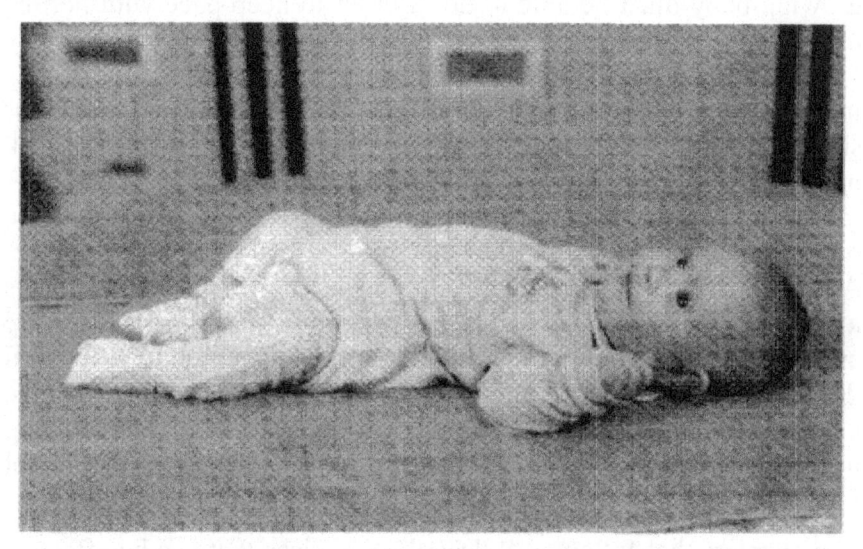

Photo 5.1. Greg, a Type 1 baby, shows overall development.

Types 2 and 3

The second and third types occur in about 50% to 65% of all babies with DS. These types are characterized by a discrepancy in the development between the upper and lower parts of the baby's body. This is the type of physical development that is generally encountered and is typical of what can be expected in babies with Down syndrome.

The Type 2 baby has a strong upper back, neck, shoulders, and arms. Like Type 1, the baby pulls to sit, is able to hold his or her head steady, and can raise up on the arms within the first 3 months after birth. But there is a noticeable weakness in the body from the waist down. When held in an upright position, Type 2 babies are unable to bear weight on their legs as babies typically do at 3 or 4 months of age. It can also be expected that these babies will have difficulty learning to crawl, roll over, and walk. With exercise, however, the impact of these problems can be greatly reduced, and close-to-schedule physical development can be expected.

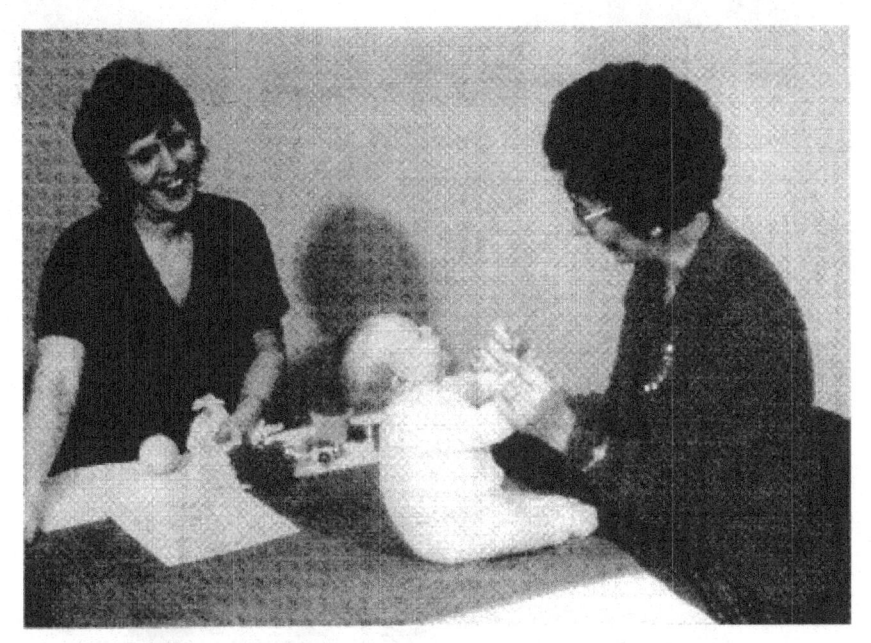

Photo 5.2. Danny, a Type 2 baby, pulls to sit at 3 months of age.

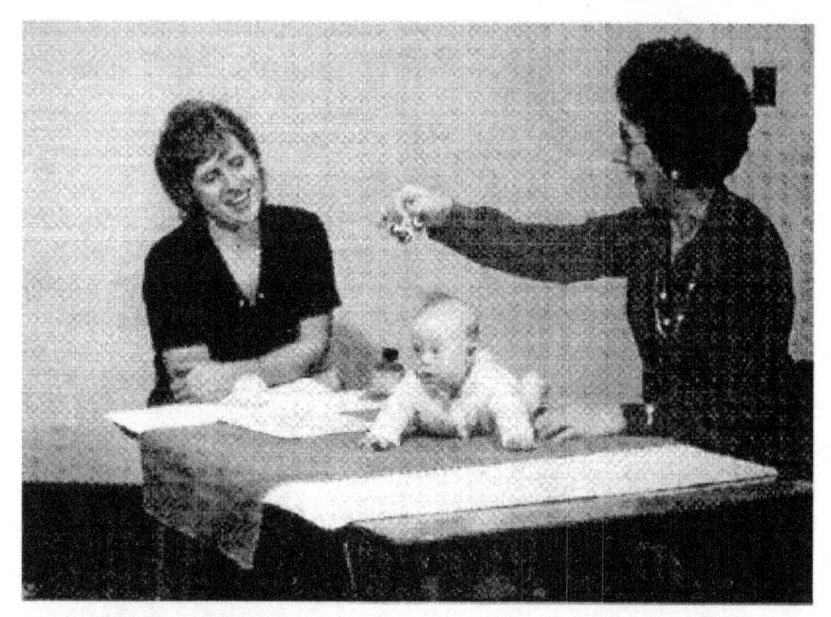

Photo 5.3. Danny is strong enough to raise himself on his arms.

Photo 5.4. Like all Type 2 babies, Danny's legs are weak and unable to bear weight.

Photo 5.5. At 3 months, Kevin, a Type 3 child, has strong legs and is able to stand firmly, with support.

Type 3 is the reverse of Type 2. The legs and lower torso are strong. The legs are sturdy, and the baby is fully able to bear weight on the feet. Any weakness that may be present occurs in the upper torso, the neck, head, shoulders, and arms. This is the baby that will have difficulty pulling to sit, raising up on the arms, and sitting independently. Without intervention and exercise, considerable gross motor delay can be anticipated. With exercise, however, rapid improvement occurs.

Type 4

The fourth type occurs in about 15% to 25% of the cases. This is the infant that is weak all over. Sometimes the arms and legs feel very flaccid, almost jelly- like. Frequently, it is found that these babies have a heart defect in addition to being born with DS. This is, of course, very disheartening and frightening to the parents. However, with the aid of current advances in medical technology and more enlightened attitudes on the part of physicians, heart defects are rarely as life- or health-threatening as they were in the past. As soon as a suspected problem is diagnosed by a pediatric cardiologist, usually at birth or in early infancy, parents can expect prompt medical intervention. Some defects must be repaired surgically; a number of other heart problems are treated with drugs. In any case, once normal heart function is restored, there is a marked spurt in the child's physical growth and general well-being. Our experience has shown that young children with repaired heart defects responded exceedingly well to physical exercises and other aspects of the program. They ate better, gained weight, and became more physically active and mentally alert. To learn more about congenital heart defects and treatment options, you may wish to refer to Van Dyke, Matheis, Eberly, and Williams (1995).

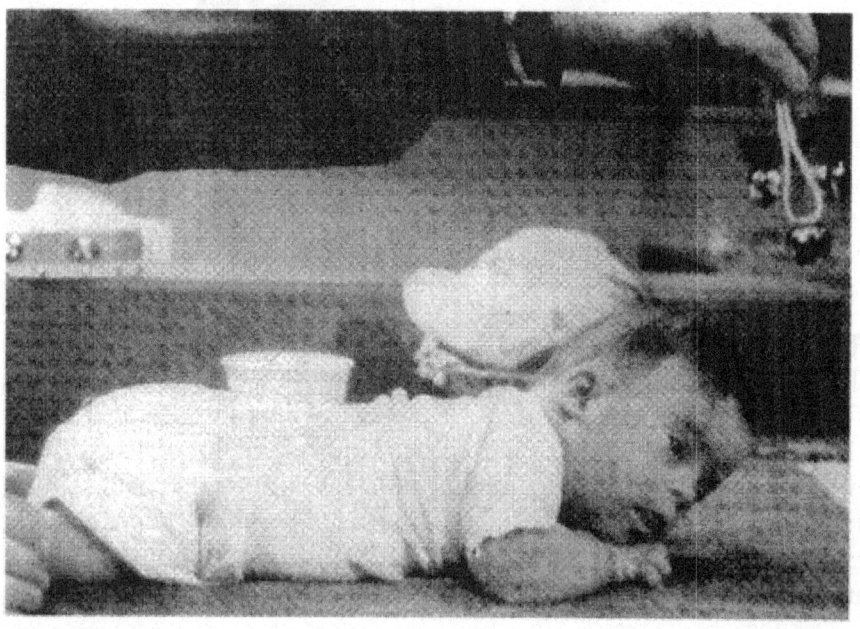

Photo 5.6. Weak in his upper body, Kevin is unable to raise his head and shoulders.

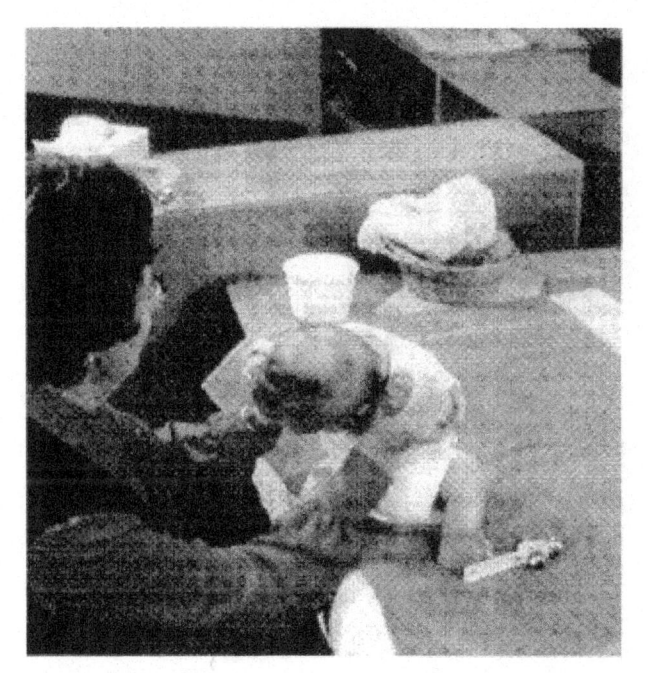

Photo 5.7. In a sitting position, Kevin slumps forward.

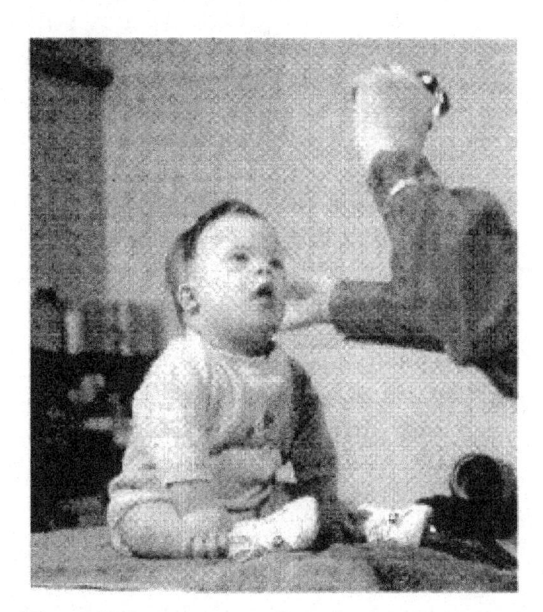

Photo 5.8. By 6 months of age, Kevin has overcome his upper body weakness and is able to sit independently.

Photo 5.9. At 12 months Kevin is ready to walk, with minor support.

Whether or not you are able to identify your baby's type of physical development as 1, 2, 3, or 4, it is still very important to begin a program as soon after birth as possible. In the past, we began seeing a baby at 5 weeks of age. Later, we encouraged parents to come to the Experimental Education Unit as soon as they were physically able to do so. The same is true of other early intervention centers. Contrary to what some people may think, there is a great deal that a newborn baby can do, and a great deal that the baby must learn during the first few weeks of life.

How Behavior Is Learned

How is it that a baby, a child, or any one of us learns new skills or behaviors? Basically, we learn from our successes and failures. Actions that result in success or the attainment of a desired goal—the fun of playing with a new rattle, the feeling of accomplishment and a mother's praise when a toddler successfully pulls on a pair of socks, or the quick relinquishment of an attractive toy by another child when he hits—quickly teach the child which behaviors guarantee success. As a result, there is a probability that these behaviors will be repeated until they become learned skills-actions which are per- formed easily and routinely. In the same way, a child, an adult, or an animal discovers which actions result in failure, or in an unpleasant or undesirable consequence, and learns that these behaviors should be avoided.

Toddlers who are never encouraged to dress themselves, whose parents become impatient because the children are not doing it "right" or are taking too much time, may cease all attempts at self-dressing. When hitting another child results in the toy being removed, or if screaming for a cookie never produces the desired treat, a toddler soon learns that such actions are unproductive. According to the principles of behavior, unsuccessful actions are less likely to be repeated and, as a consequence, will become "unlearned," or never acquired.

All behaviors are governed by these laws. The proper use of these principles, which ensures that a child experiences success when he or she engages in appropriate behaviors and failure when he or she does not, has given us a dependable technique for teaching the child who was thought to be unreachable. The "hopelessly retarded," unresponsive, low-functioning individual, especially in the case of DS, is becoming a notion of the past. We now have the techniques and the means by which to motivate these children to sit, walk, feed themselves, brush their teeth, dress themselves, use a toilet, say words, read, count, and write.

These are the principles on which the program at the Experimental Education Unit at the University of Washington was built. The exercises delineated in the following chapters have been developed in conjunction with the DS program at the university. Those listed incorporate these principles and are meant to introduce readers to simple, effective exercises that can safely enhance development, especially when no other professional help is available.

6. Gross Motor Development: Birth to 3 Months

From observation and locomotor scales developed by physical therapists and developmental psychologists, we know that during the first 3 months of life, babies are expected to achieve the skills listed in Table A.1 in Appendix A. From this list, it should be evident that even at an early age, there are many physical things that a baby is capable of doing, and there are many ways of helping a baby acquire these skills if the baby is delayed in his or her development (Winders, 1997). The following exercises will help your baby attain these abilities and prepare for new skills that should be displayed by 6 months of age.

Record of physical development. Before you begin your baby's program, review the list of skills in Table A.1 in Appendix A and check off the items that your baby can already perform with mastery. With mastery means the skill is something that you routinely observe your baby doing spontaneously and independently. For example, each skill that you check off as mastered must occur at least three times out of five tries, and for at least 3 consecutive days.

Behaviors that occur now and then, or that you have seen your baby do only once or twice, are considered emerging skills, and should be checked off as such. Skills or behaviors that your baby is not yet able to perform are checked off as program objectives.

Thereafter, whenever a new skill emerges or is mastered, check it off and date it. In this way you will have a permanent record of your baby's progress. Do not overlook your child's fine motor/cognitive program. The two programs, gross motor exercises and fine motor training, must be carried out concurrently. (See Chapter 10 for fine motor/cognitive activities.)

Lying-on-the-Back Exercises

GOALS: To develop leg muscles and to learn to push against your hand.

Leg Pushes

Place baby on his or her back. Take hold of one of the baby's legs and gently but firmly raise it, knee bent, to the baby's chest. Then, rest your hands against the bottom of the foot. Push with a light pumping rhythm against the sole of the foot. Encourage the baby to tense his or her leg muscles and push back. Praise the baby and hold that position until the baby relaxes. Rest and repeat the exercise, alternating legs. Do this five times. Be sure that the legs move straight forward and not to the side. This is important for proper hip alignment.

Kicking

GOAL: To learn to kick spontaneously, exercising the back, abdomen, and leg muscles. Play with the baby, moving his or her legs in a kicking motion, up and down, with knees bent, as well as straight.

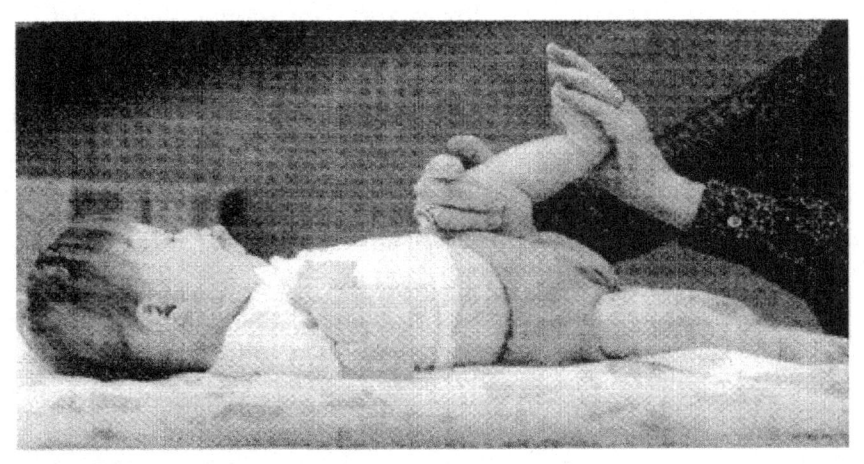

Photo 6.1. Leg pushes.

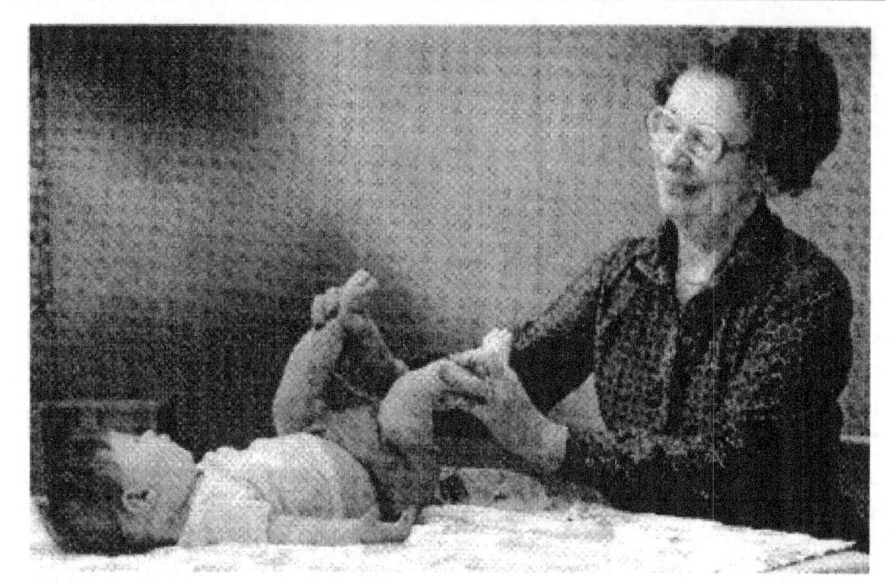

Photo 6.2. Kicking.

Pull-to-Sit Exercises

GOAL: To develop back, shoulder, and neck muscles, enabling the baby to come up to a sitting position by pulling on your hands with no active help from you. Take hold of the baby's hands and wrists. Say, "Up," and then gently and very slowly pull the baby to a sitting position. Say, "Down," and lower the baby down again, just as slowly. Don't let the baby's head drop suddenly or bump. Do five or six repetitions. Doing the movements slowly encourages the baby to use his or her muscles. First, the baby makes an attempt to pull against you as he or she comes up, and then the baby pushes against you, resisting the backward movement as he or she is lowered again.

Be sure that the baby has enough strength to bring his head forward, chin down, as he or she is raised off the mat. Be equally sure that as the baby pulls upward, he or she is using the abdominal muscles correctly. This means that the abdomen is tightened and pulled inward toward the back.

If the baby's head drops backward and remains in that position, or the baby arches the back, protruding the abdomen, he or she is not doing the exercise correctly. To correct the arched back, try holding the baby's hands with one hand, and place your other hand on the abdomen to give support as the baby pulls to sit. If problems continue, your baby may need to begin with a modified program of pull-to-sit exercises. These are described in the next paragraph.

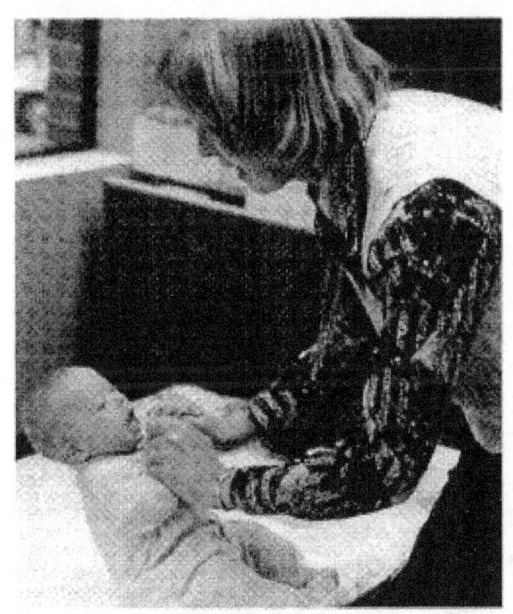

Photo 6.3. Pull to sit with no shoulder support.

Modified Pull-to-Sit Exercises

Babies who are weak may not have sufficient head control to perform the pre- ceding exercise. The task is too difficult. Their heads fall backward, and they are unable to assist in the process of coming to sit. More support is necessary. To accomplish the pull-to-sit exercise, the baby is brought forward to an upright position from his shoulders. Instead of holding your baby's hands and wrists, place your hands on his or her shoulders, slightly rotate the shoulders forward and inward toward the chest, and bring the baby to sit- ting. In this version of the pull-to-sit exercise, the baby has to exert less effort. This is a good beginning exercise for a very young or weak baby.

The same goal can be achieved in another way. As you grasp the baby's shoulders, turn him or her slightly to one side. The baby then comes to sitting not directly face up, but with the head and trunk turned to one side. Halfway through the process, as the baby is raised, the trunk and shoulders can be realigned so that the baby is again looking straight ahead.

The best way to experience these two exercises is to try them out yourself. Lie flat on your back on the floor, legs extended, arms stretched out along your sides. Now, come to sitting, upright, facing straight ahead, without using your arms in any way. You may find that this is fairly difficult to do.

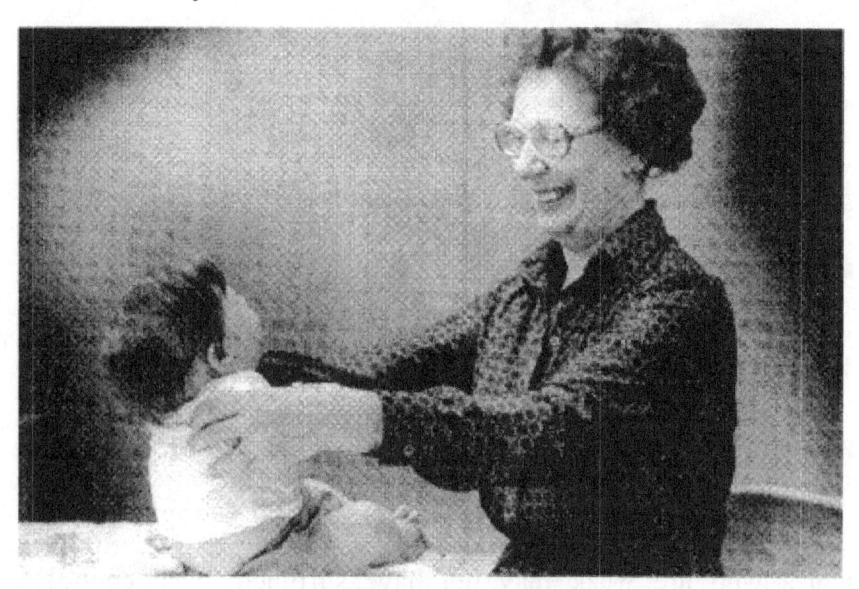

Photo 6.4. Pull to sit with shoulder and back support.

Now try the same exercise by rotating your body to the side as you force yourself into a sitting position. You may find that rotating your trunk helps you to do the task more smoothly.

Simultaneous Arm and Hand Exercises

GOALS: To develop neck, shoulder and arm muscles, to expand the rib cage, to encourage the child to bring hands together across the chest.

Let baby grasp your fingers, or narrow rubber rings or bracelets if he or she is unable to hold your finger. Cover the baby's fist with your hand for a firmer grip. Move the baby's arms rhythmically and slowly up and over the baby's head and down. Extend the baby's arms sideways and bring them together across the baby's chest. Do the whole series five times, rest, and repeat.

Talk to the baby as you work saying, "Up, down, out, together." Smile and praise the baby. As you extend the baby's arms, make gentle tugging motions, encouraging the baby to pull against you in order to maximize muscle tension and flexure.

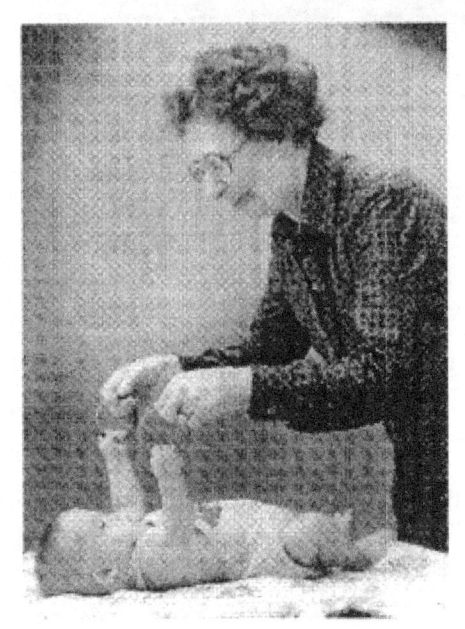

Photo 6.5. Ring grasping, using bracelets.

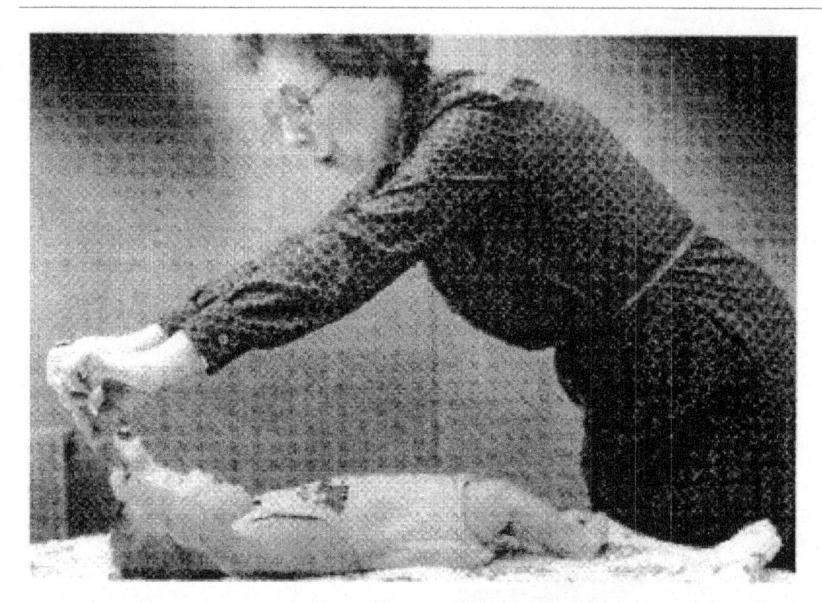

Photo 6.6. Arms up, using bracelets.

Exercises Lying Face Down

Place baby face down. Be sure that the baby's arms and hands are resting comfortably in front of him or her between the chest and chin. Proper placement of the arms facilitates head raising.

Head Lifting

GOAL: To develop the neck, back, and arm muscles, enabling the baby to raise the head and torso unaided, and to ultimately hold this position for several minutes at a time. Shake a bell or a rattle above the baby's head. If the baby doesn't lift his or her head, help the baby to do so by raising his or her chin with your hand. Say, "Look." Repeat five times. At first, a baby may not be able to hold his or her head up for more than 2 or 3 seconds. As the baby gains in strength, he or she will be able to maintain the position for several minutes.

Push-ups

Shake a bell or a rattle above the baby's head. If the baby is able to lift his or her head, but doesn't push up on the elbows or hands, place your hand under

Photo 6.7. Head up, elbows bent.

Children with Down Syndrome the baby's rib cage and gently push upward until the baby is resting on his or her elbows. Lower the baby down and repeat five times.

Head Lifting Using a Bolster

Head lifting can be achieved by placing the baby over a rolled towel or a bolster that is about 3 or 4 inches in diameter. Place the baby over the roll so that it supports the baby under the arms and chest. Encourage the baby to extend his or her arms forward over the bolster and, at the same time, to raise his or her head. Make sure that the bolster fits comfortably under the baby's arms, and that the baby is able to lift his or her head, if only for a few seconds at a time. If the baby cries, falls forward over the roll, or seems completely unable to lift his or her head, the roll may be too high for the baby and the diameter of the roll should be made smaller.

At first, allow the baby to remain on the bolster for only 1 or 2 minutes at a time. Small babies tire easily, and you don't want to place your baby in a position where the baby is too tired to lift his or her head, however briefly. Later, as the baby gains strength, you may increase the time on the bolster to 5 or even 10 minutes, or for as long as the baby is able to keep his or her head up and appears content. Make this exercise interesting by placing a mirror in front of the baby, as well as a mobile or toys.

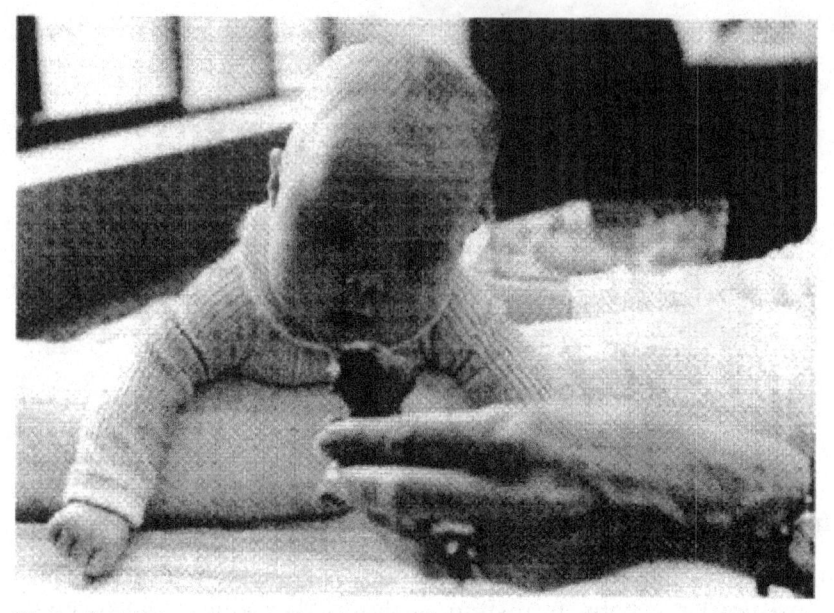

Photo 6.8. Head up prone, using a bolster.

7. Gross Motor Development: 3 to 6 Months

This next trimester of your baby's life is a period of transition, bringing your baby into the second key stage of growth. During this period, the baby progresses from an entirely horizontal period of development to one of upper trunk control and independent sitting.

In order to traverse this transitional period successfully, your baby must first master all of the initial gross motor skills that were listed in the preceding chapter. Your baby must also acquire a number of new skills (see Table A.2, Appendix A).

Remember, however, that physical development and learning are not subject to strict timetables. Each individual, with or without disabilities, has his or her own inner schedule and level of ability for learning and development. You may realistically expect to find that in some areas your baby will progress more rapidly than anticipated, and in some areas he or she may progress more slowly. If this occurs, note the strengths and weaknesses in your baby's development, but do not be unduly concerned.

The important thing is to adhere to the suggested sequence for physical growth. Keep in mind that each time you help your child attain a prerequisite skill, you are paving the way toward the attainment of new goals. These skills for the 3-to-6-month old baby, are listed in Table A.2.

Record of physical development. Before you begin your baby's pro- gram, review the list of skills in Table A.2 and check off the items that your baby can already perform with mastery. At the same time, check off emerging skills as well as new program objectives. Thereafter, whenever a new skill emerges or is mastered, remember to check it off and date it. In this way you will have a continuing record of your baby's progress. Do not overlook your child's fine motor/cognitive program. Monitor and record progress in fine motor training concurrently with gross motor development.

Learning To Sit

GOAL: To develop back, shoulder, and neck control, enabling the baby to sit with a straight back and steady head with minimal support.

Bring the baby to a sitting position and hold the baby in this position for at least a minute, or as long as you and the baby are comfortable. Give support by placing your hands under the baby's arms, thumbs facing the baby's chest, palms and fingers of your hands resting on the baby's back. If it is necessary to prevent the baby's head from falling backward, extend your fingers upward, bracing them against the baby's neck. This exercise can begin very early in the baby's life, at about 1month of age, provided you give enough sup- port to the neck and back.

If the baby is still too young or too weak to maintain an absolutely vertical position, even with support, move your arms backward slightly, allowing the baby to sit upright with a slight backward incline of about 75 degrees. During this exercise, speak to the baby, making direct eye contact. This will not only serve to develop social attentiveness, but will also encourage the baby to hold his or her head up in a midline position.

Photo 7.1. Learning to sit.

At the end of 1minute, or as soon as the baby appears tired and his or her head begins to wobble, lower your arms, permitting the baby to lie down again. Take a brief 15- to 30-second rest. Repeat the exercise three to five times.

Rolling Over from Back to Stomach

GOAL: To become progressively more successful in completing and eventually initiating the roll, and bringing the arms forward during the roll. Place the baby on his or her back. To help the baby roll over to the stomach, hold one of the baby's legs, bending it slightly at the knee, and bring it forward across the other extended leg in the direction that the baby will turn. Allow the baby to complete independently as much of the roll as he or she can. Be sure that the baby's arms are placed in such a way that he or she can bring them forward under the chin as the roll is completed. Repeat the exercise, leading with one leg and then the other. Be gentle; don't rush or force the movements.

The best way to learn how to do this exercise properly is to do it yourself. Lie on your back, swing one leg, bent at the knee, over your other leg and roll over to your stomach. Note that your arms will end up tucked under your chin and that the whole movement can be accomplished in one easy motion.

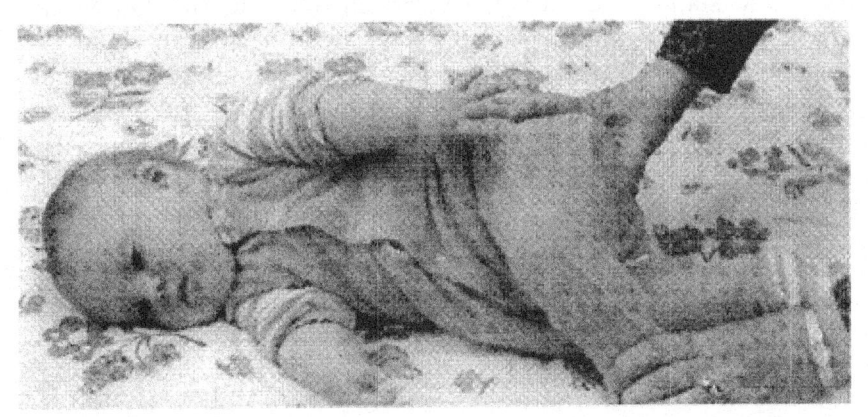

Photo 7.2. Rolling from back to stomach. The first step: the baby is placed on the side and the outside leg is flexed.

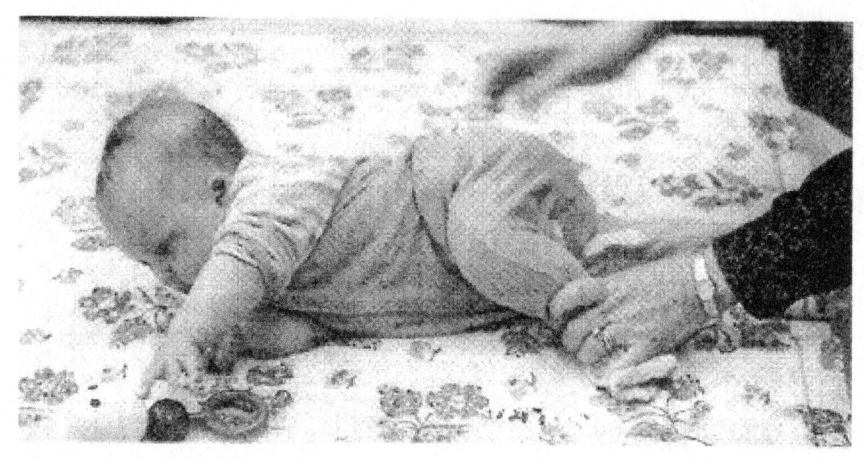

Photo 7.3. The baby continues the roll by extending the outside arm in the direction of the roll.

Bearing Weight

GOAL: To hold a weight-bearing stance (with support) for 1 minute.

Some babies as young as 2 or 3 months of age appear very eager to stand and will place their feet firmly on a table or floor as soon as they are brought to an upright position. Some babies will, in fact, struggle to stand up even when you want them to sit. Others may behave quite differently. These babies, for one reason or another, will not place their feet on a surface in a weight- bearing stance when held upright. In some cases, their legs buckle at the knees. In other instances, they will draw up their legs or curl their toes to avoid standing. Nevertheless, weight-bearing is an important skill that should develop between 3 and 7 months of age, and it should be encouraged.

Photo 7.4. The baby completes the roll and raises the body on extended arms.

To help your child develop weight-bearing, try the following procedure. Stand at a waist-high table or counter. Hold the baby in such a way that the baby is facing away from you, with his or her back against your chest. Use one arm to support the baby around the chest and under the arms. With your other arm and hand, guide the baby's legs down until the feet are able to touch the surface of the table or counter. Press the baby's feet down on the table by keeping his or her knees straight with your free arm and hand. Press the rest of the baby's body securely against your own body. Give a great deal of support. Keep the baby's back and legs straight. Hold for a count of ten. After a brief rest (30 to 60 seconds), repeat the exercise. This can be repeated two or three times a day at your convenience.

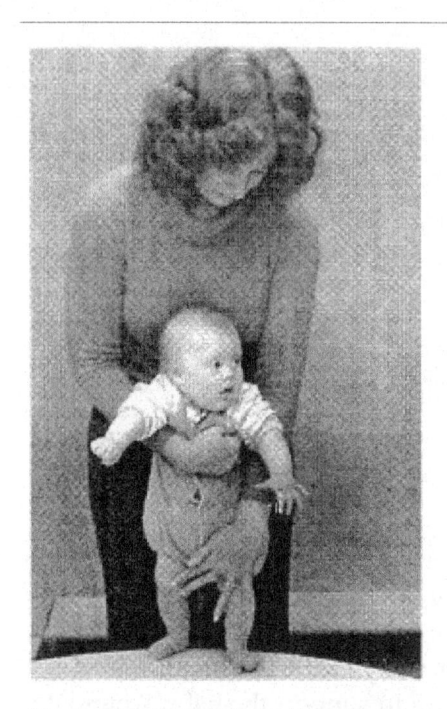

Photo 7.5. Beginning weight-bearing requires substantial adult support.

Scooting

GOAL: To brace against a hand and lunge forward toward a toy, extending the arms, back, and hips, while straightening the legs. Typically, a baby learns to scoot forward and backward very early in life. The mother first becomes aware of this activity when she suddenly discovers that the baby has moved himself to the other end of the crib without any assistance from her. Many babies with DS accomplish this feat without special instruction. However, it is sometimes helpful to give these children additional practice. Scooting is a very beneficial gross motor activity. It strengthens the whole body and provides the baby with mobility that enables him or her to reach for toys and other interesting things in the environment.

Before you begin, be sure that your baby has already developed good back and neck control, that your baby can pull to sit readily without head lag, and that when placed on the stomach, your baby is able to support the upper body on his or her elbows, with head and chest raised off the bed. If your baby can meet these requirements, you can proceed.

Select a firm (but not hard), flat, smooth, and fairly large surface. A mat- tress pad placed over a dining table or over a rug on the floor can serve nicely. Place the baby on his or her stomach, and bring the baby's arms (hands touching and elbows bent) forward in front of his or her chin. Place an enticing toy just out of reach. Stand or kneel in back of the baby. Gently bend the baby's legs at the knees and tuck them under the baby's hips, raising the hips. Keep the legs close together and tucked under by bracing the soles of the baby's feet with your hand. Give support with a steady pushing motion. The baby will brace against your hand and lunge forward toward the toy, extending the arms, back, and hips and straightening the legs. Be sure that the baby does the scooting forward. If you push too hard, the baby will simply fall forward on his or her nose. If the movement is done correctly, the baby will progress forward, keeping the head up, and moving the arms ahead as he or she scoots. In the beginning, the baby may forget to move his or her arms for- ward, and they will be pinned under the chest. So it may be necessary to realign the baby's arms after each lunge.

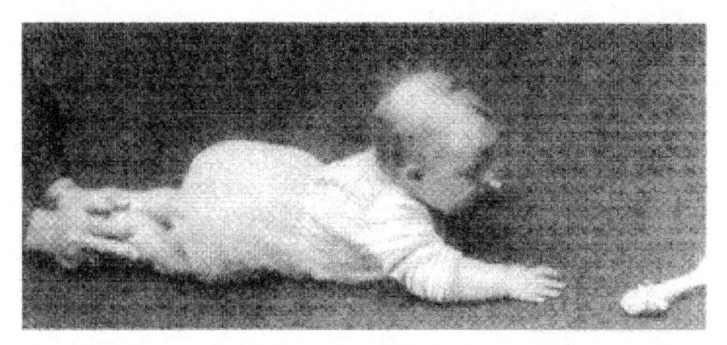

Photo 7.6. Baby is taught to scoot foward and reach for a toy.

Once you and the baby get the system going, the baby may make four or five scoots in a row, so give yourself plenty of room for these maneuvers. If you are working on a table, don't let your baby scoot off the edge!

Propped Sitting

GOAL: To develop balance and back, neck, and head control; to enable the child to sit with less and less reliance on cushions and couch for support.

Between 4 and 6 months of age, you can begin placing your baby in the corner of a couch or overstuffed chair for propped sitting. Tuck the baby comfortably into the corner of the furniture, supported securely with pillows so that the baby does not fall over. Let the baby remain seated from 1to 5 minutes at a time. Extend the time to as much as half an hour as the baby's back and neck gain strength and the baby is able to sit for a longer period without falling to the side or sagging forward. This is a very helpful exercise, especially for children that appear to be slow in acquiring the physical control necessary for independent sitting that should be achieved between 6 and 8 months of age. For the child that needs intensive practice in propped sitting and is still unable to maintain this position for more than 1or 2 minutes at a time, plan to repeat the exercise several times a day, increasing the total minutes to about 30 minutes per day.

Therapy-Ball Exercises

A large, sturdy beach ball that is from 24 to 36 inches high is a desirable, but not essential, piece of equipment. If you can obtain one without too much trouble and expense, it can be used to augment the gross motor program in many ways. Usually parents and children enjoy the therapy-ball exercise. However, when you first place your baby on the ball, make sure that he or she feels comfortable and secure, and not frightened.

Basically the benefits that a baby derives from the ball activities result from the physical sensations that the baby experiences when the ball is gently rocked or bounced, and from the spontaneous adjustments that the baby's body makes in response to these movements. These spontaneous adjustments develop a sense of balance and can also help to build muscle tone.

If your baby attends a program where he or she receives regular physical therapy, the therapist may outline additional exercises for you to follow at home. However, even without this kind of close supervision, there are many activities you and your baby can enjoy together.

GOAL: To tolerate increased therapy-ball exercise, learning to maintain balance, and head and trunk control.

Between 3 and 6 months of age, you can begin placing the baby on a therapy ball. If the baby is weak and has not yet developed good head control, limit your exercises to very gentle rocking and bouncing motions.

Place the baby on his or her back or stomach on the ball. Hold the baby securely and slowly roll the ball back and forth and from side to side. At first, limit the movements to three or four in each direction. With the baby lying on his or her back or stomach, you can also try light bouncing. About eight bounces in each position should be enough when starting therapy-ball exercises.

If at any time you notice that the baby's head or body is jiggling helplessly, or if the baby begins to cry, you are probably rocking or bouncing too vigorously. Smoothness, slowness, and gentleness are key at this stage.

Photo 7.7. Sitting on a therapy ball.

When the baby is older and stronger and is beginning to sit successfully in a propped position, you can repeat the same rocking and bouncing exercises with the baby sitting on the ball. Hold the baby at the hips, but be sure that the baby has enough control to keep his or her back straight and head steady, especially when you are bouncing the ball. Again, if you notice that the baby appears to be bouncing around helplessly, head nodding and jerking, you are performing the exercises too vigorously. Remember to gear your actions to the baby's ability to adjust his or her body to the motion, and thus remain in control.

In later sections of this book, other more vigorous, therapy-ball exercises will be described.

8. Gross Motor Development: 6 to 12 Months

The preceding section described exercises for accelerating a baby's physical development during the horizontal period, when the main portion of the baby's activities take place lying on the back or stomach. These exercises stressed the achievement of head and neck control, back, arm, and leg strengthening, as well as the muscle coordination necessary in rolling over and scooting forward. In helping a baby achieve these skills, we were looking forward to the next period of growth, when the major portion of the baby's activities should occur in an upright sitting position.

The basic skills that the baby must acquire within the next 6 months of his life are listed in Table A.3 in Appendix A.

Record of physical development. Before you begin your baby's program, review the list of skills in Table A.3 and check off the items that your baby can already perform with mastery. Check off the items that are program objectives and emerging skills, and note the dates in order to maintain a good record of your baby's progress.

The exercises in this chapter will help your baby meet the following important objectives: to sit independently, to change positions from lying down to sitting and from sitting to lying down, and to creep, scoot, or crawl.

Self-Supported Sitting

GOAL: To develop independent self-supported sitting. Baby will be able to maintain this position for 3 to 5 minutes without falling, progressing from a forward inclined back (45 degree angle) to a vertical back (90 degree angle).

Between 6 and 7 months of age, and sometimes sooner, you may find that your baby can now sit on the changing table or on the floor with very little help. If you find that holding your baby lightly at the hip level is sufficient to prevent the baby tipping to the side or falling over, you should begin self-supported sitting exercises. (If your baby isn't ready for this step, for health or other reasons, do not be concerned. Continue working on the exercises in the preceding chapters.)

The goal for self-supported sitting is to teach your baby how to sit with- out adult help, by bracing the body with his or her arms. A normal baby learns self-supported sitting by bending forward and placing his or her extended arms on the floor between the legs. A baby with DS is also able to do this, but not as efficiently. The problem that is often encountered is that in bringing the hands forward to rest on the floor, the baby with DS may lean so far forward that his or her chest is practically resting on the knees.

This, obviously, is not the best position for upright sitting. To avoid this position, teach your baby to place his or her hands on the thighs or knees for support, rather than on the floor. This will enable the baby to maintain a more upright position. Look at your child's posture while he or she is sitting. It should resemble a triangle and not an arc over an angle (see Figure 8.1). To encourage an upright head and straight back, hold an interesting toy in front of your baby, slightly above the baby's eye level so the baby must raise his or her head. Raising the head also facilitates straightening the back.

To teach self-supported sitting, kneel or sit in back of your baby. Seat him or her between your legs; this will free your hands and at the same time give the baby the support that may still be necessary. Use your hands to place the baby's extended arms on his or her knees, and brace the baby in this position, holding the baby's hands pressed down against his or her legs. If the baby slumps forward, bring the baby's shoulders back, straightening the baby's back and moving his or her arms to a point where the baby can obtain the best balance. See that the baby maintains a posture that most closely approximates the recommended sitting position. If you are working alone, sitting in front of a mirror or in front of a dangling toy or mobile may encourage the baby to keep his or her head up. Have the baby hold the braced position, with your help if necessary, for a minute or longer. Repeat three to five times in succession. While your baby is perfecting this skill, prevent him or her from getting hurt when falling over by surrounding the baby with good-sized pillows.

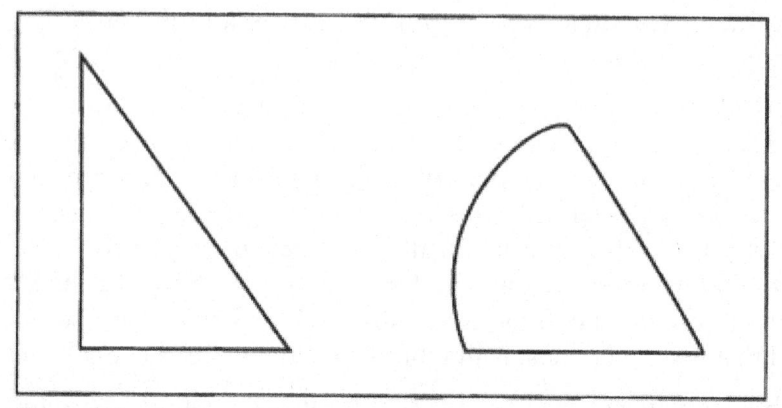

Figure 8.1. A seated child's posture should resemble a triangle rather than an arc, or curve.

Protective Extensions and Righting Reactions

At about the time that you begin training your baby for self-supported sitting, and in preparation for completely independent sitting, it is important to pro- vide practice in what are known as "protective extensions, righting reactions" and "trunk rotation."

Protective extensions and righting reactions are the reflex reactions that develop in conjunction with the maturation of the nervous system. These are the spontaneous movements that one makes with one's arms and body to pre- vent falling. Normally, as a baby learns to sit independently, it can be observed that if tipped forward or to the side, the baby will automatically put out an arm to prevent falling over or the baby may curve the body away from the direction in which he or she is tipped in order to retain balance.

Trunk rotation refers to a baby's ability to turn the body sideways and to look back over the shoulder without losing balance. A baby should be able to rotate the body in this manner, regardless of whether the baby is sitting, standing, or crawling.

Babies with DS appear to have some difficulty in acquiring these movements without prior training. The following exercises are aimed at developing these skills and other equally important advanced gross motor behaviors.

Protective Extension to the Side

GOAL: To extend an arm to the floor without help.

Sit or kneel behind the baby and seat the baby between your legs. With one hand, tip the baby to the side; with your other hand extend one of the baby's arms in the same direction that he or she is leaning until the baby is supporting his or her body with an arm extended and the palm flat on the floor. Encourage your baby to push his or her body back up into an upright sitting position. Repeat, tipping the baby to the other side. Repeat the exercise three to five times to each side every day.

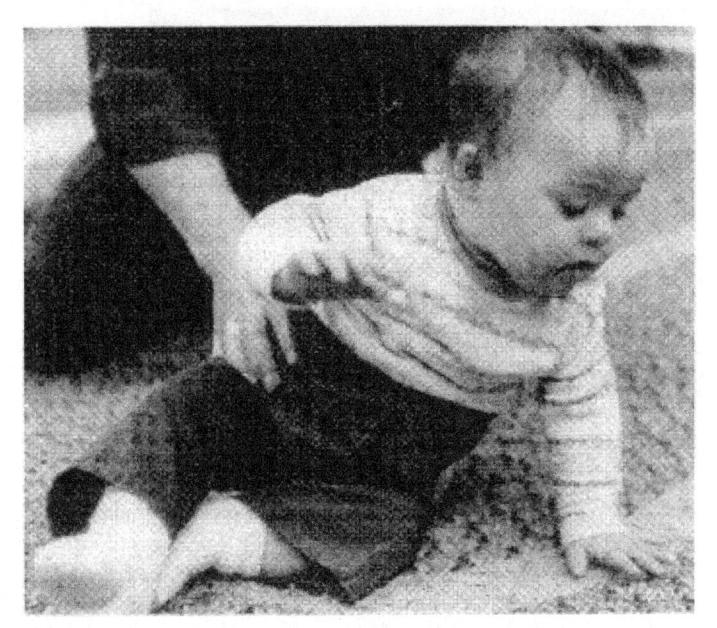

Photo 8.1. Protective extension to the side.

Forward Protective Extension

There are basic exercises to help your baby develop a forward protective extension: the wheelbarrow, the seated forward extension, and therapy-ball exercises.

Wheelbarrow

GOAL: To keep a strong back, head raised, and arms braced.

The wheelbarrow exercise can be started when the baby is about 6 months of age. The exercise develops forward protective extension and strengthens the back. To perform the exercise tip the baby forward. Encourage the baby to brace his or her hands on the floor, palms down, while you lift the baby's legs at a 45 degree angle. Support the baby at the chest, waist, and thighs. As the baby becomes stronger, reduce the support to the torso, limiting the support to the legs only.

Therapy-Ban Forward Extension

GOAL: To immediately thrust arms forward in a protective extension at any sudden forward rotation of the ball.

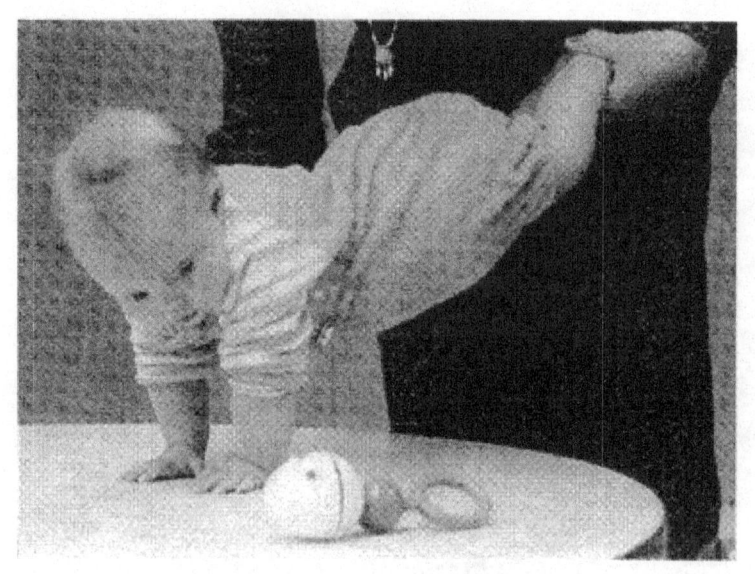

Photo 8.2. Wheelbarrow.

Lay the baby face down on the ball. Place yourself in back of the baby, and hold the baby securely by the legs. Gently rotate the ball forward, until the baby is able to reach the floor with his or her hands. At first, the baby may want to cling to the ball with his or her hands. There may be a greater tendency to do this if the baby is not used to being on the ball, or if you rotate the ball too quickly.

If the baby appears frightened, or refuses to extend the arms, place something enticing on the floor in front of the ball, and then rotate the ball forward by degrees, allowing the baby to become adjusted to each shift of position. Once babies learn what to expect, they usually enjoy this exercise, and then you can gradually increase the suddenness with which you tilt the ball forward.

Righting Reactions: Front, Side, and Back

GOAL: To develop righting reactions necessary for walking and over- all gross motor development.

Sit on a Chair

Seat the baby on your knees, away from your body. Give support by holding the baby at his or her hips. Now tilt the baby forward, to one side and then the other, and back. As the baby is tilted, he or she will try to keep the head up in a straight line. In order to do this, the baby's body will curve in at the waist, away from the direction of the tilt. For example, if the baby is tilted to your left, the baby's body will curve like the letter "C." When tilted to the right, the baby's body will curve in a reversed "C." Physical therapists call this reaction the "C Curve."

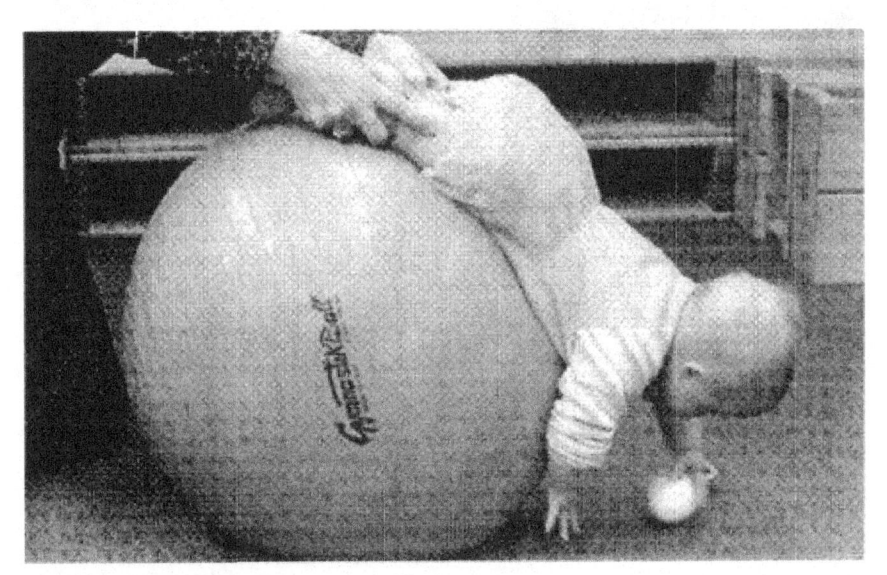

Photo 8.3. Therapy-ball forward extension.

Therapy-Ball Righting-Reaction Exercise

Seat the baby on a therapy ball. Stand in front or in back of the baby, holding the baby at his or her hips. Slowly tilt the baby forward, backward, and to the sides; give the baby time to adjust his or her body into a C curve before you shift position.

Trunk Rotation

GOAL: To rotate the trunk to look at or reach for objects that are behind the body without losing balance.

When your baby is sitting, standing, or later, holding a crawl position, encourage the baby to turn at the waist in order to reach for or look at objects that are behind the baby. The presentation of a toy, to the right and left of a baby, several times a day when the baby is sitting, standing, or crawling can aid in developing trunk rotation.

Photo 8.4. Therapy-ball righting reaction: the C curve.

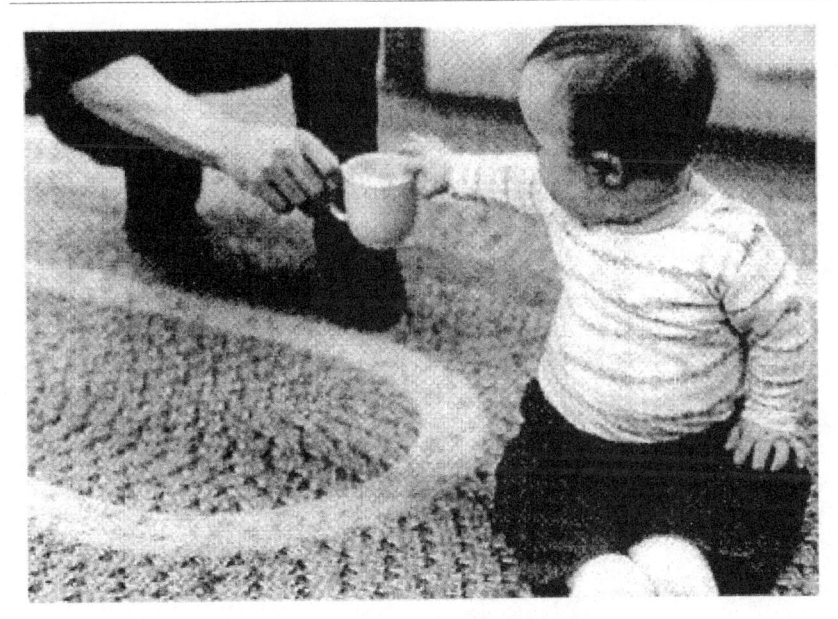

Photo 8.5. Trunk rotation.

Independent Sitting

GOAL: To gain strength, trunk control, and confidence to sit independently without supporting the body with the hands.

It is anticipated that as your child perfects self-supported sitting and acquires the related skills of protective extensions, righting reactions, and trunk rotation, your baby will also be mastering complete independent sitting. Once these prerequisite skills are learned, no particular effort is required to help your baby sit independently with his or her hands free to do other things. Your main goals during this stage of development is to provide your baby with opportunities for sitting for longer periods of time and to observe your baby's ability to maintain a sitting position while you encourage the baby to lift one hand and then both from his or her thighs in order to reach for and hold a toy. Sitting in a highchair also prompts independent sitting. If the baby is seated securely enough, the baby is then free to use his or her hands in other ways, such as handling toys and bringing food to the mouth. It is a good idea to make or acquire a low chair or stool on which your baby can sit with his or her feet flat on the floor. A small, sturdy chair with sides and a back is safer because the baby is less likely to fall off. However, many babies, once they have learned how to sit securely on the floor, have readily progressed to stool sitting with competence. Stool or chair sitting is recommended for babies with DS because it teaches them to place their feet correctly and to bend their knees. Without this kind of practice, children with DS tend to sit cross-legged, tailor fashion, or with widely spread, extended legs, which is also undesirable.

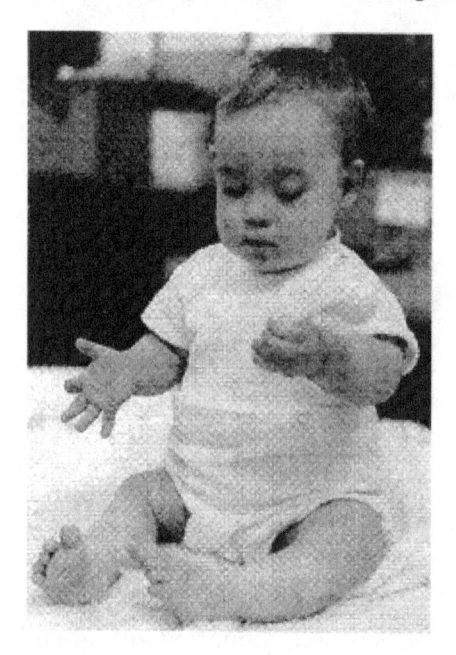

Photo 8.6. Independent sitting.

Other important skills that your baby must attain during this third period of the first year of life are the abilities to hold a crawl position, to come to sitting from a prone posture, and to pull to stand.

Crawl Position

GOAL: To get into a crawl position independently and to hold it from 1 to 5 minutes.

In a crawl position, the baby is on hands and knees, stomach and hips raised off the floor. A baby who has a weak back is unable to assume this pose. Crawling is not as important to future walking as the ability to assume and maintain a crawl position for several minutes at a time. If your baby is not crawling or holding a crawl position, this exercise will help him or her to strengthen the lower back.

To help a baby assume a crawl position, place the baby on his or her knees. Kneel behind the baby, giving support with your knees by locking them on either side of the baby, touching the baby's legs. Place one hand over the baby's thighs, and your second hand over the baby's stomach and diaphragm. Tip the baby forward, teaching the baby to brace himself or her- self with the arms. Continue to support the baby's middle and prevent the baby's legs from straightening. Hold this position for the count of ten, or for as long as possible.

If the baby has not done this before, he or she may fuss and cry at first. Be gentle and encouraging, and be sure that the baby has enough support to feel secure. Sometimes, placing a mirror or favorite toy in front of the baby helps to entertain the baby during the exercise.

This is an exercise that most children with DS find difficult to do, but it is important as a prerequisite to many gross motor skills (e.g., coming to sit from a prone position, learning to stand, walking with properly flexed knees).

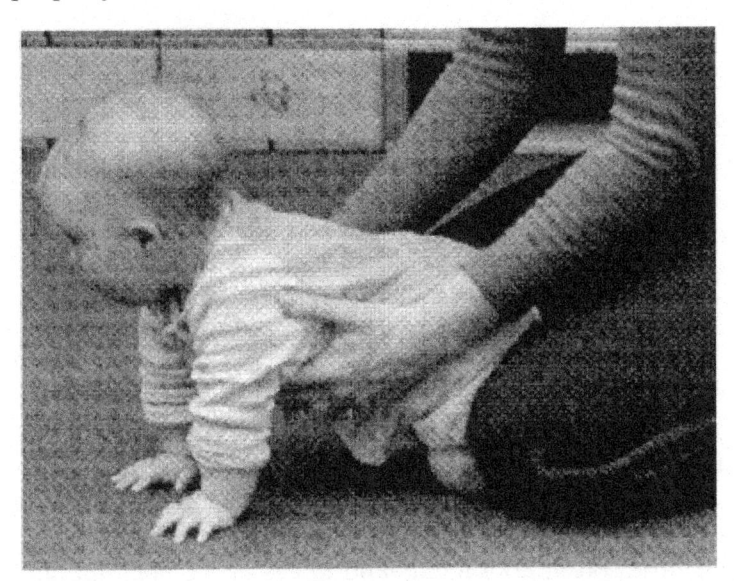

Photo 8.7. Assuming a crawl position with help.

Photo 8.8. Independent crawling.

Prone to Sit

GOAL: To come from a prone position to sitting correctly.

A very important milestone in a child's physical development is reached when he or she learns to push the body up to sitting from a prone, face-down position. Without intervention, many children with DS learn to do this in an extremely awkward and potentially harmful manner, which can result in hip dislocation. They may, for example, pull themselves up to sitting by spreading their legs and swinging them in an arc around their bodies.

Properly, a child or an adult comes to sitting from a prone position by doing what might be called a reverse of the rolling-over movement. The body is shifted to the side, legs are bent at the knees and drawn up, and the arms, in a movement reminiscent of the side-protective extension, push the upper torso into a vertical sitting position. The same sitting posture can be assumed in another way, by progressing from prone to a hands-and-knees crawl position, and from there to sitting by shifting the legs and hips sideways. In order to teach your baby the proper sequence of movements, do it yourself several times. Note carefully where you place your hands and legs and how you shift your body.

If your baby has mastered rolling over, the side and forward protective extensions, sitting without support, and holding a true crawl position independently, he or she will probably learn the correct prone-to-sit progression without your help. If your baby has not attained the necessary prerequisite skills, be prepared to teach him or her how prone to sit should be done once your baby attains the prerequisite skills or begins doing it incorrectly.

Pull to Stand

GOAL: To raise to a standing position with minimum assistance. To pull to stand independently by grasping a low chair or table for support.

Seat the baby on a low stool or box, with his or her feet firmly on the floor and knees flexed. Take the baby's hands and help the baby rise to a standing position by pushing up from his or her feet, knees, and hips. Proper posture and movement are most important; don't pull the baby. Make the baby do most of the work; simply give support. Be sure that the baby stands in a completely erect position, with back and hips in straight alignment. Do not permit the baby to lean forward from the hips, resting on his or her arms for sup- port. Such a posture forces the baby into a locked-kneed position and can indicate a lack of strength in the lower middle back. To strengthen the back, focus on pull-to-sit and crawl position exercises.

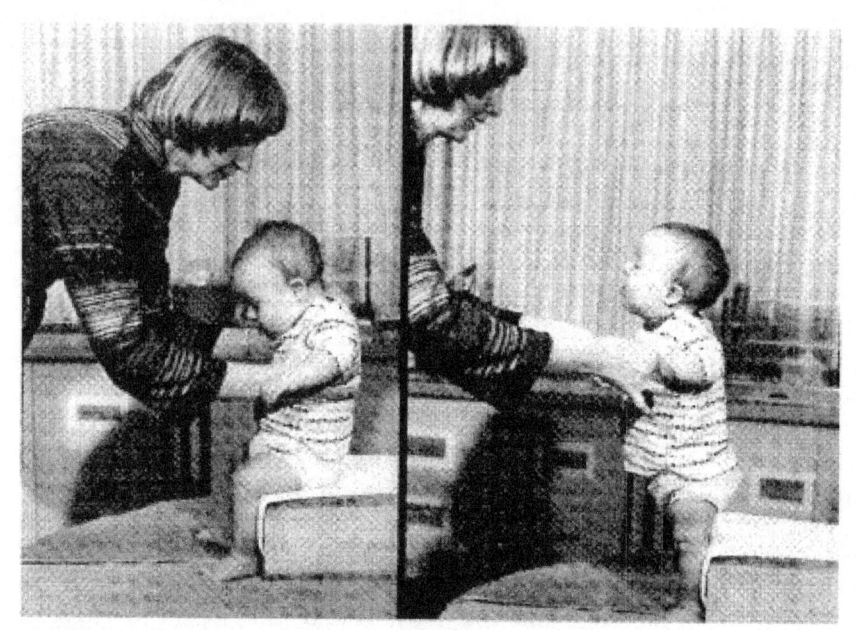

Photo 8.9. Sitting on a stool (left), pull to stand (right).

9. Gross Motor Development: 12 to 24 Months

After children have mastered the physical skills related to the upright sitting position, they are ready to embark on the fourth stage of the gross motor developmental sequence: standing and walking. During this period, the growing child must acquire the skills described in this chapter.

Photo 9.1. Board walking.

Record of physical development. Before you begin your child's program, refer to Table A.4 in Appendix A and review the list of skills, checking off the items that your child can already perform with mastery, as well as emerging skills and program objectives.

Kneeling

GOAL: To kneel while supporting the body against a table or box.

Place the child in a kneeling position as you would in preparation for the crawling exercise. Keep the child in this position, giving only as much support as necessary, for a count of ten or longer. As the child kneels, keep him or her occupied by holding a mirror in front of the child or by placing toys on a low table, box, or stool for the child to look at and touch as he or she is kneeling.

Kneel to Stand

GOAL: To assume a kneeling position, support self with hands, and push and pull self to standing.

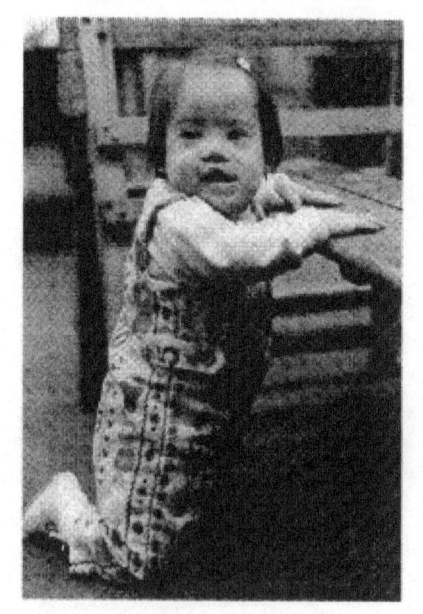

Photo 9.2. Kneeling.

Kneeling is an important preparatory step for kneel to stand. Once a child is able to kneel confidently, you should proceed to this maneuver. To accomplish the movement of kneel to stand, a child must be able to do the following:

1. Kneel with upper thighs and back straight (erect)

2. Take hold of some kind of support such as the edge of a couch, chair, or an adult's arm, leg, or clothing
3. Bring one leg up and place the foot firmly on the floor with knee bent
4. Shift weight to the raised leg and, using it as a lever, push or pull self to a standing position

Generally, if the child has the prerequisite skills of crawling, kneeling, and pulling to stand from sitting, the kneel-to-stand maneuver is quickly learned and rapidly becomes part of the child's spontaneous activity. When the child has achieved these prerequisite skills, the child is able to assume a standing position independently.

Photo 9.3. Kneel to stand.

Standing

GOAL: To stand, without fatigue, at a waist-high table for 5 to 10 minutes.

Many children need several weeks of supported standing before they are ready to begin cruising. Standing is a vital developmental function, not only as a prerequisite for walking, but as an activity that strengthens leg and back muscles and teaches balance, control, and endurance.

In order to encourage standing, let your child stand at a waist-high table to play with toys or to engage in creative activities such as water play, manipulating dough, or finger-painting. When fatigued, a standing child may lean forward, resting the upper torso against the table. This is not desirable. Instead, teach the child to lower his or her body to the floor or a stool when tired, and to pull up again when he or she is ready to resume play.

Photo 9.4. Standing at a cruising board.

Cruising

GOAL: To cruise independently to the right and to the left, using furniture or walls for support.

After a child has learned how to stand comfortably at a table or couch for 10 or 15 minutes, he or she is then ready to begin cruising.

To encourage cruising, simply move the toys slightly out of reach to the right or left. To further encourage the sideways stepping that is involved in cruising, you can physically show your child what movement to make by moving one leg and then the other in the direction of the toy. Think of cruising as a step, slide, step, slide movement. For example, the right leg steps away to the right, and the left leg slides up to the right leg, completing the action.

Walking with Support

GOAL: To walk forward spontaneously with adult support.

A child that is cruising confidently in the house is generally ready to begin forward walking with support. Children who need walking experience should be walked with support at every opportunity at least 5 to 10 steps at a time.

The child with minimal skill can be supported under the arms and elbows. The adult stands behind the child, placing his or her feet on either side of the child's feet. By placing the feet in this manner, the adult can prevent the overly wide gait that is common to young children with DS, and the adult can also encourage forward stepping by nudging the child's foot with her toe if the child doesn't move his or her feet forward independently. Toddlers who are ready for less support can be held by one or both hands. Parents and teachers should be careful not to yank or pull a child's arm over the child's head, especially if the child trips and begins to fall. Children's limbs are fragile and are easily dislocated or broken.

Independent Walking

GOAL: To walk independently with good balance and with no support.

After a child is able to stand alone without any support for at least 30 seconds, he or she is generally ready to begin walking independently. Some children are more cautious than others and may need considerable coaxing to take those first few steps on their own, but developmentally they are ready to do so. A child can be further encouraged to walk independently by having a small chair or a sturdy buggy or cart to push. The buggy or cart should be weighted down with blocks, books, or another child to give it more stability.

Board Walking

GOAL: To walk a board with legs close together, taking forward steps and following a straight line.

At the preschool level, every child in our program was given practice in walking the length of an 8-foot by 8-inch board. Board walking is an excellent exercise, appropriate at all stages of walking. The narrowness of the surface encourages the children to look where they are stepping and to attend to how they are placing their feet. Initially, even the fairly skilled independent walkers may find the board to be a challenge and will be unable to walk its length without some adult help, or without stepping off the edge.

Advanced Exercises

GOALS: To develop self-confidence and motor control, and to learn how to use equipment safely.

Advanced exercises should include practice in walking or crawling up inclined boards, sliding down boards, stepping over obstacles, stepping on or off a block, walking up and down stairs, and climbing ladders.

Exercises with Equipment Walkers

I am inclined to discourage parents from purchasing or using walkers in order to teach a child how to walk, because it may prevent the child from learning a prerequisite skill that they really need, such as cruising. If a walker is used, it is important to observe the child's posture in it. Look for the following:

1. The child must be standing in a straight, upright position.
2. The child must be supporting his or her body only with hands and arms, not by leaning the chest against the walker.
3. The child must be moving the legs in a walking motion, not simply dragging them along in a stiff-legged, locked-kneed manner.
4. Ideally, parents should consult a physical therapist or a knowledgeable, interested doctor before placing their child in a walker.

Photo 9.5. Dennis, the author's first student in the DS program, climbing a ladder.

Jump-up Swings

1. Jump-up swings should be used with caution.

2. Be sure that the child is able to reach the floor with his or her legs, and that when the child reaches the floor he or she is able to bend the knees. Bouncing up and down with stiff legs is most undesirable, especially for children with DS who are prone to poor posture and a stiff-legged, locked-kneed gait.

3. Give adequate back support, possibly with a thin, hard pillow. Don't permit the child to sit with a slumped, rounded back (this is a poor way of trying to develop a strong back and good neck and head control).

4. Use a jump-up swing only 10 to 20 minutes at a time. Make sure that your child is sitting and using it properly; then it can provide useful and enjoyable exercise.

10. Fine Motor/Cognitive Social Development: Birth to 6 Months

Sight and hearing are the two most crucial paths to early learning. Long before a baby can handle objects, sit, walk, or talk, the baby begins using his or her ears and eyes. The baby startles at sudden noises and recognizes his or her own mother's face. Daily the baby practices sharpening the senses. Yet, if these senses are not called upon to function as the baby develops, they will not operate as effectively and efficiently as they could if they are given stimulation. For example, deaf children born with normal intelligence may become developmentally delayed because they can- not hear. Working with a deaf baby to develop the remaining senses helps the child's future development.

Training in both looking and listening is important for developmentally delayed babies, and it is hard to say which causes the other-a baby looking because he or she hears, or hearing because he or she looks. Before a baby learns how to react to sound, he or she has to learn how to focus his or her eyes on objects in the line of vision. This chapter details a set of exercises that can be used with babies, toddlers, or anyone else who lacks these basic skills for learning. However, before you begin the exercises, remember to assess your child using the Record of Fine Motor/Cognitive and Social Development (see Table A.5 in Appendix A).

Exercises for Visual Responsiveness

Making Eye Contact

GOAL: To respond to parents' faces, looking into their eyes and seeking to maintain eye contact when they move out of the immediate line of vision.

Human eye contact is the first step in the development of social aware- ness. Some babies with DS respond better to and will fixate longer on a human face than on a toy. Other babies prefer rattles and similar objects. In either case, parents should make a practice of bringing their faces within 10 or 12 inches of their baby's face and of looking directly into their baby's eyes. Make a game of this activity, smiling and talking softly. Slowly move your head from one side to the other. Encourage the baby to maintain eye contact by moving his or her head in the same direction.

Stationary Suspended Objects

GOAL: To fixate on an object for 30 seconds.

Place the baby on his or her back. Hold a suspended object-a wide red bracelet dangling from a string is a good choice-in the baby's line of vision, and attract the baby's attention by tapping or shaking the toy and saying, "look," until eye contact is made. Smile and praise your baby when he or she looks. Repeat five times. Hold all objects for this exercise, and for the ones that follow, approximately 15 inches from the baby.

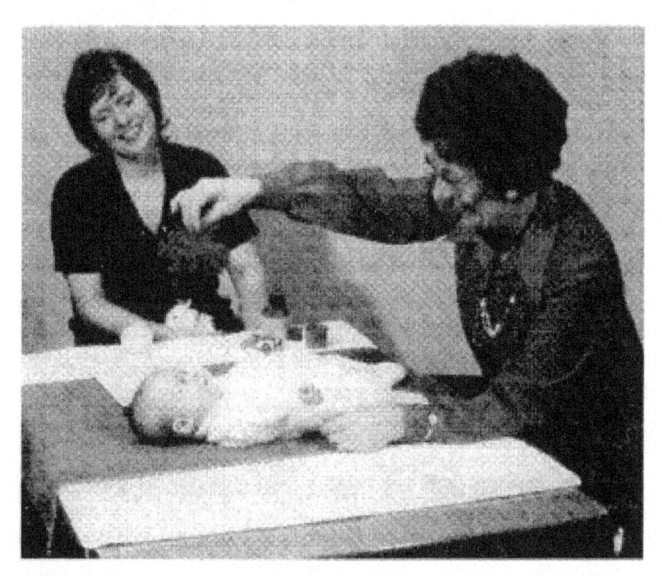

Photo 10.1. Fixating on an object at midline.

Moving Suspended Objects

GOAL: To fixate on and follow moving objects, first with only the eyes and later by turning the head and body.

After the baby has learned to make immediate eye contact, move the object slowly in an arc from left to right, and then from right to left, horizon- tally, vertically, and in a circle across the baby's line of vision. If the baby does not follow the object by moving the eyes or head, gently turn the baby's head in the direction of the object, repeating, "look," until the baby focuses on it. Praise the baby's looking. Repeat five times.

Visual Responsiveness While in Different Positions

GOAL: To learn to respond to the environment, whether lying down 'Or sitting up.

Repeat the same exercises with the baby sitting in an infant seat, sitting on someone's lap, sitting up supported by cushions, or lying face down. Pre- sent a variety of objects such as suspended toys and toys held in your hand. Vary the color and type of toy; even very young babies respond more readily to novelty in the environment.

Exercises for Auditory Acuity

Auditory Training

GOAL: To assume a listening posture, keeping very still with eyes focused into space. To move the eyes and turn the head toward the sound.

Place the baby on his or her back. Make a soft noise using a bell, rattle, or clicker, about one and a half feet away from either ear, outside the baby's field of vision. If the baby does not respond by listening (keeping very still with eyes focused on one spot), or by turning his or her head toward the sound, gently turn the baby's head until he or she looks at the object that is making the noise. Alternate sides and repeat six times.

As the baby learns to respond to sounds, gradually move farther away, up to 6 feet. Praise the baby for responding.

Photo 10.2. Turning to sound and looking.

Auditory Training While in Different Positions

GOAL: To respond to a variety of sounds whether lying down or sitting up.

As with the focusing exercise, repeat the auditory training when the baby is sitting with support, reclining in an infant seat, or lying on his or her stomach.

Teaching Responses to the Human Voice

GOALS: To attend to human speech. To respond to his or her name.

At every opportunity speak to the baby and call him or her by name. When approaching the baby's crib or playpen, call to the baby, and turn his or her head toward you if the baby doesn't do so.

Most important, remember to make eye contact with your baby. This visual interaction is the basis of all social and verbal communication, and I cannot stress its importance enough. As you talk or call to your baby, giving him or her practice in auditory acuity, don't forget to look your baby directly in the eyes as he or she responds to your voice. You can also use your own face and eyes as objects on which your baby can fixate and track as you move your face slowly back and forth, across the baby's line of vision (see the first exercise, Making Eye Contact, in this chapter).

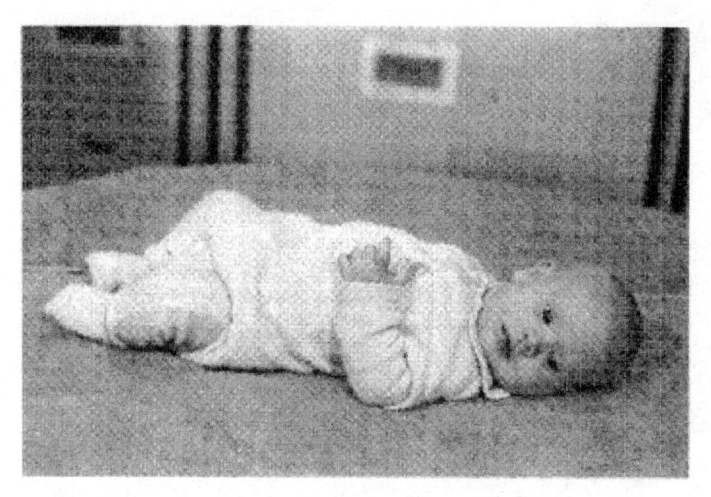

Photo 10.3. Baby assumes a listening posture.

Recent research has shown that babies with DS are sometimes slower in developing this sensitivity to human eye-to-eye contact. It is also possible that delays in language development are correlated to some extent to poor visual communication between babies with DS and the adults in their environment. It has been found, for example, that normal babies vocalize when their mothers are making direct eye contact with them, but that the babbling of babies with DS appears to be unrelated to any social interaction with their mothers. It appears, therefore, that it may be extremely important to establish this visual relationship as early as possible and to maintain and use it as a basic and essential part of your behavior whenever you care for, play, or talk with your baby.

11. Fine Motor/Cognitive Social Development: 5 to 12 Months

Between the ages of 5 and 12 months, the human baby learns many new skills. The most noticeable development occurs in the way the baby learns to handle his or her body, and in the baby's ability to coordinate the function of his or her senses of sight, hearing, touch, and so on, with the intellectual awareness of his or her expanding world. In other words, the baby's prime developmental task is the increased mastery and management of his or her environment.

Briefly, this mastery of one's environment involves three main areas: eye-hand coordination, mobility (the ability to move from one place to another independently), and language (communication). This chapter will describe early exercises for developing eye-hand coordination such as looking, reaching, grasping, and releasing. However, before you begin these exercises, assess your baby using the Record of Fine Motor/Cognitive and Social Development (see Table A.6 in Appendix A).

Eye-hand coordination entails the ability to purposefully manipulate objects in the environment. In this respect the baby progresses from haphazard swiping at objects to deliberate and accurate reaching out and grasping. The baby acquires the ability to hold or release at will and learns to place things into predetermined locations, be it his or her mouth, or a cup or box. The baby also masters the more complex task of placing one object upon another, as when stacking blocks.

Learning Principles and Techniques

Any effective program of instruction, be it college algebra or the development of eye-hand coordination in a baby, is based on specific learning principles and techniques.

The Course of Instruction Is Programmed

One begins with a simple task that the baby is physically capable of per- forming, and with each success, one moves to progressively more difficult tasks. For example, if the baby has the potential for moving his or her arms, hands, and fingers, the baby is potentially capable of reaching out and grasping objects, although he or she may not yet have the ability to do so skillfully. Therefore, the first step in such a program might be the simple movement of arms and hands, and the final step would be reaching for and grasping of objects.

The Program Is Precise

The parent or teacher determines beforehand precisely what the baby must do. The demands or criteria for performance are consistent. For example, if, during a training session, you want a baby to pick up a certain object with his or her right hand only, do not allow the baby to randomly switch from using the right hand to using the left.

The Program Employs Proven Teaching Techniques

Proven teaching techniques include cueing, shaping, and reinforcement. Examples of procedures for cueing, shaping, and reinforcement follow.

1. The parent holds up a rattle and says, "Look." (*Cue*)
2. The baby looks. (*Positive response*)
3. The parent smiles and says, "Good." (*Reinforcement*)

or

1. The parent holds up a rattle and says, "Look."(*Cue*)
2. The baby does not look. (*Negative response*)
3. The parent repeats, "Look," and physically turns the baby's head until eye contact is made. (*Shaping*)
4. The baby now looks. (*Positive response*)
5. The parent smiles and says, "That's right. Now you're looking." (*Reinforcement*)

Remember that a positive response is always reinforced (acknowledged) in some way that is *pleasing* to the baby.

Reinforcement tells the baby that he or she is successful, and that his or her actions are correct. Reinforcement gives the baby a sense of achievement and accelerates learning.

Each baby has individual preferences for reinforcers. Although many babies work well for adult attention-a smile, a word, a nod, a pat-some require a more tangible consequence for a positive response. In such cases, a bit of a favorite food (one-fourth teaspoon), such as fruit, cereal, milk, or ice cream, paired with loving attention can be a very effective way of increasing the rate of positive responses.

A positive response is reinforced, but a negative response is ignored or shaped because a verbal correction such as, "No, don't do that," is a form of adult attention that could be reinforcing to the baby. It is imperative that reinforcement be given only for positive, or desired, responses to avoid con- fusing the baby. An example of ignoring a negative response follows.

1. A mother hands a ball to the baby and says, "Put the ball in the box." (*Cue*)
2. The baby takes the ball and flings it to the floor. (*Negative response*)
3. The mother makes no comment, drops her head, and does not look at the baby for 15 to 20 seconds. (*Ignoring the negative response*)
4. The mother makes no comment, picks up the ball, and repeats the cue. "Put the ball in the box." (*Cue*)
5. The baby takes the ball, but before it can be thrown, the mother physically helps the baby place the ball in the box. (Shaping and positive response)
6. The mother says, "Good," and gives the baby one-fourth teaspoon of applesauce or two hugs. (*Reinforcement*)

Progress Is Recorded

To program appropriately—to assure success as the baby moves through a progression of learning tasks—it is extremely important to have a record of the responses that a baby makes. Data-taking is not difficult; simply note every cue you give the baby and the baby's response, whether positive, negative, or shaped. A page in a notebook and a coding scheme are all you need. In order to use data profitably, you must be able to figure out what they mean. The sample in Table 11.1 shows that eight cues were given. The baby made six (75%) positive responses, two (25%) negative responses, and three (38%) shaped responses. One day's data shows only how the baby performed on that particular day. A week's record, however, should indicate whether or not progress has been made. If the record shows that after several days the baby is making a positive response 75% to 80% of the time, as compared to 30% on the first day, you can be assured of progress. You may also decide to begin teaching a new task.

Table 11.1
Code

Check Mark	✓	Cue
Plus Sign	+	Positive Response
Minus Sign	−	Negative Response
Plus Sign and s	+ s	Shaped Response
Slash	/	Reinforcement

Example

Task: Grasping a Toy	Date: 2/15/99
Cue: "Take"	✓ ✓ ✓ ✓ ✓ ✓ ✓ ✓
Response:	− +/ +s/ − +s/ +s/ +/ +/

Note. Reinforcement is given only after a shaped or positive response but never after a negative response. Be sure to label the tasks and date your record sheets.

Other Points To Remember

Novelty. All children like novelty, and very young children have short attention spans. When presenting objects and toys during training sessions, avoid presenting the same stimulus more than three times in succession. With some children (until they have established a 75% to 100% rate of positive responding on cue), twice in a row may be sufficient since they may refuse to respond by the third trial.

Preparedness. Be prepared before beginning to work with the baby. Have materials, data sheet, and pencil close at hand. At first plan to spend at least 10 uninterrupted minutes per session. After your baby has mastered the first exercise, you may extend the time to 20 minutes, and finally, to a maximum of 30 minutes.

Beginning Eye-Hand Coordination Exercises

The basic purpose of early eye-hand coordination exercises is to teach the skills of looking, reaching, grasping, and releasing in a variety of positions, using a variety of materials.

Materials

The following is a list of materials you might find useful in teaching eye-hand coordination. A rattle with a sturdy handle, 3 to 4 inches long

- A matching pair of jingle bells (Triple bells on a handle are available in music stores or through child-craft equipment companies.)
- Six or seven small and large rings, 2 and 3 inches in diameter, such as dime-store bracelets or canning jar rings, to dangle or hand to the child
- Household objects or small toys, such as plastic measuring cups, spoons, pill bottles without the lids, small dolls, or stuffed animals
- Three or four 1-inch cube blocks
- A variety of containers, such as shallow baskets 6 to 8 inches in diameter, shoe boxes, pint and quart cottage cheese cartons, and jars or cups 1 to 3 inches in diameter

Look, Reach, and Grasp

GOAL: To look at, reach for, and grasp a toy whenever and however it is presented.

Hold a rattle in front of the baby. Say, "Look." If the baby does not look at the toy immediately, shake the rattle, and turn the baby's head (shape) until the baby is looking at the toy. As the baby looks, move the rattle toward his or her hand, either right or left, and say, "Take."

The baby will reach and grasp the toy. If the baby doesn't reach, shape by curling the baby's fingers around the toy, making sure that the baby is holding it. Reinforce the response. Take the toy back and repeat the procedure two more times. Record on your data sheet. Work for approximately 10 minutes, changing objects, hands, and positions. Use beads, bells, and rings with and without string attached to them. Try dangling one ring at a time or two rings at a time, one for each hand. Reinforce after each positive or shaped response.

Positional Changes. Do this exercise with the baby lying on his or her back, sitting with support, and lying face down. Present objects directly in the front of the baby, to either side, above shoulder level, at waist level, and below waist level.

When a positive response is occurring with 90% to 100% accuracy with- out shaping (check your data), proceed to the next exercise.

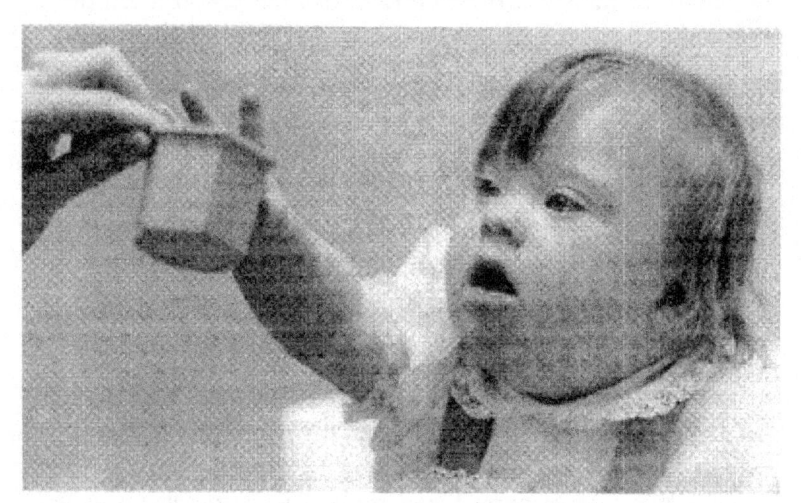

Photo 11.1. Looking and reaching.

Independent Look, Reach, and Grasp

GOAL: To look at, reach for, and grasp a toy independently.

General procedures are the same as in the first exercise, but this time the baby is in a sitting position and the toys are placed in a container such as a basket, carton, cup, or jar. The baby is required to look, reach, and retrieve a toy from the container.

Variation 1. Place one object at a time into the container. As the baby removes the toy, reinforce the response. Let the baby hold the toy for 15 to 30 seconds. Remove the toy from the baby's grasp. Reinforce the release. Repeat the process with new objects five more times.

Variation 2. Place several toys in the basket at one time and allow the baby to select the toys one at a time until all the toys have been handled. Cue and shape when necessary, and reinforce positive responses. Remember to change containers and the arrangement of toys after every third response, and to take data.

Toy Manipulation

GOAL: To look at, grasp, and manipulate a toy. Place one or several objects in front of the baby on a flat surface such as a table or highchair tray. Repeat the basic techniques. Cue by saying "Look," and "Take."

Photo 11.2. Grasping and removing objects from container.

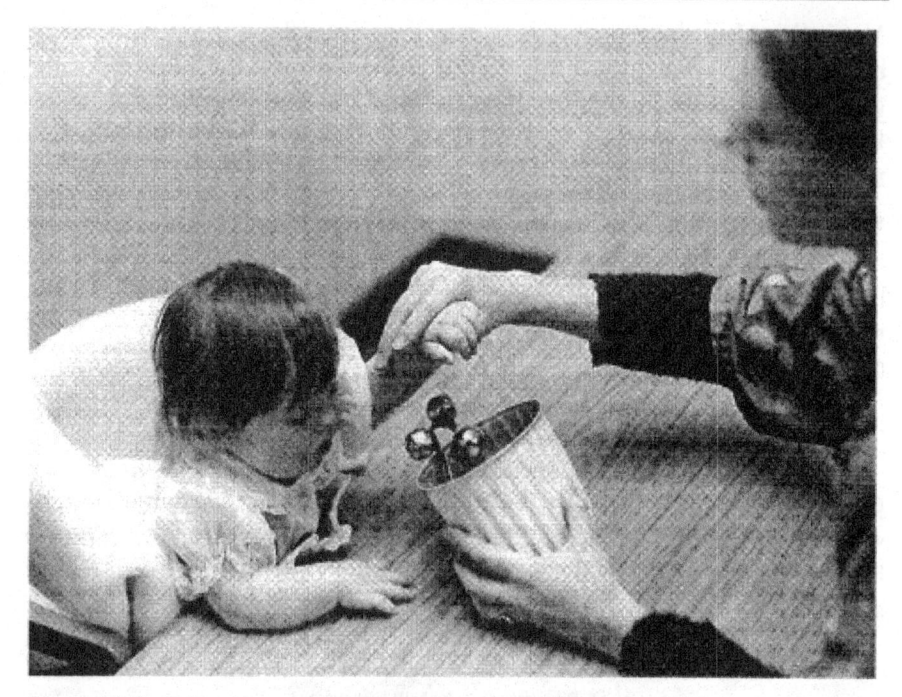

Photo 11.3. Releasing an object into a container (shaping).

Shape when necessary, reinforce, and allow the baby to hold and manipulate each object for 1 to 2 minutes. In manipulating the toy, the baby may transfer the item from one hand to another, shake or bang it on the table, or drop it and select another toy. Reinforce all of these activities. Look, Grasp, Place, and Release

GOAL: To look at and grasp a toy, and then to place it on a table or into a container, and release it.

As the baby sits in a highchair or at a table, present him or her with a variety of toys in a container. Cue the baby by saying, "Take" and "Put." The baby removes the toys and places them one by one in another container or on the table. In the beginning, much of this activity may have to be shaped. To facilitate the release and placement of toys, cue the baby to look at and reach for the next object. Coordinated Manipulation of Two Objects

GOAL: To look at and grasp two objects, one in each hand, in one simultaneous, coordinated movement. To retain the objects, lift them off the table, and bang them together in a clapping motion. Between 8 and 12 months of age, after a baby has mastered the preceding fine motor activities, he or she is ready to work toward another milestone in development. This new skill involves the ability to simultaneously pick up two small objects, one in each hand. This ability to reach out with two hands and to pick up two objects, in one coordinated movement, indicates increased maturation of the central nervous system.

Step 1. To help your baby perfect this skill, place two small identical objects in front of the baby on a flat surface such as a table or highchair tray. The reason for selecting identical objects is to prevent the baby from reaching with only one hand for an object that may be more appealing to him or her. For this reason, 1-inch wooden blocks are a good choice. Moreover, this early manipulation of blocks will lay the groundwork for other basic block-play activities such as banging, stacking, and building.

If the baby makes no move to pick up both blocks at the same time, give physical assistance. First, place the blocks in front of the baby, and then with your two hands, place the baby's hands, palms down over the blocks. If the baby grasps the blocks correctly (with both hands at the same time), rein- force. If not, give further assistance by curling the baby's fingers over the objects. Reinforce the shaping.

Repeat the exercise three or four times, using pairs of different colored blocks for novelty. Keep your help to a minimum and be alert to any correct, self-initiated response that your baby may make. If, after 4 or 5 days of practice, your baby still seems unable to coordinate a two-handed movement independently, it may be that he or she is not developmentally ready for this task. Temporarily discontinue this exercise, and try again in a month.

Step 2. In the sequence of normal development, once a baby has learned to pick up and hold two objects in a coordinated two-handed movement, he or she begins bringing the two objects together, touching one to the other and then lifting them up and banging them together in a clapping motion. A baby with DS does not always progress spontaneously to block-banging. However, this is a skill that is readily acquired with some demonstration, shaping, and encouragement. In fact, this is one of many basic milestones that all children seem to enjoy.

In addition to scheduled work sessions, it is very important to give your baby plenty of opportunity to handle toys and objects independently. Give the baby rattles, plastic dishes, containers, balls, stuffed toys, squeaky toys, and wooden spoons for waving and banging. To be safe, do not give anything small enough to be inserted completely into the mouth. Also, to preserve novelty and interest, do not let the baby handle the lesson materials during these free play periods; similar, but not identical, objects may be given.

It has been said that play is a child's work, and that is certainly true. During these play times, your baby will be practicing the skills you have been teaching. Your baby will be looking at, reaching for, grasping, combining, and releasing objects. As it was pointed out in the preceding sections, typically developing children acquire these abilities in the natural sequence of their maturation. Without special training, children with disabilities are generally less successful.

As your child matures chronologically and developmentally, he or she will need new and more demanding experiences in order to continue to progress. The next chapter describes exercises and skills your child will need to master as he or she moves from infancy into toddlerhood.

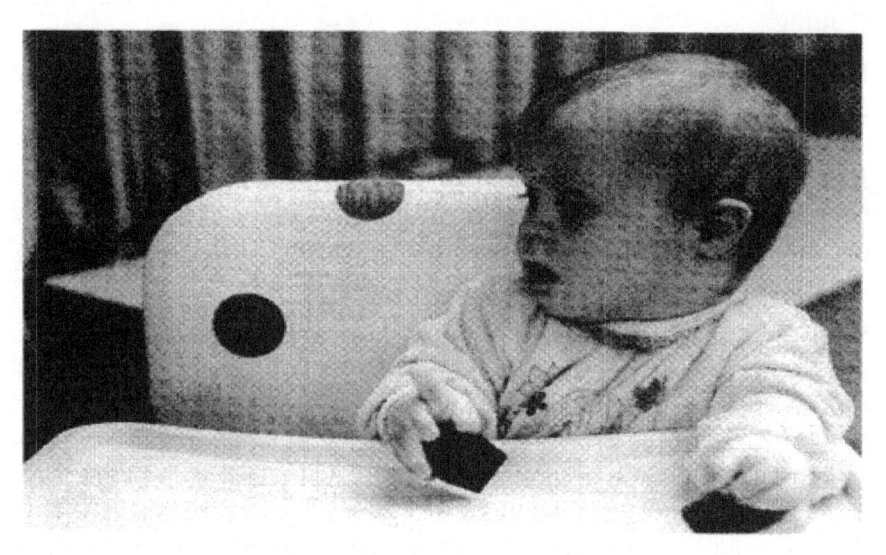

Photo 11.4. Grasping two objects simultaneously.

12. Fine Motor/Cognitive Social Development: 12 to 24 Months

Once the child has learned how to look at, reach for, grasp, and release objects, he or she can begin discovering new ways of using objects and toys. The child can also begin learning about shapes and colors, and developing new skills which require a more precise use of the fingers and wrist. The ability to do these things is extremely important, for they are the building stones for all future learning-language, reading, writing, and arithmetic.

This chapter will describe several exercises designed to develop these skills. The same procedures of program, structure, and reinforcement that are described in Chapter 11 should be used. These techniques are based on proven learning principles and assure effective teaching. Teaching the tasks described in the following pages will ensure a smooth transition to the more difficult tasks ahead. However, before you begin these exercises, remember to assess your child according to the Record of Fine Motor/Cognitive and Social Development (see Table A.5 in Appendix A). At this time, you may also wish to begin monitoring your child's overall development by referring to Tables A.6, A.7 and A.8 in Appendix A.

Preparation

As with the earlier exercises, you will need a place and a time to work, a favorite food reinforcer (if praise alone isn't effective enough), and a few materials. Work habits, procedures, and programming must also be considered.

Place To Work

As a general rule, the child will perform these exercises in a sitting position. A highchair with a tray or a nursery school table (not over 24 inches wide) and a low chair would be best. If necessary, give additional support to the child with blankets or pillows. Make sure that the child is sitting both comfortably and securely, with both feet resting on the floor or on a footstool, and high enough to be able to rest his or her elbows on the table without straining.

Time

Select a time of day when the child is rested and when you can expect to have 10 to 20 minutes without interruption. Don't be concerned if it is difficult for you to work every day. Three or four well-structured, relaxed sessions a week are enough and are much more valuable than seven that are hurried or disorganized. Work Habits

AB the child gets older and you begin teaching him or her progressively more complex skills, the establishment of good work habits becomes increasingly essential, since work habits will reinforce the foundation of future learning experiences. The development of good work habits depends on parents and teachers and the amount of discipline that all of you are willing to apply to yourselves.

Guidelines for Programming

Know your goals. Know what you are trying to teach and precisely what response you want from your child, and then accept no other.

Structure the task. The task must be structured in such a way that your child is able to, and will make, the desired response. I use the word will because you must be able to depend on your child making the correct response whenever you require it, at least 80% of the time. Only then can you be sure that your child has learned a task.

Structuring a learning situation correctly means breaking down a task into a series of small steps, which, when learned separately, will assure eventual mastery of a new skill.

Guarantee that a correct response is rewarded. You must make certain that making a correct response will be rewarding to the child, whether this reward comes simply from the process of "doing," from your praise, or from some other kind of reward. In other words, as a teacher, you must be sure that a correct response guarantees your child the glow of success. Feedback for success helps to develop a feeling of self-worth and achievement in a child.

You must be efficient. Stick to the task at hand and remain in control of the session. This is when the ability to view yourself objectively becomes so important. Try to listen to yourself and notice what you are doing. Are you talking too much, over prompting, saying "no" too many times? Are you able to give just enough help to enable your child to complete a task without stifling your child's initiative and learning?

For example, suppose you hand your child a ring to put on a stick, but your child throws it instead. What do you do? Scold your child by saying, "No, no, that isn't nice!" or "Don't do that. That's naughty!"? Scolding only brings attention to the very behavior you wish to eliminate. A better procedure would be to ignore the throw. Calmly hand your child another ring. Say, "Put the ring on the stick," and at the same time take hold of your child's arm before he or she can throw, and gently but firmly guide your child to make the desired• response. Then, reinforce your child's correct response and record your data.

Materials

The following materials can be used during the intermediate eye-hand coordination exercises.

- Six or seven small and large rings, 2 and 3 inches in diameter (approximately), such as dime-store bracelets in several colors and canning jar rings of metal or rubber

- A stick or peg on a pedestal made with a piece of doweling, 7 inches long by one-half to 1inch thick, inserted into a 5-inch square piece of wood for stability

- A set of nesting cups and blocks in a variety of shapes and colors (The Learning Tower, a set of 12 nesting cups by Child Craft, is a good choice.)

- A dozen 1-inch colored, wooden blocks

- Several small, pellet-size objects such as marbles, screws, cloth-covered buttons, or raisins

- A variety of containers such as cottage cheese cartons, glasses, or jars that are 2 inches in diameter, and pill bottles that are about 1 inch in diameter

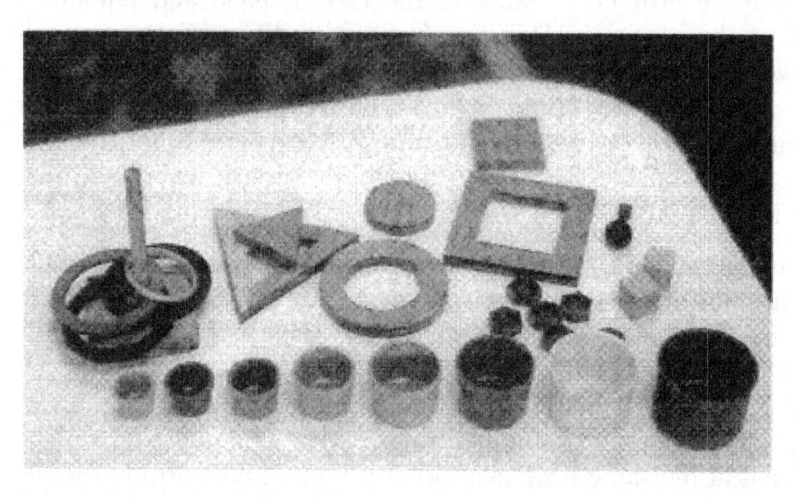

Photo 12.1. Basic materials for fine motor/cognitive development.

General Procedures

Collect all the necessary materials, pencil and paper for your data, and a special reinforcer that you might want to use. Seat the child in a quiet corner in a highchair or at a small table at a comfortable height. The edge of the table should be level with the middle of the child's torso. (Too often a small child is expected to work at a desk that comes up to his or her chin!) If the child is sit- ting so that his or her legs do not reach the floor, place a stool or box under the child's feet for support.

If you have completed the earlier exercises, the child should readily make eye contact with materials and reach for, take, and place objects. How- ever, some of the new exercises may be difficult for the child at first, so be pre- pared to give physical assistance (shaping) for several sessions before the child is able to make any correct responses independently. Do not allow your- self to become discouraged or tense if progress seems slow. If you have done your homework (studied and applied the techniques on early eye-hand coordination), the child should be ready to learn the new tasks. All you have to do is recognize progress. The data that you keep will help you to do that.

Intermediate Eye-Hand Coordination Exercises

Rings on a Stick

GOALS: To place rings on the stick without help 80% to 100% of the time. To take the rings off the stick.

Photo 12.2. Rings on a stick.

Place the stick and pedestal in front of the child. Hold up a ring. Say, "Look. Put the ring on the stick." Demonstrate the action for the child. Pick up a second ring and hand it to the child. Say, "Put the ring on the stick." Shape if necessary. Reinforce the response. Continue until all rings have been placed on the stick.

Developing the Pincer Grasp and Wrist Control

GOAL: To pick up an object and drop it into a container using the pincer grasp. Use the cloth-bound buttons and other small objects. Place a container, carton, jar, or bottle and one of the objects in front of the child. Say, "Put the button in the jar." Demonstrate the action. Retrieve the button and repeat the verbal cue. Shape, if necessary. Reinforce the child's response and record.

At first the child will probably use his or her whole hand to grasp, but as you continue working and shaping, the pincer grasp (a grasp using only the thumb and forefinger) will develop. Begin with the blocks and larger buttons, then progress to the pill bottle and the smaller objects. Total number of responses per session should be 10. There are several variations of this exercise.

Variation 1. Present objects first to one of the child's hands, then to the other.

Variation 2. Present two objects at one time to develop grasping with both hands simultaneously.

Variation 3. Let the child retrieve an object by reaching into the container, or by tipping the container and dumping the block or button on the table.

Variation 4. Place a jar or bottle upside down over an object. Let the child retrieve the toy by lifting the container in an upward lifting movement of his or her wrist.

Nesting and Stacking

GOALS: To place a smaller nesting cup into a larger one, to remove cups from the nest, and to stack cups.

Nesting. Begin by giving the child two nesting cups at a time. Some• times it is difficult for a small child to nest a cup into another that is only slightly larger, as they may fit very tightly, so begin by presenting a significantly smaller cup each time.

Once this step has been mastered, the cups may be presented in sequence, and more than two cups at a time can be placed in front of the child. However, in order to avoid errors and frustration at the early stage, place the cups in a horizontal row moving from the biggest to the smallest. Learning the difference between big and little will come later; for now, the child must concentrate on looking and using his or her hands and fingers.

Photo 12.3. Nesting cups.

Removing cups. This is a fairly easy task and children enjoy taking the cups out one at a time. Present only two at a time if you want to teach your child to take them apart and to put them together again in one operation.

Stacking. The same cups can be used for stacking. Turn them over and show your child how to place one cup on top of the other. Begin with only two or three cups.

Block Stacking

The placing of one block upon another, especially the small 1-inch size cubes, to make a tower of three, four, and eventually ten blocks is a fairly complex task, and more significant developmentally than it may appear to be. For this reason, the skill with which a child is able to perform this task is used in many standardized tests as a measure of a child's physical and mental development.

In order to stack objects successfully, the child must have acquired certain capabilities. Mentally, the child must be able to perceive a new dimension in his or her relationship to objects in the environment. The child has already learned that objects can be seen, grasped, held, and released. The child has also learned that things can be placed into and taken out of containers. Now the child must discover, independently or through guided practice, that one object can be placed on top of another.

Even if a child has the cognitive understanding that certain objects can be stacked, he or she might not be physically ready to do so. Building a tower with 1-inch blocks requires more than just the handling of blocks. It requires the precise control of the thumb, fingers, and wrist. If a child uses his or her whole hand to grasp the block with a closed fist, the child will be unable to place it on top of another block, because the child's closed fingers will get in the way.

In order to stack, a child must be able to lift a block using only the thumb and first two fingers. The child must also be able to use his or her wrist in con- trolled upward and downward movements. Then, even if a child is able to pick up a block correctly and correctly place it on top of another block, the child must also be able to release the block so carefully and precisely that it doesn't fall when the child moves his or her hand away. This is the final and most important step in the sequence of block stacking. Beginners may have trouble with this last step because they may fail to release the block before removing their hands, so that the block and hand move off the stack together. Or beginners may simply lack the ability to voluntarily release the block.

It should be evident by now that the purpose of all of the preceding exercises was to lay the groundwork for this major milestone in your baby's development. Rings on a stick gave practice in visual perception, grasping with fingers, up-and-down wrist movement, and voluntary release. The handling of buttons and other small objects gave further practice in thumb and fingel grasping. The stacking and manipulation of nesting blocks offered other preliminary practice.

Assuming that your child has by now successfully placed one inverted nesting block upon another, you may wish to begin stacking solid blocks. Break the task into several small steps. Repeat three to five times a session

Step 1

GOAL: To pick up a block, place it on top of an inverted nesting block, and to release the block.

Demonstrate placing a 1-inch block on a large inverted nesting block. If the child doesn't repeat the task correctly, shape, and reinforce. If the child had trouble releasing the block after it has been placed on the inverted block (fol example, if the child removes his or her hand too quickly or prematurely) restrain the child's hand and arm until the child's fingers have released the block, and only then permit the child to move his or her hand away.

You can vary this exercise by giving the child many different objects to place and release, and by using a variety of objects as the base. In addition to the inverted nesting blocks, you can use boxes or larger blocks. It is also good idea to vary the height and placement of these objects, so that the child develops a finer perception of height and distance.

Step 2

GOAL: To pick up a block and independently place it on top of another block, removing his or her hand after releasing the block, with an adult steadying the block tower if necessary.

Once the activities in Step 1 have been mastered, you can progress to the actual stacking of blocks. Begin with two blocks. Demonstrate placing one block on top of the other. Then, place one block on the table and hand the second block to the child. As the child moves to place one block on top of the other, steady the bottom block with your fingers. As the second block is placed, hold it also, so that when the child moves his or her hand away, the blocks remain standing. Such a procedure serves as a model of what you want the child to accomplish, and gives the child a sense of success.

Do not repeat more than three times in a session. Although many children appear to enjoy block stacking, they can become frustrated when required to repeat it many times and, as a result, may throw or scatter the blocks.

Step 3

GOAL: To build a straight tower of four 1-inch blocks without assistance, gradually improving the skill to complete an eight-block tower.

Introduce a third and then a fourth block. Start out by holding the bot- tom block as described in Step 2; however, as the child gains control and confidence, allow him or her to place the first block independently. Hold the tower steady as the child places the next block. After the child is able to make a three-block tower without assistance, add the fourth block. If necessary, hold the blocks as before, until this step can also be performed independently. Unless the child indicates a desire to repeat the task many times, limit the activity to two trials per session.

Also, after a tower has been built, don't permit your child to knock it down. This behavior encourages random throwing and scattering of blocks which may not be desirable. Instead, teach your child to dismantle the tower by carefully lifting the blocks, one by one, and dropping them into a designated box or similar container.

After your child has mastered Step 3, you can continue adding blocks, until your child can successfully build an eight-block tower. Normally, a child is able to build a tower of four blocks between 16 and 26 months of age, and an eight-block tower between 20 and 36 months of age.

Future Exercises and Activities

It is important to expose your child to many different materials and toys during free play periods. However, as your child learns to use toys more effectively, it becomes less important to avoid using his or her lesson materials during these times.

If possible, add other instructional materials such as large and small pegs and peg boards, form boxes and form boards, plastic and wooden stacking rings, simple one-piece puzzles without knobs, and puzzles with knobs for easier handling. Include balls for tossing, bouncing, catching, rolling, and kicking. Also include nontoxic felt marking pens for marking and scribbling and plenty of sturdy paper. All of these materials can provide developmentally important experiences, but be sure to teach your child how to use them correctly.

If your child is unable to attend a preschool, it would be a good idea to give him or her play dough for practice in rolling, patting, and pounding. Water play and easel painting offer additional benefits to the growing child.

Exposure to books and pictures is vital. Try to include 10 to 20 minutes of looking at books in your daily schedule. Looking at pictures and listening to simple comments such as "This is an apple," "Here is a boat," "The cow says moo," and "The lamb says baa-baa," promote attending skills and language development. Chapter 14 describes language acquisition activities in some detail.

Photo 12.4. Looking at pictures.

However, since language does not develop in a vacuum, but is related to mental growth, it is necessary to first consider other experiences relative to cognitive development and the role of discrimination learning as a basis for intellectual achievement. These aspects of a child's progress are discussed in the next chapter.

13. Cognitive Development and Discrimination Learning

The word *cognition* refers to the act, power, or faculty of comprehending, perceiving, and knowing. Cognitive development refers to the mental development that takes place as the child learns to interact with his or her environment with increasing understanding. Everything that your child has learned to do during the first year of life is directly related to his or her future intellectual growth. As your child matures to toddlerhood, it becomes important to add new experiences to this basic learning. The goal of these new experiences should be to expand the child's cognition by exercising his or her attending, observational, and perceptual skills.

The word *perceptual* refers to a person's ability to become aware of the world through his or her senses of sight, smell, hearing, touch, and taste. Even at birth, a baby has the ability to perceive and to react to sights, smells, sounds, textures, and foods. For example, a baby will frown and blink if a light is too bright, startle at a sound, turn away from an unpleasant odor, cry if a wet diaper becomes uncomfortable, and refuse a distasteful liquid. How- ever, the baby's perception is more an instinctive or reflexive reaction to a stimulus, rather than a conscious awareness of an occurrence about which he or she can make a judgment. The baby has yet to learn, for example, that the response that one makes to the sound of a ringing telephone is different from the one that is made in response to the ringing of an alarm clock.

The baby has no labels, no words, and no meanings for the things that he or she perceives. As the baby matures, he or she gradually begins to under- stand more about things that can be seen, heard, touched, felt, and tasted, and how one should respond to those things. Much of this learning occurs accidentally through trial and error, play, and direct teaching.

This brings us to discrimination learning. The ability to discriminate is the ability to perceive sameness and difference, and the significance of these attributes in the environment. The mature individual is able to make judgments, solve problems, and, in general, behave appropriately. Our lives, as adults, revolve around this ability to discriminate accurately. Frequently; we are called upon to interpret very subtle differences, requiring extremely fine perception and discrimination abilities.

Very often the skills of the physician, the pharmacist, and the nurse depend on their ability to make these fine discriminations. However, regard- less of profession, occupation, or day-to-day activities, nearly everything we do, if we are to do it correctly and successfully, depends on our ability to discriminate what we perceive, from taking the right bus on the way to work to putting the right amount of seasoning in the stew. Many developmentally impaired children and adults are unable to make correct decisions because of deficits in their discriminatory skills. However, it is possible to teach discrimination, and both typical children and children with special needs can benefit from such training. The following section will describe exercises for discrimination learning between the ages of 15 months and 3 years.

Early Discrimination Learning

The goal of early discrimination learning is to teach shape, color, object, and picture recognition. The focus is on visual (sight) and auditory (hearing) perception. Although the formal program is designed to teach these specific skills, it should be recognized that everything else that your child experiences, either during your work sessions or independently, also contributes to the refinement of his or her perceptual and discriminatory skills. Every time your child hears a new sound or your voice, handles an object, or tastes a different food, he or she is receiving additional information about the environment. Later, programs can be expected to build on these experiences. For the present, however, it is sufficient to begin a basic program of shape, color, object, and picture recognition.

Discrimination learning has five basic steps:

1. Matching
2. Selecting

3. Sorting
4. Labeling
5. Generalizing

Matching

The ability to match involves visual discrimination and the cognitive ability to follow a verbal direction. The latter could be called auditory discrimination. A child matches correctly when he or she recognizes two or more shapes, colors, objects, or pictures as being identical. There are two levels of matching.

Level 1. At this level, the child matches only one set of identical items: the child has one picture of a horse, and he or she places a second identical picture on the first one.

Level 2. The child matches two or four sets of identical items. For example, there are four pictures of four different animals placed in front of a child: a horse, a cat, a fish, and a duck. The child then places a picture of a horse on the horse, a picture of a cat on the cat, and so on. Level 2 requires more difficult discrimination because the child must keep from being distracted by the other pictures as he or she makes the correct match.

Selecting

In making a selection, the child must respond to the verbal cue, "Give me ____." The child must be able to select the correct shape, color, object, or picture from one or more items that have been placed on the table in front of him or her. This is an exercise in auditory and visual discrimination. There are two levels of selecting.

Level 1. At this level, the child selects from only one set of identical items. For example, there are two identical pictures of a horse in front of a child, and the teacher says, "Give me horse," or the teacher might hold up a picture of a horse and say, "Take horse."

Level 2. The child selects from two to four sets of identical items. Again, this is a more difficult task because the child must not be distracted by the competing pictures or objects as he or she makes a selection.

Sorting

Sorting is basically an independent task that involves classification, putting like things with other like things. For example, the child may be given a handful of different colored blocks—red, blue and yellow—and three containers of the same colors. The child must then place all the red blocks in the red container, all the blue blocks in the blue container, and all of the yellow blocks in the yellow container. More advanced tasks would involve sorting different classes of objects into sets. For example, given a variety of blocks, pictures, and spoons, the child would have to put all of the blocks in one pile, all of the pictures in another, and all of the spoons in a third. This is a task requiring a fairly high level of cognitive development, and probably would not be introduced until kindergarten or first grade.

Labeling

Labeling refers to the naming of objects. Since it is harder to learn and to remember what a particular color, shape, or object is called, labeling should be viewed as a skill that a child acquires gradually over a long period of time. How well and how quickly a child learns to name things depends on how well he or she is able to perceive and distinguish things in the environment, and on the amount of auditory information that the child is able to receive and process. Auditory information refers to what parents, teachers, and other adults say to a child. This is why, as you work with your child on picture, object, color, or shape recognition, it is important to name these objects. How- ever, care must be taken not to overwhelm the child with too much information. Parents are cautioned to speak slowly, distinctly, and in short, simple phrases.

Labeling, the ability to name things spontaneously, is a major step in expressive language (speech) development. The first words that a toddler says are generally names of people, animals, and things: *mama, dada, bow wow, cookie*. Possible strategies for language development are described in Chapter 14.

Generalizing

The ability to generalize, that is to transfer information received in a specific instance or situation to other situations or environments, is yet another important milestone in a child's early cognitive growth. Having learned how to match, select, sort, and label geometric shapes, colors, and pictures during the learning sessions, a child must now be able to transfer this knowledge to the world at large. Cognitively the child must, for example, develop the ability to recognize a circle wherever it may occur, regardless of size, color, or location. That is what is meant by the term *generalization*. Of course, the ability to generalize refers to everything that the child has learned through instruction or independently.

The ability to generalize evolves through a process of mental maturation and experience. All young children encounter some difficulties in attaining this level in their intellectual functioning. Having learned what a cat is, toddlers may "over-generalize" and refer to all four-legged animals as cats, or sometimes the process of generalization simply does not occur. One four year old child, without DS but with mental retardation, had successfully learned to recognize and label colors wherever they might appear in the classroom. Green was her favorite color, and she readily identified a green book, scarf, block, or color chip indoors, but on a nature walk, she failed to identify the green colors of the grass, shrubs, and trees. Her knowledge and concept of the color green had not yet transferred fully to the world at large.

All children need practice in developing these generalization skills. Children with developmental delays in particular, who may be slower in making the transition from the specific to the general, or from the concrete to the abstract, can benefit from special programming. It should be remembered, however, that generalization is the final step in the hierarchy of discrimination learning, and practice in generalization naturally follows specific training in matching, selecting, sorting, and labeling. Every time your child engages in play activities, you are providing opportunities for generalization.

The following exercises are designed to teach your child a few of the basic discrimination skills. However, keep in mind your child's individual rate of development, and do not attempt these tasks until your child is performing the intermediate eye-hand coordination tasks described in Chapter 11. Also, note the suggested ages when these more advanced activities might be introduced. Before you begin these exercises, remember to assess your child according to each Record of Overall Development (see Tables A.7 and A.8 in Appendix A).

Materials

The following materials can be used during the exercises in this chapter.

Geometric shapes. Although it is possible to buy kinesthetic geometric templates or form boards, a set can be made out of heavy cardboard, Masonite, or plywood. Cut three solid shapes (a circle, square, and triangle) about 5 inches large and one-half to 1inch thick. From the middle of each of these, cut a second, identical shape so that the smaller shape can be fitted into the larger one like a jigsaw puzzle. Make all of the shapes the same size and color, preferably a neutral shade of tan or beige.

A set of nesting cups. These are available in a variety of colors. The Learning Tower, a set of 12 nesting cups by Child Craft, is one of many from which to choose. Nesting cups are used to teach color discrimination as well as other fine motor/cognitive skills.

Four sets of small colored objects. Plan to use several objects that are the same color as the nesting cups you choose. Buttons, small plastic toys, blocks, and trinkets can be used. Since the goal is to teach the concept of color, select colors that are bright, true, and identical within each set. Avoid gradations and variations in hue. Size, shape, and the identity of the objects are less important; in fact, the greater the variety of objects used, the better. The use of identical as well as different objects will help your child to generalize the concept of color.

Paired objects. Plan to use 5 to 10 pairs of objects common to your child's environment such as a pair of the child's shoes, mittens, cups, spoons, small toy animals, cars, apples, bananas, crackers, and so on.

Two small trays or inverted shoe-box tops. If you use trays, be sure that they are solid, neutral colors and similar in appearance. Bright colors and designs, or markedly different trays, can be distracting and confusing to your child.

Pictures. Plan to use 5 to 10 pairs of identical pictures from two sets of Whitman Pre-Primer Flash Cards. These can be found in most toy departments or school supply stores. It is, of course, possible to make your own sets of matched pictures; however, as your child gets older, the Whitman, or similar sets of flash cards, will continue to be an important instructional tool in his or her educational program.

Matching and Selecting: Level 1

Introduction to Shape Discrimination: 15 to 18 Months

GOALS: To match and select geometric shapes, and to generalize this perceptual skill to one-piece puzzles and form boards. Begin with the circle. Take the center piece out of the geometric form board and place the cutout in front of the child. Say, "Circle." Hold up the inset piece. Say, "Look, circle. Put the circle in the circle." Show the child how to do it by doing it yourself. Pick up the inset piece again and hand it to the child. Say, "Circle. Put the circle in the circle." Help the child make the correct response. Don't allow errors such as placing the circle on the table, holding on to it, or throwing it. Physically assist the child when necessary in order to eliminate the errors. Reinforce the response and record data. Repeat the exercise three times only and avoid drilling.

Photo 13.1. Shape and color matching.

After your child is able to place the circle correctly without help for three successive sessions, introduce the square, using the same procedures. After the child has mastered square placing, introduce the triangle.

Every other day or so, review circle or square placing. If the child is able to do this correctly, don't require more than two responses per session on the review tasks. After the child has learned to place all three shapes without any physical assistance from you, continue to present each one separately on a review basis, once or twice every 2 weeks. Meanwhile, let your child work with simple one-piece puzzles and commercially available form boards and boxes.

Introduction to Color Discrimination: 20 to 24 Months

GOALS: To match and select colors, and to generalize this recognition to the environment. To attempt to name the colors. .Begin the exercise with a red cup from the nesting set, and six red objects. Eventually you will use four different colored cups from the nesting set.

Say, "Red," and place the cup in front of the child. Hold up an object. Say, "Look, red. Put red in red." Demonstrate by dropping the object into the cup. Pick up the second object and hand it to the child.

Say, "Red. Put red in red." Don't allow the child to make any errors. Shape, if necessary. Reinforce the response and record. Repeat until all the red objects have been dropped into the cup. At the end of the task, put out your hand with your palm facing up.

Say, "Give me the red cup." Wait 15 seconds. If there is no response, repeat the verbal cue and shape. Reinforce and record. Do not repeat this exercise until the next day.

After introducing your child to the color red for three consecutive lessons, repeat the procedure with another color, perhaps a yellow cup and yellow objects. However, do not neglect red. Review the exercise with red objects every other day, with no more than three red objects.

If all goes well, after a period of another 3 or 4 days, you can introduce the blue cup and the blue objects, then the green cup and the green objects. Again, it is necessary to maintain a schedule of review. This time, review the exercise with red as well as yellow objects, and eventually blue and gree1 objects as well. In order to avoid drilling, use only three objects for each of the colors you are reviewing and review the colors on alternate days.

You can later develop your own schedule for review with the focus OJ labeling and generalization. As you work with your child, encourage him to her to repeat the names of the colors after you. If your child has difficulty saying the word, combine signing with what you say. (Chapters 14 and 15 contain information on signing and total communication.) Also, if your child is unable to say the word exactly, praise him or her for any approximation o attempt to repeat what you say. Or modify the word so that your child can imitate you. For example, if your child says, "Ellow," instead of "Yellow," say "Yes, that's right, yellow," emphasizing the y sound, but at the same time, accepting your child's attempt to pronounce the word. If your child doesn't even attempt an approximation, make it easier for him or her by breaking the word down phonetically, and teaching your child to make the sound for a particular letter such as b (bah) for blue. These language activities are important steps in labeling and general speech development.

As your child acquires these basic matching skills, you can reinforce and expand what he or she has learned by pointing out these colors whenever they are encountered in the environment. "Here is your yellow shirt," you might say, "and your blue tennis shoes," or you might offer a choice, "Which do you want, the red ball or the yellow ball?" A13 you label colors in the environment, or offer choices in colors, you are laying the groundwork for generalization, language development, finer discrimination, and cognition.

Matching and Selecting: Level 2 Introduction to Object Discrimination: 24 to 36 Months

GOALS: To match at least five different pairs of objects at the same time. To repeat the object names on cue, and eventually to name them spontaneously.

The procedures for conducting this exercise are similar to those describe1 in the two preceding exercises for teaching shape and color recognition. However, since the child is now older, and since objects may be easier to dis criminate than colors, the child is required to match two different object simultaneously.

Plan to use the two trays or shoe-box tops and two pairs of objects-two shoes and two cups, two cars and two identical toy animals, or two apples and two bananas. Place the trays on the table in front of the child. Select two pairs of objects, such as the shoes and the cups.

Step 1

Pick up a shoe. Say, "Shoe," and place it on one of the trays. Hold up the other shoe. Say, "Shoe. Put shoe with shoe." Demonstrate by placing the shoe with its mate on the tray. Retrieve one of the shoes and hand it to the child. Say, "Shoe. Put shoe with shoe." The child should place the shoe on the tray with the other shoe. Do not allow errors. Shape, if necessary. Reinforce, and record data. Encourage the child to repeat the word shoe.

Hold your hand out toward the shoe in the tray. Say, "Give me a shoe." Wait 15 seconds. If there is no response, repeat the verbal cue, and shape. Reinforce, record, and leave the shoe on the tray.

Step 2

Pick up a cup and say, "Cup." Place the cup on the second tray. Hold up the second cup and say, "Cup. Put cup with cup." Demonstrate. Retrieve one of the cups, and hand it to the child. "Cup. Put cup with cup." The child should place the cup on the tray with the other cup. Do not allow errors. Prompt and shape, if necessary. Reinforce, and record. Encourage the child to say the word cup. Hold out your hand toward the cups on the tray. Say,

"Give me a cup." The child must now discriminate between a cup and a shoe, so do not allow errors.

Prompt or shape, if necessary. Reinforce, and record data. Encourage the child to repeat the word cup. Leave one cup on the tray.

Step 3

Repeat Steps 1 and 2, but do not demonstrate. Hold up a shoe. Say, "Shoe. Put shoe with shoe," and hand the shoe to the child. The child puts the shoe with the other shoe on the tray. The child must discriminate between shoe and cup, so do not allow errors. If errors occur, then shape, reinforce, and record. Ask the child to give you a shoe and repeat Step 3.

If no error occurs, proceed to Step 4. If an error occurs, repeat Step 3. If an error occurs one more time, then shape, reinforce, and record. Say, "Give me a shoe." Prevent errors, and reinforce the correct response. Say, "Give me a cup." Prevent errors, reinforce the response, and end the session for the day.

Repeat Step 3 the next day. If errors persist, your child may not be ready for Level 2 Matching. Move back a step, and allow your child to practice Level 1 Matching. Follow the procedures outlined in Level 1 Matching by using only one pair of objects at a time. Above all, avoid drilling or becoming impatient or frustrated with your child. To be successful, learning must be a gratifying experience for both you and your child.

However, if your child has successfully learned to match shapes and colors at Level 1 Matching, no great difficulties should be encountered in performing any of the steps in Step 3; therefore, after completing Step 2, a child should be able to complete Step 3 with equal ease.

Step 4

The child must now discriminate using the cup instead of the shoe. Hold up a cup. Say, "Cup. Put cup with cup." The child takes the cup and places it with the other cup on the tray. Do not allow errors. If errors occur, refer to correction procedures described under Step 3.

Repeat the exercise over a period of 2 or 3 days, using the same set of objects, but changing the order in which they are placed. Never ask the child to do the entire exercise more than once per session.

Every 2 or 3 days, introduce new pairs of objects, but don't forget to review the ones the child has already learned. Remember that the goal is to work on vocabulary as well as on perceptual skills. This is why it is important to reintroduce the objects already learned on a regular basis. Introduction to Picture Discrimination

GOALS: To select and match at least four different pairs of identical pictures. To repeat, or attempt to repeat, the names of the objects, and to eventually name them spontaneously. This exercise repeats the procedures that were described in the previous lesson. The only difference is that 5 to 10 pairs of identical pictures are used instead of objects. Again, select pictures of objects that are familiar to your child. Some of the pictures may represent the same objects that were used in the previous exercise. However, for the sake of novelty and to expand your child's vocabulary, do not neglect to add several new items. Pictures of a baby, a house, a tree, a car, and a bird may be good choices. In the beginning, avoid pictures that are similar in appearance, such as dogs and cats, apples and tomatoes, or balls and balloons.

It is expected that once your child has mastered the exercises for shape, color, and object discrimination, it will no longer be necessary to repeat these exercises except perhaps once every 2 weeks. However, the work with pictures should continue as a regular part of your child's education. As soon as your child is able to match a picture spontaneously for 3 consecutive days, introduce a new pair of pictures. Keep a list of words that your child can say or communicate through sign language.

Review newly acquired words on a daily basis, or every other day, as the list gets longer. Remember to generalize; let your child hear and say these words at every opportunity in different environments. As soon as your child has a spoken vocabulary of 20 to 30 nouns, you may wish to introduce other parts of speech.

Photo 13.2. Picture matching.

Photo 13.3. Alicia reads and matches words.

(For ideas and teaching procedures for more advanced language and pre-academic skills, refer to Teaching Reading to Children with Down Syndrome. This excellent book by my colleague, Patricia Logan Oelwein, is based on her work with children attending the Model Preschool Program for Children with Down Syndrome at the University of Washington.) At the same time do not overlook Chapters 14 and 15 in this book. These contain procedures to help you teach your children pre-spoken verbal skills, such as babbling and vocal imitation. Without these early exercises, it may be impossible for children with DS to repeat or speak words independently.

14. Early Intervention for Language Development

It was pointed out in Chapter 2 that one of the major deficits affecting children with DS lies in the area of language development. Deficits can occur in articulation as well as in the time when speech begins. Standardized tests, such as the *Bayley Scales of Infant Development-Second Edition* (Bayley, 1993), frequently indicate noticeable delays by the time a baby is 6 months old.

It hardly seems possible that such a young child could already exhibit a language delay, or that a parent should even begin giving thought to a child's progress in this area at such an early age. But it is possible, and it is true because language, like everything else related to a child's growth and development, is a gradual process of evolving skills beginning at birth.

Too often parents and teachers do not become concerned about a child's lack of speech before age 3 or 4. Such a view overlooks all the prerequisite skills that a baby should be acquiring from birth. These skills are the fore- runners of meaningful speech, which generally begins emerging shortly after a child's first birthday. Early training in language development, therefore, is as essential as the exercises for neck control, sitting, looking, reaching, and standing. These statements are made not for the purpose of alarming parents, but rather to create an awareness. They are an attempt to alert parents and to tune them in to the earliest beginnings of language development.

Language and speech involve more than saying words. Language is communication, and communication is the means by which we express our needs, share our experiences, and reveal our emotions.

Communication begins with the baby's first cry, the first penetrating eye-to-eye look with a mother, the first smile, and the first reaching out for and grasping of a father's finger.

Communication is both verbal and nonverbal, and involves the abilities to receive, understand, and express ideas, information, and emotions. These abilities to comprehend what is being communicated, and to communicate ill return, are called *receptive* language and *expressive* language.

When you lean over your baby's crib and say, "Come," and the baby holds ou1 his or her arms to be picked up, your baby is showing both receptive and expressive language development. The baby's active response indicates that he or she understands what is meant by your words (receptive), and that he or she is also able to communicate the desire to be lifted from the crib (expressive)

This is where training for future language begins, with parental awareness of the baby's earliest efforts at communication. It also focuses on increasing and refining the baby's ability to communicate verbally as well ae nonverbally. Chapter 10 describes exercises for social and visual responsiveness and development, and stresses the importance of establishing good visual attentiveness and auditory responsiveness in a baby. These skills are so basic to language development that it may be helpful to review that section, especially the final three paragraphs of the chapter, and to use tha1 information as your first step in language intervention.

In order to increase a child's expressive communication skills, you mus1 first be aware that these behaviors are occurring and, second, you must respond to them. Moreover, you must respond verbally as well as with your actions; it is very important to pair your gestures with words. One way to bridge the gap between gestures and speech is to provide the verbal input f child needs in order to begin speaking. When your baby holds out his or he1 arms to be picked up, you should say, "Up" as you take your baby in your arms, and "Down" as you set the baby down. If your baby points or reaches for a toy such as a ball, you must respond by saying, "Ball. You want the ball?" and then help your baby to obtain it.

Responding positively to a baby's communication gestures reinforces this behavior, and it teaches the baby that communication gives him or her control over the environment. The baby learns that communication is useful and rewarding and should be resorted to routinely. In addition to responding to your baby's nonverbal communication when it occurs, you should also encourage and elicit more communication every time you are in contact with your baby by creating needs for him or her to communicate.

For example, you should teach your baby to reach for a bottle of milk at feeding time. As you bring the bottle within reach, give the verbal cue "Bottle" emphasizing the "b" sound, and teach your baby to reach for it. Many of the tasks that you will be doing in developing eye-hand coordination will be helping to develop receptive and expressive language skills as well.

Mother-Child Verbal Interaction

In order to assess mother-child verbal interaction among children in the Down Syndrome Infant Learning Program, two 5-minute pre- and post-trial observations were taken on verbal exchanges between eight mother-child dyads (Dmitriev, 1979).

Observations were made under specified conditions. After placing her son or daughter in a highchair or infant seat, the mother was asked to show pictures to her child. Ten familiar drawings (e.g., a smiling face, cat, dog, ball, car) were selected from the *Peabody Picture Vocabulary Test-Revised* (Dunn & Dunn, 1981), Level I, for this purpose.

Mothers were instructed to show and name the pictures for 5 minutes. During this time, maternal speech and infant vocalizations were tallied. Mother and child utterances that occurred within the same 15-second interval were counted as co-occurring responses. Maternal repetition of a baby's vocalization, a baby's self-initiated sounds, as well as the total individual verbal output by mother and baby were also recorded.

Since the mothers tended to speak in phrases such as "Kitty, look at the kitty. Here's a ball, say ball," each phrase rather than each word was counted as an instance of maternal speech. If a mother paused at the beginning of a new 15-second segment of recording time and the infant was the first to vocalize, the mother's first utterance following the baby's vocalization (if the utterance occurred within the 15 seconds) was counted as a maternal response. Data were also taken on the number of times that a mother or child imitated a word or sound uttered by the other.

Pre-trial Results

Pretrial data showed that there were far too many words spoken by the mothers, suggesting that few babies had opportunities to respond within the 15-second intervals. We also found that the mothers rarely imitated their baby's initiated verbals.

Post-trial Results

After discussing the pretrial findings, we cautioned the mothers to use fewer words and to allow their babies to make responses. We also reminded them to repeat their baby's spontaneous verbals.

We were pleased that the post-trial data showed that once the mothers used fewer words, the babies' verbals increased by over 50%. Although the mothers still failed to echo their babies' vocal sounds with any consistency, this exercise suggested that adult speech can elicit babbling as long as verbiage is limited to short phrases or single words, and is paced to accommodate the rate and promptness of a baby's response. Table 14.1 illustrates our findings.

Table 14.1

Individual Data: Pre- and Posttrial Scores on Initiated Verbals, Responses, and Imitation for Each Mother–Child Dyad

Subjects	Verbals Pretrial	Verbals Posttrial	Maternal responses and imitation of child-initiated vocalizations Pretrial	Posttrial
Name: R. D.				
Mother	69	45	1	0
Child: 20 months	4	1	7	7
Name: D. J.				
Mother	20	43	0	2
Child: 19 months	0	5	4	24
Name: E. B.				
Mother	101	65	0	1
Child: 14 months	0	5	19	13
Name: E. I.				
Mother	82	77	0	4
Child: 13 months	0	16	10	5
Name: M. P.				
Mother	76	80	0	2
Child: 13 months	2	10	3	19
Name: M. O.				
Mother	57	44	1	2
Child: 13 months	2	2	9	17
Name: R. O.				
Mother	108	104	0	2
Child: 11 months	0	15	4	5
Name: A. S.				
Mother	97	49	0	3
Child: 10 months	0	4	4	4

Babbling as a Prerequisite Skill

In the past, authorities in the field of language development tended to dismiss babbling as an infantile vocal exercise unrelated to future speech. More recent research supports the view that babbling serves an important function as a prerequisite for talking. Babbling, and similar vocalizations that babies engage in, are vocal exercises that can impart strength and agility to the mechanisms of vocalization and articulation. Singers, lecturers, and actors, who use their voices professionally, routinely perform vocal exercises in order to improve their oral production. Babbling also gives auditory feed- back, that is, it accustoms the child to the sounds and variations of human speech. Furthermore, a positive relationship has been found between a baby's rate of babbling at 3 months of age and the baby's subsequent development. It has also been reported that a baby's babblings appear to be significantly related to preschool language development (Ferguson, 1978; Smart & Smart, 1973).

It has been my observation that, although babies with DS are able to babble very much like normal babies, their babbling is not as sustained, nor as frequent, as that of typically developing babies. It can be expected, for example, that babies will engage in these vocal exercises for many minutes without stopping. Few babies with DS do this without adult stimulation and encouragement.

It has been suggested that babies with DS babble less for at least two reasons. The first may be related to the baby's general hypotonia (muscle weakness), which, by affecting the baby's vocal apparatus, makes it harder and less intrinsically rewarding for babbling to occur without additional reinforcement.

The second reason has to do with the phenomenon of auditory feedback. It has been determined that babies like to hear themselves make sounds. Hearing themselves appears to be highly reinforcing to babies, so they tend to continue their vocal exercises just to keep themselves entertained. Unfortunately, as we already know, children with DS don't always hear as well as they should. Hearing can be impaired by the smallness and irregularities of the ear canals common to the syndrome, or it can frequently be caused by middle ear infections resulting from colds and allergies. Moreover, babies with DS rarely babble as loudly as, or even as shrilly as, some typical babies do. So there is a probability that babies with DS cannot hear their vocalizations. Therefore, babies with DS are not motivated to continue the activity long enough to discover, reproduce, and practice sounds that they will need later for intelligible speech.

As pointed out earlier, the incidence of hearing impairment is extremely high among children with DS. Remember also that even after an infection has been treated with antibiotics or decongestants, it may be 3 to 6 weeks before normal hearing is completely restored. As concerns your own child with DS, be aware of the possibility of an ear infection if he or she has frequent colds, appears irritable, or does not respond when spoken to, and seek a doctor who is sympathetic and knowledgeable.

Hearing is essential for speech to develop. Children who are deaf, for example, might make vocal sounds in early infancy, but usually cease all vocalization after 6 months of age and, without treatment and hearing aids, never learn how to speak. There are a number of things you can do to stimulate your baby's vocalization. Before you begin the exercises on babbling, however, remember to assess your child according to the Records of Physical Development located in Tables A.1 and A.2 of Appendix A.

Visual Reinforcement of Babbling

There is no question that appropriate adult-child verbal interaction increases a baby's babbling. At the same time, several investigators, including myself, have discovered that a visual reinforcer such as a light that automatically turns on at the sound of a baby's voice, can be an even greater stimulus for sustained verbal output.

In my study, I used a voice-actuated switch that turned on a goose-necked reflector lamp as soon as a baby made a vocal sound. The lamp remained lit for as long as the baby continued to vocalize. By turning off whenever the baby stopped babbling and relighting as soon as vocalizations resumed, this voice-actuated apparatus became an intriguing stimulus, which even very young babies learned to control with the sounds they produced. These voice-actuated switches are available in stores selling electronic equipment.

To make the lighted reinforcer even more interesting, I attached several pictures (one at a time) to a translucent lamp. The illustrations that I selected were a stylized smiling face, a black mask, and a circle cut out of a colorful piece of gift-wrapping paper (see Figure 14.1). The light behind the pictures gave them an attractive luminated brightness. Under these conditions, the data showed a significant increase in babbling among all 10 of my subjects who were 4 to 20 months old. I also learned that the younger children responded better to the black-and-white drawing of the smiling face. Children who were 12 months of age or older preferred the more complex design of the red and yellow gift-wrapping paper.

Early Babbling

GOALS: To increase the amount of babbling and the number of different sounds that the baby is able to initiate and imitate accurately.

Make eye contact with the baby and then talk and babble to the baby; make the sounds ah, baba, dada, and mama. Talk directly to the baby, keeping your face and lips about 8 or 10 inches away from the baby's face. As you talk, watch the baby's face. Is the baby making lip movements in an attempt to imitate you? If so, smile, nod, speak, and encourage participation.

Figure 14.1. Pictures of a face (a), a mask (b), and a circle of gift-wrapping paper (c) that were used as luminated visual reinforcers.

Pause after talking to the baby, and give the baby a chance to vocalize in response. Try to establish a give-and-take pattern, a dialogue, with you and the baby taking turns. If the baby begins babbling, don't interrupt, but continue to encourage him or her by maintaining eye contact, smiling, and nod- ding. When the baby stops, repeat his or her sounds and try to get the baby talking again. Modulate your voice. Experiment with pitch and loudness to discover what works best. Repeat the exercise. Practice for 5 minutes at a time, at least three times a day.

It is best to begin this type of vocal interaction at birth and to maintain it, modifying the exercise as necessary, until true speech begins to occur. However, this procedure is recommended for any child who is not babbling or imitating sounds, whatever the child's age.

Babbling in Response to Objects and Pictures

GOAL: To look at objects and pictures and respond by touching and babbling. New and interesting toys, colorful shiny mobiles, and pictures tend to elicit vocalizations in babies. Be aware of objects that motivate your baby to babble. Make these things available when you are not around to talk to your baby. At other times, look at pictures together. Select fairly large, well- colored (realistic) illustrations of familiar objects and animals.

Encourage your baby to point to or touch the pictures. Babies usually begin pointing to a picture by touching and patting the page with their hands. This is a typical response and should not be discouraged. Pointing with an index finger will come later.

Your present goal is to motivate your baby to babble and to repeat the sounds you make. Name the pictures, and repeat and reinforce any vocal response that occurs. The previous section on mother-infant interaction shows how vital it is not to overwhelm a baby by speaking too rapidly or by using too many words. Single words, spoken with pauses, are more likely to elicit verbal sounds from a nonspeaking child.

Figures 14.2 and 14.3 show samples of the results of my study. In both cases there was a dramatic increase in babbling under the reinforcement condition (the light was turned on). See graphs B1 and B2 in each figure. Com- pare these graphs to graphs A 1 and A2 in each figure, which illustrate the amount of vocalization that occurred during the baseline 5-minute intervals without lighted visual feedback. These sample data are representative of the performance of the entire group of children in this research project.

Developing Meaningful Speech

GOAL: To repeat and imitate modeled sounds and words.

The next step after babbling is the development of meaningful speech. As pointed out earlier, speech is more than the utterance of words; it is a complex system of receptive language, cognitive, and social development. Nevertheless, even if a child masters all of the necessary skills, there is no guarantee that speech will occur. This, in fact, appears to be the problem with children who have DS. Invariably, their receptive, social, and cognitive performance greatly surpasses their speaking ability.

When a child's earlier babbling does not spontaneously evolve into meaningful speech, it becomes the task of the parent and the teacher to mold the child's articulations into words. This procedure relies almost exclusively on the child's ability to imitate. Imitation plays such a major role in the acquisition of articulate speech that this topic will be discussed separately in the next chapter.

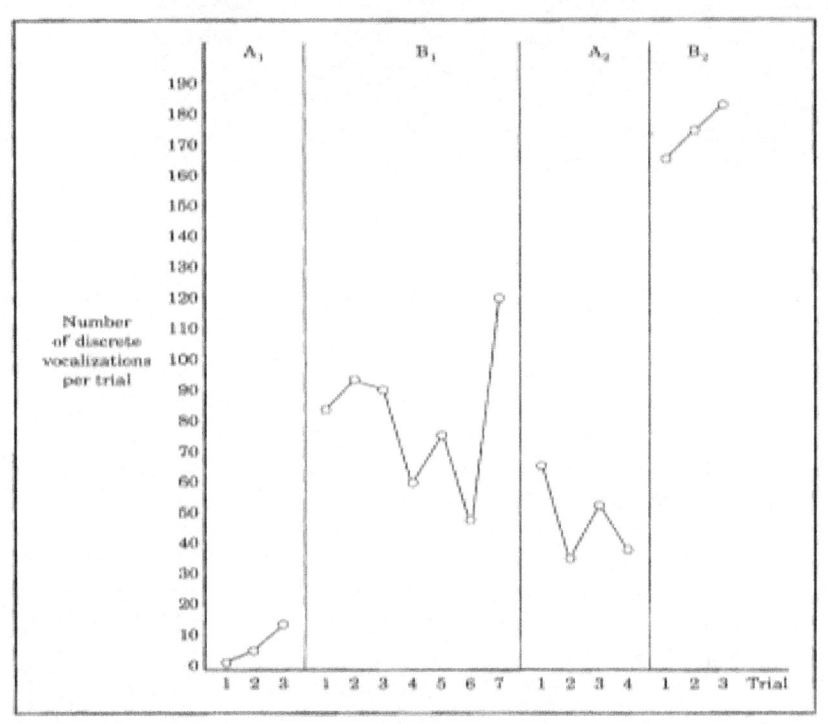

Figure 14.3. Number of discrete vocalizations per 5-minute trial under baseline A_1 and A_2, and treatment B_1 and B_2 conditions.

Total Communication

No discussion on language development in children with special needs would be complete without mentioning "total communication" as a useful and powerful technique.

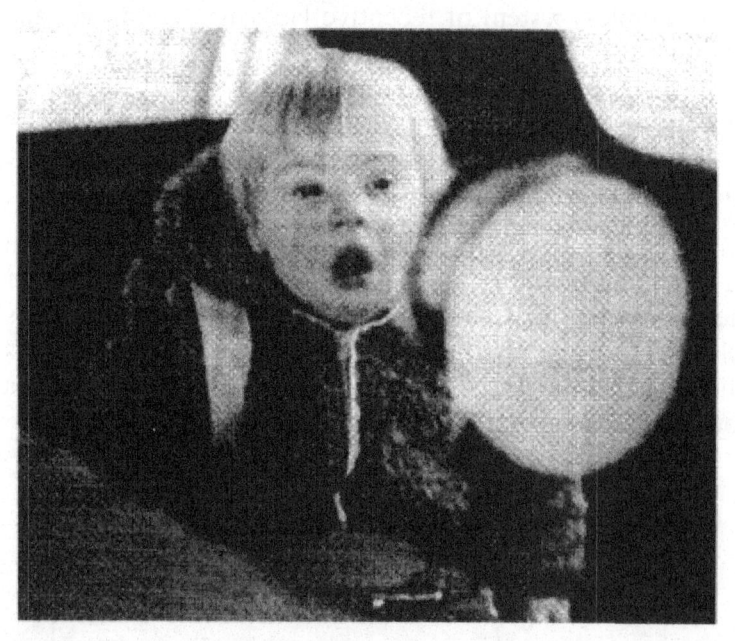

Photo 14.1. D. J. vocalizes as he fixates on the luminated visual reinforcer.

Total communication is a system that combines spoken words with signs (gestures). The terms *sign* and *signing* apply to the accepted system of hand and finger gestures used to teach language to the deaf and hearing impaired. This method of combining signs with spoken words has been very effective in developing spontaneous speech in basically nonverbal children with DS, and is used routinely with individuals or groups of children who need this kind of instruction.

It has been found that many children who fail to communicate verbally can readily learn to sign. In many instances, we have noted that the silent, and frequently rebellious and "stubborn" child, becomes compliant and out- going once he or she understands gestures. It appears that children who make no attempt to speak have not learned that words or sounds can be used to express ideas, or to obtain items and services from the environment. Signing, as a system of more basic self-expression, is easier to comprehend.

Initially, many parents are concerned when they see total communication introduced into their child's program. They are fearful that their child will become so dependent on signing that he or she will never learn to speak. This certainly is not the case. The whole purpose of total communication is to help the child learn to use speech meaningfully. Moreover, every sign that a child sees or learns to make is used in conjunction with a spoken word. As children acquire this mode of communication, they generally progress very rapidly to speaking. And, as their verbal skills improve, they no longer find it necessary to rely on signs.

Imitation, the subject of the next chapter, is also a factor in acquiring speech. Learning how to sign is important not only as a means of helping a child to communicate, but also as an exercise in developing imitative skills. For more information on signing, refer to Bornstein and Saulnier (1984).

Photo 14.2. A boy who is hearing impaired reads and signs the word *apple*.

15. The Importance of Imitation

Imitation is the ability to observe the action of another child, person, animal, or object, and then to reproduce that action precisely as performed by the model. This ability is an extremely important aspect of learning.

Yet, important as it is, imitation is frequently overlooked by parents as well as teachers as an essential skill in a child's early development.

Books and articles about children with DS frequently stress that these children are great "mimics" and "comics." These observations, like many other myths, are misleading. From our experience at the DS program, we have found that most babies and preschoolers with DS do not imitate readily. Because of this deficit, much learning that occurs spontaneously in the typically developing child, who begins to imitate before 1year of age, can fail to take place.

The children with DS who have been called mimics are generally much older and have, in most cases, been residents in an institution. The institutionalized individuals whom I have observed have indeed learned to imitate. They imitate gestures and rituals, but without apparent purpose or meaning. It appears that this skill has come too late in their development; their ability to imitate has not helped them learn social and intellectual skills as it normally does in early childhood. It has not taught them expressive language or the simple skills of everyday life. More importantly, the mimicking is not used appropriately in relation to what the situations demand.

What, then, is the actual relationship between imitation and learning? Does imitation facilitate learning? What imitation does foster is awareness. In order to imitate, a child must observe and be able to react to what he or she sees and hears. Attention and awareness are the keys to learning. This is the role that imitation plays in learning; imitation helps to develop the important prerequisites for acquiring new skills-attention and awareness.

The child who does not do what is expected in a specific situation, who is not "with it," or who seems unaware or shut off in another world, might well be a child who has never learned to imitate. Such a child is not "tuned in" to the actions of others; he or she is not picking up important nonverbal cues from the behavior of others that should indicate to the child how he or she should act.

For example, a preschool teacher announces that it is time for juice and guides one or two children to their places at a table. Other children notice what is going on and follow suit *without additional teacher direction*. They are, in fact, imitating the modeled behavior of the teacher and their classmates. They are able to respond correctly, even if they did not hear what the teacher said and did not know what they were supposed to do next.

This type of appropriate imitative behavior appears to occur spontaneously at what might be considered an almost subconscious level. But the child who has not learned how to pick up on these behavioral cues continues with whatever he or she is doing, seemingly oblivious to what is going on.

The extent to which a child is able to respond appropriately to what he or she sees, hears, feels, tastes, and smells indicates how well and to what degree the child is able to function independently. Imitation is one of the basic ways by which a child learns to respond correctly.

It would be impossible to list the extensive general and specific kinds of learning that can occur through the imitation of modeled behavior. In fact, this is learning that continues throughout life. Every day, we have the opportunity to learn new skills and to learn how to act in new situations by observing the behavior of others.

Children, like adults, learn many self-help, social, academic, and play skills through imitation. In all of these areas, the ability to imitate is helpful, but not crucial. For language development, however, the ability to imitate is absolutely essential. A child who hears, but is unable to reproduce (imitate) the sounds of words heard, will never be able to talk. Moreover, all children of the world learn to walk and eat and work in basically similar ways; only the spoken languages are different. A child that does not hear language will never learn to speak.

There are some specific exercises and procedures which can be used to help develop imitative skills. In order to teach imitation, begin with large gross motor movement and, whenever possible, combine movement with sounds (words). Give physical assistance (shape) if the response does not occur spontaneously. Begin training when the baby is 8 months old and continue until he or she is able to repeat modeled words. This usually occurs between 36 and 48 months of age.

Imitation-Level 1: 8 to 18 Months

Tapping on a Table

GOAL: To imitate tapping on a table readily and without shaping. Seat your baby at a table or in a highchair. Sit across from the baby. Be sure that he or she is able to attend and make eye contact with you.

Say, "Tap the table." Demonstrate tapping with your palms, saying "Tap, tap, tap," in a precise rhythm.

If the baby responds, even with a slight, tentative tap (maybe only one hand at first), show delight, praise the baby, and repeat the tapping two more times. If the baby makes no response, repeat the exercise, and shape by taking the baby's hands and going through the motions of tapping, saying, "Tap, tap, tap." Then repeat again.

When your baby masters tapping, you can create other simple gross motor actions like stamping feet and swinging arms. After you are satisfied with your baby's responses, you may go on to Level 2 Imitation.

Do not be discouraged if learning to imitate does not occur as rapidly as you would like. Some children, depending on their age and development, require several weeks of practice before they grasp the concept of imitation. This is why it is important to keep these lessons interesting, lively, and brief-no more than 5 to 10 minutes a session. Also, avoid relying too heavily on shaping. Give your child a chance to make spontaneous responses at the beginning and end of each session. Discontinue shaping as soon as spontaneous responses begin to occur.

Imitation-Level 2: 18 to 36 Months

These exercises require finer observational skills and, therefore, are introduced after a basic ability to imitate has been acquired. At this level the basic exercises can be supplemented with any number of simple finger plays and nursery rhymes. Use the same procedures of demonstrating, praising, and shaping that were used in Level 1.

Pointing to Body Parts

GOAL: To point to body parts on cue. Point to a part of your own body and have the baby point to his or her corresponding body part-eye, nose, ear, mouth, chin, or foot. If the baby does not imitate readily, use a doll or stuffed toy. Point to the doll's ear and say, "Ear point to the ear."

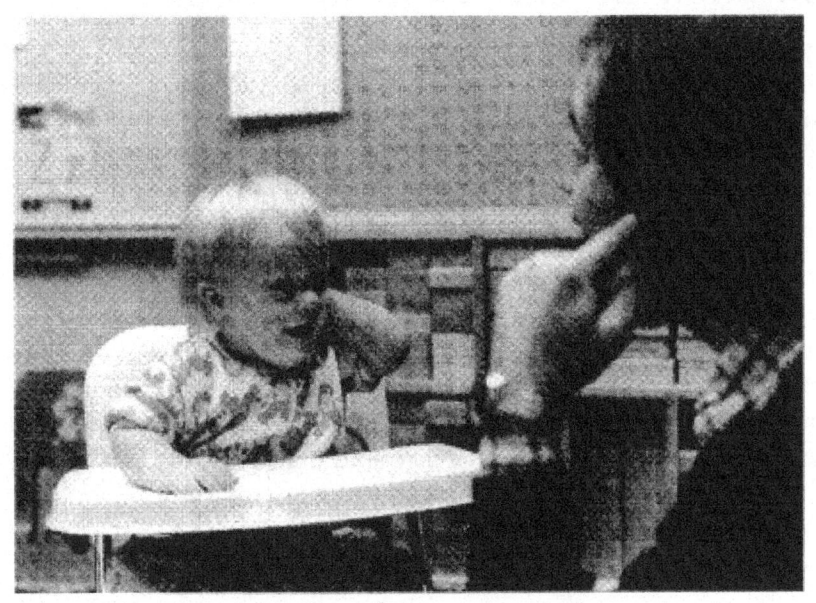

Photo 15.1. Motor imitation and learning of body parts.

Combine Gross Motor Movements with Words of a Song

GOAL: To combine movements with words of a song, when the baby is alone or in a group.

Combine your movements with the words of songs, for example, "Wheels on the Bus Go Round and Round" or "Put Your Hands Up High, Put Yow Hands Down Low." Encourage your baby to imitate your movements.

Finger Plays

GOAL: To imitate hand and finger movements as suggested by the words of a finger play.

You can do finger plays with your baby such as "Teensy Weensy Spider,' "Open Shut Them,'' or "Way Up High in the Apple Tree." Encourage yow baby to imitate your movements by praising any attempts by the baby.

Imitation-Level 3: 24 to 48 Months

If your baby is just babbling or not imitating the sounds you make, or if you wish to increase his vocabulary and improve articulation, some of the exercises at this level may prove particularly helpful. Do not repeat any exercise more than three times in any one session since babies can become easily bored. However, exercises can be repeated two or three more times during the day.

Shaking a Rhythm Instrument

For this exercise, you need two bells, two rattles, or any other two identical musical toys or instruments. First, sit on the floor or at a table facing your baby. Give one of the toys to the baby, and take one for yourself. Hold up the toy and shake it vigorously. Say, "Shake, shake the bell" (name whatever toy you're holding). Demonstrate again, saying, "Shake, shake, shake."

If the baby imitates or attempts to imitate, praise the baby, and repeat two more times. If there is no response, place the toy in the baby's hand and shape, gently shaking the baby's hand that is holding the toy. Praise the baby, and repeat two more times.

Clapping Hands

Sit facing your baby. Clap your hands and say, "Clap." Demonstrate again, shape if necessary, praise the baby, and repeat.

Combining Sounds with Gestures

GOAL: To imitate vocal sounds and gestures. Face your baby. Tap your hand against your open mouth to make a wah-wah-wah sound. Tap your hand against your baby's lips to encourage your baby to make the sound. Also bring his or her hand against your lips to further demonstrate. Shape by placing your baby's hand against his or her lips as you make the sound.

Imitating Vowel Sounds

The *a* Sound

Put your index finger on your chin, drop your jaw, and say, "Ah." By now your baby will no doubt readily imitate the motor response. If your baby does not say "ah" at first, don't press it. Praise a response, and repeat the motion and sound for three total trials.

The e Sound

Make this a long e sound. Put your fingers on the corners of your mouth and make an exaggerated grin. Say, "ee." Praise motor response even if no sound occurs at first. Repeat three times.

The i Sound

Point to your eye and say, "I." Repeat three times

The o Sound

Make a short emphatic o sound, and sign a circle with your third finger and thumb as you make the sound. Praise any motor response, and repeat three times.

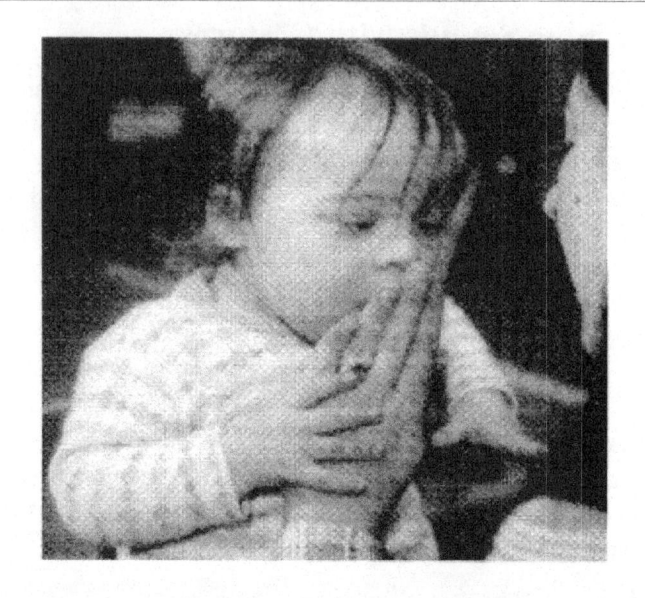

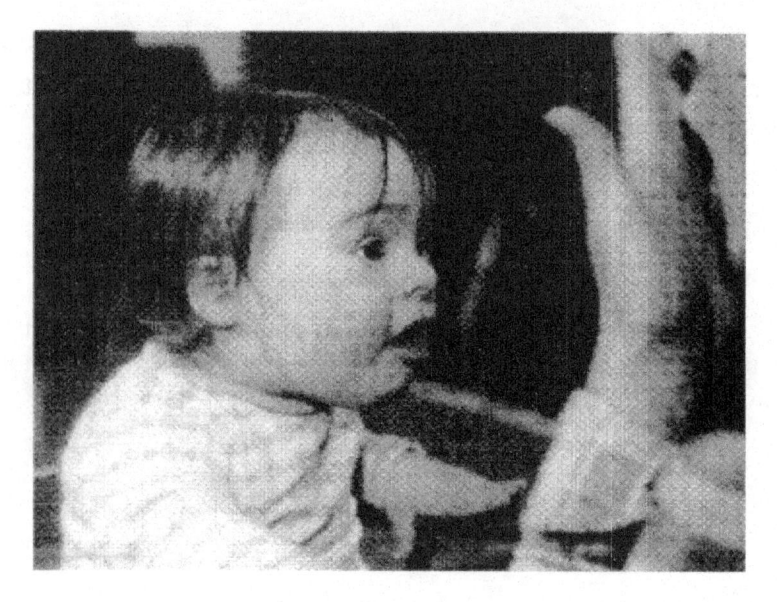

Photos 15.2 and 15.3. Alan learns to imitate gestures and vocal sounds

The *u* Sound

Make a long exaggerated oo sound, cupping your hands close to your mouth and moving out from your lips as you make the sound. Praise any motor response. Repeat three times.

Again, it may take several days before a sound occurs. Once it does, praise the baby. A bit of your baby's favorite food as an added reward might be a good idea. If a sound does occur, repeat one more time for a maximum of two times. If the baby does not repeat the sound, do not urge him or her; simply move on to something else. Intersperse the language imitation with other imitations that your baby enjoys doing. One child I knew liked to blow out a lighted match. This was a good reinforcer for a correct response and also a good exercise in breath control.

The following case study describes procedures for more advanced speech development. However, as the prerequisite for therapy is the ability to imitate, this is where we must begin.

Joy

Subject: Joy was a 3-and-half year old girl enrolled in the Down Syndrome Preschool Program.

Problem: Although Joy babbled and made verbal responses on cue, very few of the sounds she made could be interpreted as words, or even approximations of words. The main difficulty appeared to be that she did not echo modeled speech and, therefore, her babbling could not be transformed into understandable English.

Target behavior: Joy would learn to echo modeled speech. In Phase 1, she would echo all vowel sounds and a few words that stressed these vowel sounds (e.g., *i* = *"eye"*). In Phase 2, she would echo specific consonants: m, n, k, b, d, and p, and combinations of consonants such as *er*, as in cracker, and *sh*, as in shoe. In Phase 3, she would echo words based on these sounds.

Techniques and measurement: Joy received 10 minutes of individual instruction two to three times a week. A motor response was paired with a desired verbal response. For example, to produce the vowel sound a, Joy imitated the motor response of putting a finger on her chin and dropping her jaw. In order to produce the sound n, Joy imitated the motor response of placing her hand over her nose. Joy was given a marble to drop in a jar for each approximation or correct response.

Data were taken on the number of sounds or words presented, the number of correct responses, the number of approximations, and the number of times Joy did not respond.

Instructional materials: After Joy had learned to echo vowels and consonants, pictures were used to illustrate the modeled words.

Evaluation: The program proved to be very effective. Joy learned readily. It appeared that once she mastered the basic principle of imitating, she quickly generalized to situations outside of the laboratory. Her mother reported much improvement in her speech once it became possible to correct her babbling. Joy also began answering questions (e.g., "What did you do at school?" Joy's answer: "Play."), and volunteering two-word phrases such as "Sit down," "Jim cry," and "Help me."

Results: On the day of her first session, Joy was able to repeat only 45% of the 10 modeled vowels or words correctly. By the end of Phase 1, Joy echoed 28 sounds and words with 100% accuracy.

With the beginning of Phases 2 and 3, when six new combinations of consonants and words were presented, Joy's accuracy dropped to 57%, but by the end of the quarter, six sessions later, Joy's vocabulary had increased to 47 words and she was responding with 80% accuracy (see Figure 15.1).

Discussion and follow-up: These procedures were continued during the spring quarter, with the emphasis on increasing the complexity of Joy's vocabulary and improving the pronunciation of such consonants as b, d, and p, which still presented difficulty at times. Spontaneous speech was also emphasized.

Midway through the spring quarter, Joy had completed eight additional speech lessons. On the day of her last training session, Joy echoed 45 new sounds and words without error (see Figure 15.1). This gave her a repertoire of 92 verbalizations which she was repeating on first trial with 78% accuracy.

Ten of these words were spontaneous namings of pictured objects. Outside of the laboratory, Joy had a much higher rate of both spontaneous and echoed speech, but the exact number was difficult to record. Nevertheless, it was evident that Joy was continuing to make good progress.

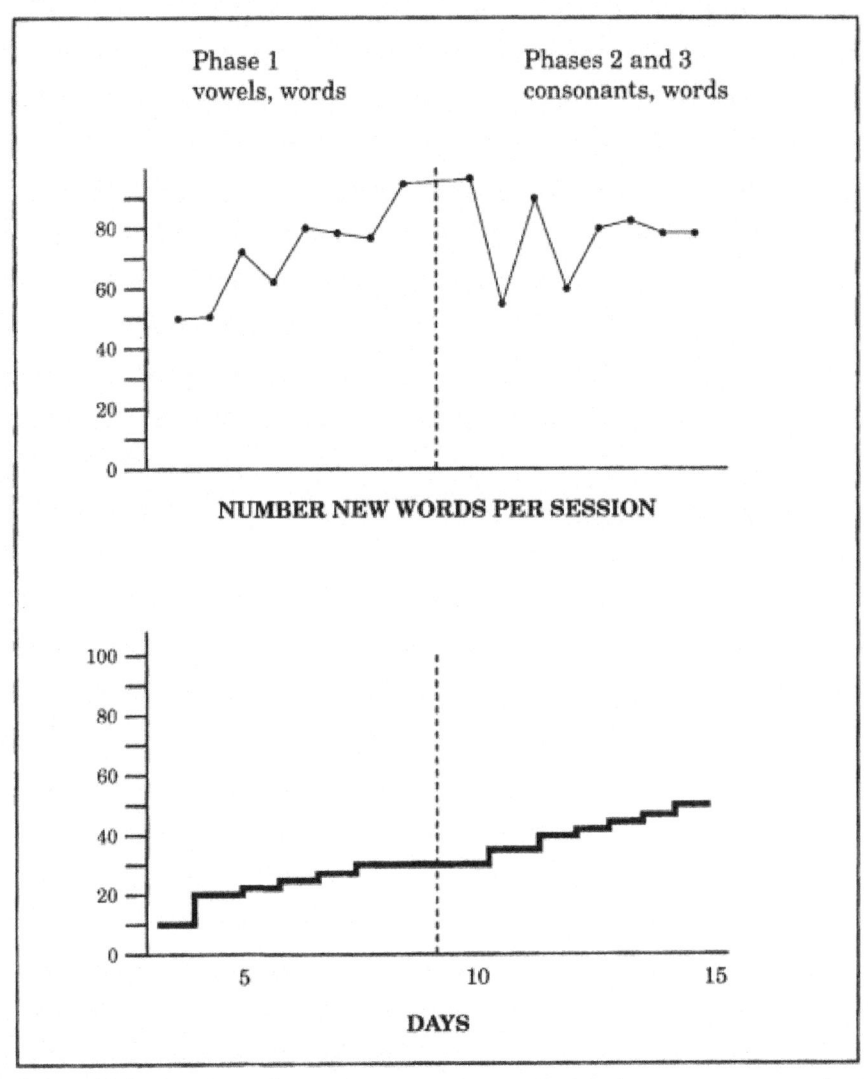

Figure 15.1. Joy during language program: percent correct responses per session.

A Sequence of Imitation Skills

The following list summarizes the sequence of imitation skills as they occur among typically developing children. The imitation exercises in this chaptel are designed to help your child with DS follow the same developmental schedule. Child imitates a visible familiar response. Examples: waving hands, banging on table.

1. Child imitates a visible unfamiliar response. Example: touching elbow.
2. Child imitates an invisible familiar response. Example: raising hands.
3. Child imitates an invisible unfamiliar response. Example: pulling an earlobe.
4. Child imitates a familiar oral motor response. Examples: opens mouth, clamps lips together.
5. Child imitates a familiar sound. Examples: "da-da," "ha-ha."
6. Child imitates an unfamiliar oral motor response or vocal sound. Examples would be sounds that a particular child does not use in his babbling, "ma-ma," "boo-boo," "ee-ee," "ah-ah" (Uzgiris, 1973, pp. 599-604).

16. The Development of Eating Skills

Self-help skills such as dressing, toileting, and eating are acquired in concert with overall physical and mental maturity. It is unrealistic, for example, to begin toilet training until there is evidence that a child has achieved bladder and sphincter muscle control. By the same token, a child must master specific fine motor abilities and cognitive understanding before he or she can become successful at removing and putting on clothing. These developmental milestones apply to the process of consuming nourishment as well. The progression from a liquid diet to semisolid food and, finally, to solid food is governed by a specific maturational timetable. In other words, sucking, mouthing, chewing, and swallowing depend on the child's physical readiness as well as practice, training, and timeliness.

Proper nutrition is essential for good health and optimum development. Without conscious guidance, however, children with DS are apt to develop poor eating habits. For this reason, I wish to devote a separate chapter to this particular aspect of a young child's development.

Feeding Problems

In some cases, feeding difficulties begin at birth, especially when it is necessary to care for a newborn who is too weak or lethargic to take a bottle or nurse well, a problem common to most premature babies. Whatever the rea- son for the problem, this period can be difficult for a mother. It is discouraging to have a baby who will take only an ounce of milk at a time, takes almost an hour to consume that tiny amount, and needs to be fed again 60 minutes later. Mothers who have gone through this process have learned, however, that the struggle, patience, determination, and love that characterize motherhood bring their rewards. Inevitably, the day comes when the baby begins putting on weight and gaining strength, and gradually the nightmare of the early feeding problems disappears. Again, parents must often seek the help of a pediatrician to ensure that the baby gets all the nutrition he or she needs. However, in this case as in all matters concerning their child, parents must also have faith in their own observations and judgment.

In the past, before early intervention programs were established, even healthy, full-term babies grew up with many feeding problems. It was not uncommon for these children to remain on bottles and soft foods until age 5 and even beyond. Worse, the older these children became, the harder the struggle to introduce solid food. Any attempt to introduce these foods usually resulted in choking, gagging, and even vomiting.

Prevention of these problems before they occur is the best way to avoid future trouble. This is accomplished by introducing the baby to spoon-feeding, finger-feeding, and soft and solid foods as soon as the baby is developmentally ready. Usually a baby is ready to accept solid food when there is a decrease in the sucking and tongue projection responses. When this happens, the baby can take food into the mouth without pushing it out with the tongue. In the case of a baby with DS, this developmental process is often delayed due to the general muscle weakness in the jaw, lips, and tongue. Waiting for these areas to develop on their own, however, is not always advisable and can result in serious feeding problems. Early practice results in developmentally appropriate eating skills. Therefore, the following procedures are suggested.

Spoon-Feeding

GOAL: To grasp a spoon with the lips and retain it in the mouth. Between 3 and 6 months of age, begin feeding your baby small amounts of cooked cereal, applesauce, and other similar foods from a spoon. Select a spoon that has a fairly shallow bowl, one that is slightly smaller than a regular teaspoon. If the tongue projection and sucking response are so strong that a spoon cannot be inserted easily into the mouth, first push the tongue inward with the tip of the spoon as it is placed in the mouth, then permit the baby to suck the food off the spoon, as long as the tongue does not protrude beyond the lower lip. Normally, when a child takes food from a spoon, he 01 she does so by a coordinated movement of the upper and lower lips. The lips are extended and puckered as in a kiss, and then drawn back, pulling the food off the spoon and into the mouth. To help your baby develop these movements, try the following exercises. You may do these exercises before meals or any time during the day at your convenience.

First, model little kissing movements with your lips. Help the baby to pucker his or her lips by bringing the baby's lips together gently with your fingers. Pull them out slightly in a pucker and then release. Repeat two or three times per day. Reinforce the baby's response. Next, smear a spoon with jelly or peanut butter, or use a small lollipop (do not use honey since it can cause botulism, a fatal illness, in young children). Place the spoon or lollipop in the baby's mouth and slowly draw it out, running it up against the upper lip. Repeat five times, then do the same with the lower lip, if this can be accomplished without tongue protrusion. As your baby learns these movements, it will become increasingly easier for him or her to take food properly from a spoon and to control the tongue protrusion.

Finger-Feeding

GOAL: To pick up and eat finger foods. Between the ages of 6 and 8 months, babies normally begin bringing everything to their mouths: blocks, rattles, balls, and so on. This is the ideal time to introduce finger foods. Finger foods are edibles that a baby can easily pick up with the fingers and place in his or her mouth. Oven-dried toast, animal crackers, Cheerios, peeled Vienna sausages, and banana slices are good choices. As finger dexterity develops, pieces of cheese that crumble easily, large-curd cottage cheese, or cooked vegetables such as string beans and carrots can be added to the diet.

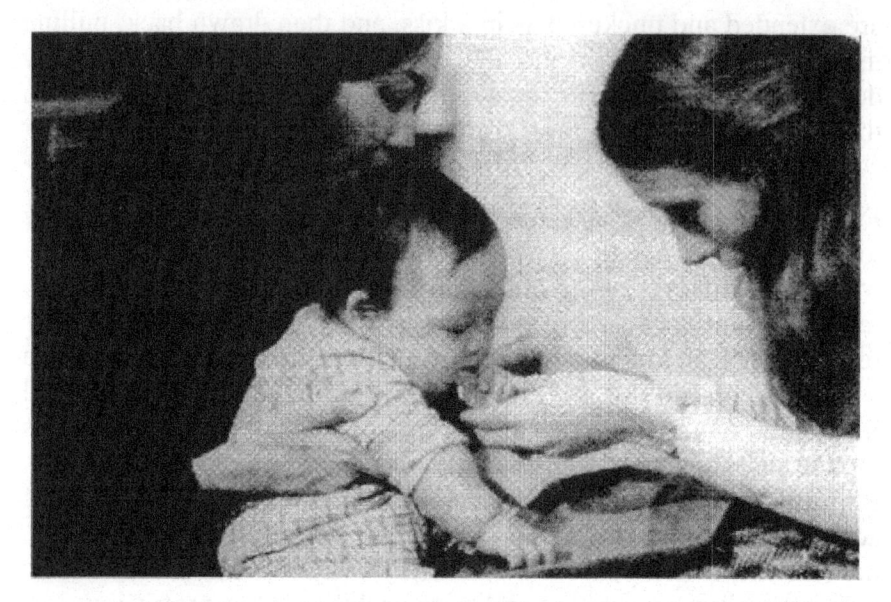

Photo 16.1. Joey gets his first taste of a cracker.

Sometimes a baby with DS does not begin bringing toys to his or her mouth until 12 or 14 months of age, but waiting for this skill to emerge spontaneously is not recommended. A mother need not begin teaching her young child how to put toys into his or her mouth, but she should introduce finger foods around 8 months of age.

Begin with a piece of toast or an animal cracker. Let the baby grasp it, and then physically help the child to bring it to his or her mouth. Do not force the whole piece into the baby's mouth. Simply let a comer of the cracker or toast remain between the baby's lips until it softens, breaks away, and subsequently is eaten. If your baby has already learned to taste different foods from a spoon, this new step should not cause any great difficulties. Usually babies are fond of animal crackers and similar finger foods, and learn to feed themselves in this manner very quickly. If additional practice is needed, shape the response with a suitable food two or three times before each meal, when the baby is hungry. Finally, avoid foods that come in very small bits (e.g., raisins, coconut, corn), foods that splinter such as soda crackers, and foods that have membranes such as orange slices or grapefruit segments. These and similar foods may cause choking in a baby who is just learning how to handle solid foods.

Solid Food and Chewing

GOAL: To accept, chew, and swallow a variety of suitable solid foods. The newborn and the young baby use the lips and tongue in involuntary sucking movements to obtain food. Gradually these movements are replaced with voluntary movements. Over time these movements diminish, and the tongue projection of the very young is replaced with the deliberate movements of the mouth which are necessary for the proper chewing and swallowing of food. About the time that finger foods are introduced, you may also begin adding table foods that can be fed from a spoon. These are solid foods such as well-cooked and mashed vegetables, spaghetti, macaroni, bananas, cooked peaches and pears, and such soft meats as peeled frankfurters, ham- burger in sauce or gravy, fish fillets (watch out for bones), liverwurst, and scrambled or soft-boiled eggs.

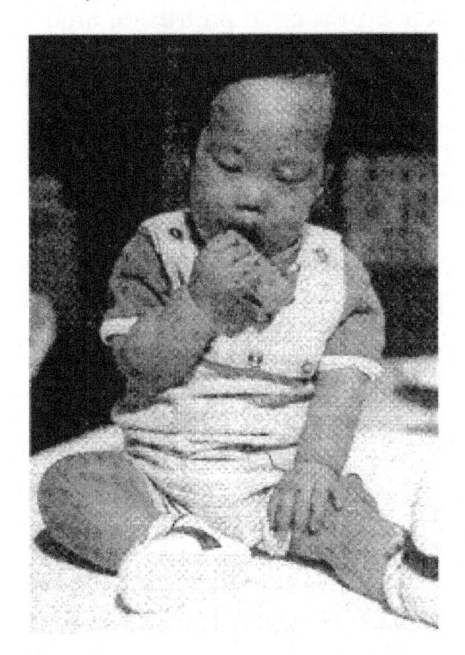

Photo 16.2. At 14 months, Joey eats a cracker with confidence.

It may be necessary to show the child how to chew. This may be done by placing your hand under the child's chin and gently rotating the jaw. Placing food between the cheeks and the gums, where the back teeth will eventually emerge, encourages chewing movements. Since the appearance of teeth in a child with DS is usually delayed, give foods that are solid, but soft enough to be chewed by the gums alone. It is important to give your child this experience with chewing because, as specialists point out, there is a critical period for learning to eat solid foods. After this period has passed, it is much more difficult to learn this skill, and problems with refusal, gagging, and vomiting can develop. Moreover, many of the muscles used in chewing and swallowing are used in speech. Thus, advanced eating skills, the ability to chew and swallow foods of varying textures and solidity, has a positive effect on future verbal articulation.

Tongue Protrusion

Closely related to the muscular development of the mouth, throat, and jaw is the relatively high incidence of tongue protrusion among children with DS. Old textbooks on the subject of DS invariably contained pictures of persons with open mouths and enlarged, protruding tongues. Such illustrations, although undoubtedly based upon actual individuals, were nevertheless another example of the misconceptions and prejudices surrounding this genetic disorder. Tongue protrusion is not an inescapable aspect of DS. In fact, children who have the advantage of well-structured, early intervention rarely develop this problem. If they do, it can be remedied. Basically, tongue protrusion can be attributed to one or more of four causes.

Poor Muscle Tone and General Weakness

As pointed out earlier, hypotonia (muscle weakness) inherent to DS can affect a child's body in many ways: the whole body can be involved in which case the baby will be weak all over; only the lower parts of the body-hips, legs, and knees will show weakness; or the weakness will center mainly in the upper torso-the back, shoulders, arms, and neck.

When the upper part of the body is involved, the weakness may also affect the development of the facial muscles, including the jaw, lips, and tongue. Poor muscular strength in these areas causes the chin to drop down, the mouth to open, and the tongue to come forward. Exercises that strengthen the neck, back, and shoulders also help to strengthen the muscles that control the chin and the tongue. If a child is sitting upright with a straight neck and firm back, it is much less likely that the child's chin will drop down than if the child is slumped forward, with a rounded back and drooping head.

Physical therapists talk about the "pull of gravity." A weak child slumps forward because he or she does not have the physical strength to counteract the pull of gravity and keep his or her body erect. Likewise, gravity causes the lax jaw to drop open. Obviously, in this case we must help the child develop sufficient muscle strength to be able to withstand the pull of gravity and, thereby, eliminate the potential problem of tongue protrusion.

Improper Feeding Patterns

An earlier section in this chapter discussed the importance of introducing solid food and of teaching the child the proper use of lips, tongue, and jaws in eating: lips remove the food from the spoon, the tongue remains in the mouth, and the jaws move to chew the food. These skills prevent feeding problems, assure better nutrition, and also help to prevent and eliminate tongue protrusion, because all of these skills are related to better control of facial muscles.

Enlarged Tonsils and Adenoids

I have seen children with protruding tongues whose tonsils are so enlarged that it would be extremely difficult for them to breathe with their tongues inside their closed mouths. This is another example of a situation in which parents and their children are at the mercy of the medical profession. It is a sad fact that not all doctors are sensitive to the needs of a child with DS. Many dismiss the suggested surgery with the statement that "all young children have large tonsils." AB a concerned parent, seek the opinion of another doctor who might be more inclined to listen sympathetically and to consider the specific needs of my child.

Bad Habit

In many instances, however, a protruding tongue is the result of a bad habit. AB you work on developing muscle control and good eating skills, you may also need to teach your child to remember to keep the tongue in and the mouth closed. The most successful procedures that I have observed were based on modeling and behavior modification. Simply telling children to put their tongues in and close their mouths tends to call attention to the problem, and is, therefore, less effective.

Teaching Tongue-in Behavior

Modeling tongue-in behavior is related to the child's general ability to imitate gestures and facial expressions. Teaching tongue-in skills is simply another behavior that you teach your child to imitate. If tongue protrusion is a problem, the following procedures may help to eliminate the behavior.

If a parent is serious about eliminating tongue protrusion, the proce-dures must be carried out in a serious, systematic manner. At first, it may appear that being systematic is going to involve a large amount of extra work. This is a false impression. Experience has shown that a systematic approach is, in fact, more efficient and effective. It eliminates guesswork, and the results are quicker and more consistent.

Assuming that you are indeed serious about eliminating your child's tongue protrusion, follow a program using the following four steps: time, baseline, intervention, and maintenance.

Step 1: Time

Plan to spend two, 10-minute periods a day working on the program.

Step 2: Baseline

Whenever a teacher or a parent is engaged in teaching a new skill, or in eliminating an undesirable habit, it is essential to have specific before and after measures. Reliance on a subjective impression that "things are improving" can be very deceptive.

Before beginning the intervention program, note the number of minutes during a 10-minute period that your child's tongue is visibly extended past the lower lip. This can be done during the 10-minute periods that you have selected for implementing the program. Select 10-minute periods when your child normally plays independently or is seated in a place where he or she will remain. This will make the observation much easier and more reliable. A good way to measure the time that the tongue is visible during a 10-minute period is to use a stopwatch. Start it and let it run for as long as the tongue is out. Stop it when the tongue disappears, and start the stop-watch again whenever the tongue is visible.

At the end of 10 minutes, write down the total number of seconds or minutes recorded on the stopwatch. You may find, for example, that the tongue was out 7 minutes, or 70% of the time. Seventy percent indicates that during the time you were watching your child, his or her tongue was out most of the time, and an intervention program certainly might be in order. On the other hand, you may find that the tongue was out far less than you previously thought. You might decide that tongue protrusion is less of a problem than you had thought.

A single baseline measure, however, is not a sufficient measure, since it may not give you a true picture of the behavior. It is, therefore, recommended that you repeat the observation during the second 10-minute period that day, and at least two more times the following day. If you are interested in obtaining a really accurate measure of the frequency of your child's tongue-out behavior, you may wish to take additional baseline measures at random times throughout the first, second, and third days of baseline measure.

At the end of each observation, write down the date, time, total number of minutes of observation, and number of seconds or minutes that tongue protrusion occurred. After you have collected the baseline data, you can obtain an average by adding the times recorded by the stopwatch and dividing the sum by the number of entries (observations) that you have made. The resulting figure should indicate the observable incidence of tongue protrusion. Having obtained and recorded these baseline measures, you can now begin a program of intervention.

Step 3: Intervention

Intervention procedures are based on two techniques: modeling and continuous reinforcement. Modeling means that you demonstrate a tongue-in, closed-mouth appearance which your child must imitate.

Continuous reinforcement means that as long as the child imitates, or maintains the closed- mouth behavior, something pleasing or rewarding to the child is taking place.

Deciding on how continuous reinforcement is to be provided and what to use as a reinforcer depends upon your child's preferences. One mother used several interesting toys. During intervention, mother and child, a 10-month- old girl, sat on the floor facing each other. At the beginning of the 10-minute intervention periods, the mother would make eye contact with the child and demonstrate (model) a closed mouth. For the period of time that Tammy imitated her mother, keeping her mouth closed, she was allowed to play with the toys. If tongue protrusion occurred, the toys were immediately removed and the mother would again model the closed-mouth behavior. After Tammy had learned to imitate the closed-mouth appearance, it was no longer necessary to model a closed mouth every time tongue protrusion occurred. Removal of a toy was enough to remind Tammy to close her mouth.

Continuous reinforcement can also be provided by bouncing a child on your knee, on a therapy ball, on a trampoline, or by swinging the child in a swing. Basically, the reinforcement should be something that the child enjoys and something that can be quickly administered or withdrawn (stopped), depending on whether the tongue is in or out of the mouth.

To ascertain whether your procedures are effective, it is essential to continue using the stopwatch to measure the incidence of tongue-out behavior. If you are consistent in your procedures, and very precise in delivering and removing reinforcement contingent on your child's tongue protrusion, you should see positive results after one or two sessions. However, the program must be maintained for several weeks, until the closed mouth has become established and the muscles have strengthened sufficiently to help your child keep his or her mouth closed automatically. A session-by-session stopwatch record will help you to continue with the program until the problem of tongue protrusion is truly eliminated.

Step 4: Maintenance

After a new behavior or skill is achieved, it is important to see that the behavior is maintained. After you have achieved satisfactory tongue control during the intervention sessions, you need to find out if an improvement is occurring at times when you are not directly modeling and reinforcing the desired behavior. By now you should have become a skilled observer of your child's behavior, so it should not be very difficult to take some random measures of your child's tongue behavior at various times during the day.

If your data show that your intervention procedures have generalized, and there is little evidence of tongue protrusion throughout the day, you may begin decreasing the intervention periods to one session per day. If the reduced intervention does not result in a return of tongue protrusion, you can, after 3 to 4 days, reduce the intervention to once every other day. If the improvement is maintained after 3 days, you can reduce the intervention sessions to once every third day. If progress is satisfactory, you can continue reducing the number of sessions per week. By the time you are running the intervention program only once a week, it should be possible to discontinue the program entirely.

If your random measures taken prior to the maintenance phase of the pro- gram show that tongue-in behavior during the intervention sessions has not generalized to other times during the day, it may be necessary to establish an awareness training in addition to an intervention program. Awareness training involves a procedure by which you can remind the child to close his or her mouth. This can be done in several ways. You could catch your child's attention and simply model a closed mouth. If your child complies, smile, and if you think it necessary, deliver some form of quick additional reinforcement, such as a hug. If your child does not comply, deliver a consequence by briefly turning the child away from whatever he or she is doing, or, if the child happens to be playing with a toy, by removing the object until the child remembers and closes his or her mouth.

Finally, the key to success is a relaxed, but systematic and precise approach. Once you have decided to eliminate tongue protrusion, view the procedure as a learning experience that may extend over a number of weeks. Maintain the project as part of a regular daily routine. Don't become careless in your procedures, or try it for a few days, drop it, and then try it again. You either do it, or you don't. If you start the program and discover that you have neither the time nor the inclination to carry it out as it should be done, it is better to postpone the intervention until you feel that you can do it properly. If your child is attending a developmental center, enlist the cooperation and help of the teachers. Above all, remember to keep accurate before and after measures. Records of your child's progress in learning to keep his or her tongue in will give you much needed feedback and encouragement and help you.to carry out the program to a completely successful conclusion.

Part III: Toddlerhood and Beyond: Social and Behavioral Competence

17. The Process of Socialization

Human beings are social animals. Since prehistoric times people have banded together to live in some kind of communal arrangement. From the most primitive to the most highly developed, these social groups have evolved norms, or standards of behavior, that governed their daily lives.

Photo 17.1. Kari pours juice.

From the moment of birth, the human baby is dependent upon social contact with other human beings. The baby's survival and future success depends on how well he or she learns (e.g., assimilates the norms of the social group to which he or she belongs).

A child growing up in the United States, for example, learns to speak English. The child learns how his or her parents behave with one another, and how children are expected to treat parents and one another. Later the child learns what people in his or her own social group believe, what values they hold, and what laws and customs govern their actions. Children growing up in other lands learn the language and norms specific to the cultures into which they are born. This process of assimilating a given society's values and rules is called socialization, and it is the means by which a child becomes integrated into the community.

Socialization is a long and complex process. Like everything else that a child learns, either spontaneously, by example, or by direct teaching, the acquisition of social competence is a learned behavior. At the same time, socialization follows a predictable timetable that is dependent on and correlated with a child's overall development, which also follows a predictable sequence. For example, a child is unable to learn the self-management skill of buttoning a shirt until the child's fine motor abilities are sufficiently advanced to enable him or her to grasp a button with two fingers.

Social acceptance, by peers and by society as a whole, is essential to one's self-esteem and success in life. Initial acceptance generally depends on a per- son's appearance, manners, athletic and artistic abilities, academic achievement, and general behavior. For children with OS or other disabilities who, as a result of their differences, may encounter rejection and prejudice, it is important to develop these attributes that society values.

The hopes and expectations that parents of children with OS experience are no different from the usual concerns of all loving and conscientious parents. They want their child to do well. They want their child to have physical, mental, and social skills. They hope that at least in some area their child will excel. They have pride in their children, and they want the pride to be justified. They recognize and encourage traits that will bring success and approval to their child and praise to themselves. They want their child to achieve in schoolwork, art, music, and sports; in appearance and socially, they want them to be well behaved and well mannered. In most cases these goals, or at least some of them, are not difficult to attain if training and guidance begin in early childhood.

Appearance and Good Manners

An attractive appearance and good manners can be easy to achieve. Neat, clean clothing and an attractive haircut enhance the appearance of any individual. Short hair is generally not becoming to children with DS. Little girls look best with long hair that is braided or curled. Boys also look best with hair that is styled to cover their ears and the backs of their necks. In some cases a side part is becoming.

Good manners can be taught. Parents who are aware that society will judge their child with DS by how he or she behaves may have to pay more attention to teaching appropriate behavior than they might with their typically developing offspring.

If the parents are realistic in their expectations, taking into account the child's age and general development, I see nothing wrong with insisting upon good manners. A parent who insists that a 2-year-old say "thank you" and "please" before the child can say "milk" or "cracker" may be a little pre- mature in their expectations. However, by age 5 or 6 every child should possess basic social skills that include saying "please" and "thank you," eating neatly, using a handkerchief or tissue properly, and showing consideration for others.

At about this same time in the child's development, parents should stress that it is not polite for little girls to sit in a way that exposes their underwear, and that it is equally inappropriate for boys and girls to hug and kiss anyone other than immediate family members. Sometimes, because children with DS are responsive to affection, well-meaning friends and even acquaintances will encourage this sort of hugging and kissing. Such inappropriate adult behaviors can become confusing to a child and lead the child to expect to be hugged by total strangers. Sometimes parents have to be reminded that they must teach their children with DS the same rules of social behavior that they would automatically expect from their typically developing children.

Photo 17.2. Jason and Cody.

Achievements in Academics, Art, Music, and Sports

The purpose of early intervention is to prepare children for success in the future. The question is no longer whether or not a child with DS can learn to read or succeed academically. Reading is a skill that is usually easily mastered. Other subjects may be more difficult; nevertheless, all of our former Early Intervention Program children graduated from high school and are now gainfully employed. Many are now living independently, with only minor support from their parents or other responsible individuals. In addition to being able to hold paying jobs, people with DS often have a wide range of abilities. Some can work with clay and create ceramic pieces, play piano or guitar, sing, dance, swim, bowl, play tennis, ride horses, and ski. Because so much potential for success and achievement exists, it is up to parents and teachers to encourage its development so that in later life, individuals with DS can enjoy a variety of artistic and athletic activities, reaping the benefits of shared fun and friendship with their peers.

Jason and Cody, the two young men pictured in the photograph, attended an early intervention program modeled after the one at the University of Washington. Both Jason and Cody are employed and live in their own apartments in a complex housing people with special needs.

Problems

Sometimes, however, in spite of their sincere desire to foster their children's social and behavioral development, parents encounter problems which they are unable to resolve. The following three excerpts are from letters that I received from parents who were troubled by their children's inappropriate behaviors, and they are typical of the many questions I am asked.

> At what age do you start addressing socially acceptable behavior? My daughter, for example, at age 2, likes to hug other children. It's nice that she's loving, but other 2-year-olds don't do this, and most children don't like her behavior. Any suggestions or comments?

> My 4-year-old son stuffs food into his mouth and barely chews, so that he chokes badly, quite often. How can I prevent this from happening?

> Although my 4-year-old son feeds himself and walks well, he isn't toilet trained, and refuses to put on any of his clothing. Is this normal for a DS child?

The problem described in each of these letters suggests a deficit in the child's social development. The exuberant 2-year-old who hugs friends and strangers alike, needs to learn less aggressive ways of initiating interaction. A smile, a simple greeting, or a proffered toy are better ways of approaching other children. Hugs should be reserved for family members.

The 4-year-old who stuffs food into his mouth should have been taught better eating habits when he was first introduced to finger foods and other solids. Obviously, cramming food into one's mouth can be dangerous, and it is certainly neither attractive nor socially acceptable.

Photo 17.3. Debbie plays her guitar.

Toilet training is difficult for some children, those who are typically developing as well as those with DS, especially boys. However, the fact that the 4-year-old refuses to attempt self-dressing is a definite deficit in his self-management social skills. Moreover, the boy cannot be expected to use the bathroom efficiently until he is able to manage his clothing independently.

In response to these letters, I made the following suggestions. The best way to deal with the problem described in the first letter is to prevent its occurrence. Parents must learn to anticipate what their child may do and deter an undesirable act before it happens, even if it means physically restraining a child. In the case of the hugging 2-year-old, parents need to put her arms down before she grabs anyone, say "No," very firmly, and then prompt her to say "Hi" or initiate some other socially acceptable response.

Above all, once parents or teachers begin modifying a "bad" behavior, they must be consistent in preventing it, in teaching a child how to behave appropriately, and in remembering to recognize and praise the child whenever the desired behavior occurs.

The second letter described the poor eating habits of a 4-year-old boy. A strategy for teaching better self-feeding skills would begin by placing single, bite-size bits of food on his plate and withholding a second portion until the first has been properly chewed and swallowed. Single slices of a hot dog, cheese cubes, small chunks of fruits or vegetables that can be eaten with a fork or with fingers, paired with verbal encouragement and praise, would be a good way of teaching the boy a more appropriate way of handling his food. The mother who is concerned over her son's refusal to dress himself should begin teaching self-dressing skills by first showing him how to pull off his shoes, socks, and underpants. These are tasks which can be broken down into small steps. A parent can, for example, pull a sock halfway down the foot and then shape the child to remove it completely. The removal of shoes and pants can be taught the same way. After undressing is mastered, the process is reversed and the same step-by-step method can be used to teach self-dressing. Pants, for example, can be pulled up over the legs, allowing the child (with help) to pull them up the rest of the way.

Other important social skills involving play, peer interaction, toileting, and general behavior management will be addressed in the following chapters.

18. The Toddler and Social Development: 18 to 36 Months

Toddlerhood is a highly significant period in the life of a growing child. It is the bridge between infancy and early childhood. It is a time for change and learning, for exploring the world, for satisfying curiosity, for greater independence, for separation from mother, and for forming friendships.

What is true for children in general is equally true for the toddler with DS. Paralleling typical development, these youngsters can show a sudden spurt in physical and intellectual growth. In order to maximize these emerging skills, all children can benefit from participation in an early preschool pro- gram. However, not all programs are created equal, and parents must be aware that not all preschools meet the special needs of the child with DS. As explained earlier, children with DS require direct instruction and intervention in order to meet crucial developmental expectations. In too many instances, left to their own devices, children with special needs remain isolated, even in group situations. The following is a letter from a mother who poignantly describes what happened when she planned a birthday party for her daughter, Allison.

> Last July when Allison turned 4, I invited several normal children from her integrated preschool class to a birthday party. It was a disaster. The children ignored Allison. They played with her presents and when she tried to join in, they pushed her away. They were noisy and rude.
>
> Later when I visited the preschool I saw that Allison is always alone. Although the teacher talks to her, the children never do, and they never include her in their games. Allison is a sweet, well-behaved child. This is breaking my heart. How can I help her?

Allison's isolation is fairly typical of what can happen to a child with DS within a group of nondisabled peers. One can expect average preschoolers to be verbal, noisy, active, and aggressive. Caught up in the excitement of a party, they can be particularly thoughtless and unruly.

Compared to her classmates, Allison has yet to learn a number of important social skills that would enable her to deal with the situation. Moreover, instead of inviting several children, Allison's mother should have asked only one child to the party, preferably one of the younger and quieter children in the school. Additionally, the mother should have planned simple activities that the children could share, and which the mother could supervise.

Ways of helping a child develop friendship-building skills as well as strategies for dealing with the problems described in the letter and other similar concerns will be discussed in subsequent chapters.

If your 3-year-old child with DS is enrolled in an inclusive preschool, make sure that activities are planned in such a way that your son or daughter is consistently involved in whatever the other children are doing. All children, whether they have special needs or not, must be taught to share, to take turns, to play side by side, and to work on projects as a group.

The schedule should be balanced to include quiet periods for listening to stories or engaging in other quiet activities such as easel painting, scribbling, pasting, puzzles, pegs, and block play. There should also be opportunities for active play outdoors as well as singing and moving to music. Self-management skills such as coat removal, toileting, and hand-washing, as well as eating and drinking, should be given equal attention.

In a well-organized preschool, free-play activities are centered on groups of two (with a maximum of three children) because, left on their own, pre-schoolers are unable to function in larger groups. The children are closely supervised, and teachers are sensitive to individual needs. Conflicts are resolved calmly and fairly, and children are taught how differences can be settled without aggression.

If no suitable preschool is available or if the parents prefer to keep their child at home, progress can be maintained if parents remain sensitive to developmental expectations and continue to help their child achieve the next level in his or her social development. Table 18.1 lists the basic skills, including toilet training, which your toddler should begin to master by age 3.

Table 18.1
Record of Social Development: 18 to 36 Months

Communication/Interaction	Date assessed	Plus/minus	Date established
Responds to "Hello," "good-bye"			
Responds to "What is your name?"			
Responds to "How are you?"			
Verbalizes or gestures for food, toys, etc.			

Self-Management/Initiation	Date assessed	Plus/minus	Date established
Takes off jacket			
Undresses fully			
Puts on socks			
Puts on hat			
Puts on shirt and pants with help			
Sits on toilet			
Bowel movement controlled			
Uses toilet			
Stays dry during the day			

Play Skills	Date assessed	Plus/minus	Date established
Entertains self for 10 minutes			
Initiates own play			
Plays in housekeeping corners with dolls, dishes, dress-up clothes			
Plays with blocks, cars, small animals, or dolls			
Plays in water			
Plays in sandbox			
Plays side by side with one other child (Parallel play)			
Shares			
Takes turns			

Goal: By the end of 36 months at least 80% of these skills should be achieved.

Toilet Training

Toilet training should begin when the child is physically ready. This means that the central nervous system is sufficiently mature to control the elimination sphincters (muscles that control the bladder and rectum). The following behaviors are generally indicative of readiness.

Goal: By the end of 36 months at least 80% of these skills should be achieved.

- Bowel movement occurs at a predictable time.
- The child is dry when he or she awakens from a nap.
- The child indicates when he or she is wet or soiled.
- The child remains dry at least 2 hours during the day.
- The child is walking with confidence.
- The child will sit on a toilet for 3 to 5 minutes.

Children with DS are usually ready for toilet training between 24 and 30 months of age. However, do not make the mistake of waiting too long. As soon as bowel movements are regulated or the child wakes up dry after a nap, begin placing the child on the toilet. Children with DS who are not at least partially toilet trained by 3 years of age may be harder to train. Also, some children, whose training begins on a potty chair, may later refuse to use a regular toilet. A child's toilet seat which fits over the toilet can prevent this problem. It is also a good idea to provide a set of steps which can be placed in front of the toilet bowl. The steps are helpful if the toilet is too high for the toddler to sit on independently, and they can also provide a footrest once the child is seated. A flat surface upon which the child can place his or her feet makes the child feel more secure and is likely to result in more successful toilet training. For more information on this subject, refer to Foxx and Azrin (1973).

Play Skills and Social Development

Toddlerhood is also a time for children to learn play skills, to begin social interaction with other children, and to experience new materials. Play is an integral part of a child's physical, mental, and social development. Play, shared with other children, accelerates the socialization process by helping the child master higher levels of competence in interactions, communication, assimilation, flexibility, and compliance.

Activities that are most likely to promote the desired socialization components are doll, housekeeping, and dress-up play; block play with cars, toy people, and animals; painting at an easel; and outdoor play with tricycles, slides, water, and sandboxes. A toddler playing in the housekeeping comer, dressing-up to "go to work," feeding a doll, or rolling out play dough to make "cookies" is assimilating the norms of society. The same holds true for other activities. Through play with blocks, cars, toy people, and animals, the child is reliving what he or she has seen and experienced: buildings, houses, highways, traffic, farm animals, and fenced pastures. In this way children learn and assimilate the realities of their existence.

Water play that involves dipping and pouring teaches self-management skills, which can be transferred to eating skills such as pouring juice or dip- ping a spoon into a bowl of soup.

Painting at an easel is another activity that has much to offer in terms of social, physical, and cognitive development. For example, it encourages standing and large, free arm movements, which are important skills for the child who may still need to strengthen the back and legs and develop the necessary stamina for both standing and walking.

Holding a brush, as the toddler paints, prepares him or her for holding spoons or forks for eating, and pencils and crayons for scribbling and writing. Cognitively, painting teaches colors and the thrill of creating bright patterns on paper. Best of all, painting is an activity that stimulates creativity and imagination, and furthers the social components of assimilation and communication by allowing the child to express through art what he or she sees and feels. A black blob of paint can be an airplane, a yellow patch can be the sun, and a streak of gray can be rain or sadness, which the child cannot yet express verbally. In this way, the young child learns yet another way of communicating with others.

Dealing with colors can also teach flexibility or an alternate way of achieving a desired result. I remember an incident at a preschool for children with Down syndrome that illustrates this point. One spring morning the class took a nature walk. They gathered dandelions and handfuls of lush, green grass. Upon returning to the classroom, Jamie and two other youngsters, Beth and Angie, elected to go to the easels.

Jamie selected a cup of yellow paint and began splashing great yellow dots on his paper.

> "Those look like dandelions," the teacher said.
> Jamie nodded.
> "Grass," he said. "Grass is green."
> "Want green," Jamie demanded.
> "I'm sorry," the teacher apologized, "there's no more green."
> "Green!" Jamie threw down his brush, splattering the floor.
> The teacher handed Jamie a paper towel.
> "Pick up your brush and wipe the floor. Then we'll make green."
> Jamie looked at the teacher who stood waiting for him to comply, then did as he was told.
> The teacher smiled.
> "Good boy, Jamie. Now let's make some green." "Green?"
> "Yes, watch carefully."
> Taking Jamie's cup of yellow paint, she added a few drops of blue paint.
> "Now mix it up, Jamie."
> The boy stirred the paint and looked up questioningly.
> "Is it green now?" the teacher asked.
> Jamie grinned and showed his cup to Beth.
> "Green," he said.

Jamie's interchange with the teacher is an example of how a child learns assimilation, compliance, flexibility, and communication. Jamie's yellow blotches, which the teacher recognized as dandelions, showed an assimilation of the children's morning experience. When Jamie's desire for green paint was not met and he threw down the brush in frustration, the teacher deliberately ignored this display of anger and gave him something positive to do instead. In dealing with developmentally delayed children, or any young child for that matter, it is best to circumvent potential tantrums and displays of obstinacy by suggesting an alternative, appropriate behavior. Such strategies bypass attention to misbehavior and encourage compliance, which can then be reinforced with praise. Furthermore, these strategies teach a child to be responsible for his or her own actions: spattered paint needs to be wiped up. Finally, mixing yellow and blue to make the desired green paint teaches flexibility by showing the child that there may be an alternative solution to a problem.

Outdoor play in the sandbox, on a slide, or on a tricycle gives the child skills that can be shared informally with any number of children in his own backyard or in a park. These are accepted activities for children in our society, and the mastery of these skills enables the child with DS to interact successfully with normal peers.

With parental help toddlers with DS can become competent tricycle riders. If the child is unable to reach the pedals comfortably, the pedals can be raised by fastening a pair of wooden blocks on either side of the pedals. Tri- cycle riding is an excellent physical activity for strengthening legs, and it also gives the child with DS a much needed sense of mastery and the ability to participate as an equal with other children.

Play exerts such a major influence on a child's overall social development that I believe it is important for parents to understand that play skills, like other areas of the child's growth, begin developing at birth and progress in a predictable pattern, from the simple manipulation of objects to highly creative and imaginative uses of materials. I term this progression "Stages of Play." It is possible to classify these stages in the following four main categories.

> Stage 1: This is the manipulative period. Babies hold objects.
>
> Stage 2: This is the exploratory period. The baby gums, looks at, and shakes toys.
>
> Stage 3: This is the constructive period. The child does something with the toys: puts two objects together, stacks blocks, nests cups, pushes a car, and so on.
>
> Stage 4: This is the creative/dramatic period. Play materials are used in a variety of imaginative ways such as blocks being used to build houses, roads, and fences. Children dress

up and role play. Children's artwork becomes representative, and children are able to talk about and describe their work.

Photo 18.1. Tricycle riding.

Most children, by the time they are 3, show signs of approaching Stage 4 in their play. From then on, the creative/dramatic aspect of their activities continues to develop, becoming increasingly complex and innovative. At the same time, pretend play with other children becomes a major part of a child's peer interaction.

By observing your child's play, whether in isolation or in a group, you should be able to determine the level of his or her performance. If play appears to be slow in progressing from one stage to the next, it is important to show your child how he or she can use toys more effectively in order to assure the child's progression to a more advanced level.

Table 18.2 gives examples of how children generally interact with common play materials at each of the four main stages of play.

Table 18.2

Stages of Play: How Materials and Objects May Be Used at Each Stage

Water play	1. Hands in water
	2. Holds objects in water
	3. Dips and pours
	    a. Pours into another container
	    b. Blows bubbles with straw

Car play	1. Takes cars out of basket
	2. Holds, examines cars
	3. Pushes car
	4. Pushes car while walking or crawling
	    a. Pushes car down or across a board
	    b. Car and another car or toy are used in play

Dough	1. Holds dough
	2. Pats dough
	3. Rolls with hands or rolling pin
	4. Uses cookie cutter
	    a. Places "cookies" on tray, etc.
	    b. Decorates cookies

Blocks	1. Takes from shelf
	2. Holds
	3. Stacks less than three blocks
	4. Stacks more than three blocks, makes a tower, bridge, or train
	    a. Any combination of two structures: e.g., train and tower, tower and bridge
	    b. Combination of all three structures
	    c. Blocks and other toys

Housekeeping play	1. Holds dolls or dishes
	2. Puts doll in bed or covers
	3. Pushes doll in buggy
	4. Puts dishes on table or stove, dresses doll
	    a. Feeds doll or pretends to eat from dishes
	    b. Puts on dress-up clothes

Photo 18.2. Parallel play at the water table.

Photo 18.3. Painting at the easel.

Photo 18.4. Julie and Mike engage in creative/dramatic play.

19. Playmates and Social Development

The art of making friends and learning how to interact with playmates is an essential component of the socialization process. The ability to make friends and to get along with people is a skill we all need to learn in order to function well and happily, both as children and as adults. If your child with DS has brothers and sisters close in age, he or she has the advantage of having constant companions from whom the many interactive behaviors that develop between playmates can automatically be acquired. Yet, as a parent, you cannot rely on siblings to be your child's sole associates. That would not be fair to the child with DS or to the other children in the family.

Photo 19.1. Playmates.

It is not within the scope of this book to examine the complex relation- ships that may exist between children and a sibling with a disability. For more information, refer to *Living with a Brother or Sister with Special Needs* (Meyer, Vadasy, & Fewell, 1985). It should be enough to say that whether or not your child with DS is the only child in the family, it is important to allow the child to make his or her own contacts with other children. Between the ages of 18 and 24 months, most children are ready to play with other toddlers for short periods of time. Generally, toddlers play well with older children, following their lead. In the case of the child with a disability, how- ever, an older, typically developing child may become too bossy or impatient with the slower pace of the younger child. In such a case, a slightly younger companion, or one closer to your child's age, may be a better choice. In order to give a child with DS the opportunity to play with other children, it may be necessary to invite likely candidates into your home for an hour's play once or twice a week.

In the beginning, unless you are present and are comfortable with the playmate's mother, I would riot recommend allowing your child to play outside of your home because, if the playmate is a normal child, situations may arise which the playmate's mother may not know how to handle. Moreover, you would not be in a position to guide their play as you might wish.

On the other hand, do not overlook the advantages of including other children with DS among your child's playmates. Experience has shown that early contacts with peers who also have DS can develop into strong, satisfying, and lifelong friendships.

When I began the Model Program for Children with Down Syndrome at the University of Washington in 1971, our first class consisted of 11 children between the ages of 18 and 36 months. To this day, 22 years later, these young people are still friends. They bowl, swim, party, and go to dances together. One couple has been dating since high school and may eventually marry. This same camaraderie has developed among the parents of my former students.

Teaching Social Interaction Between Young Children

When you invite a similarly aged child to play with your toddler, you are doing so for specific reasons: to give both children and yourself a pleasant experience and to teach social skills that include the following.

1. Mannerly interaction

   - Greeting a guest: Learning to say "hello," "come in," and so on.

   - Showing hospitality: Learning to offer toys, food, and so on.

2. Play interactions

   - Parallel play: Children engaging in identical activities independently, yet side by side

   - Cooperative play: Children engaging in a joint activity such as teeter-totter and block play, when each child adds blocks to the same structure

     - Turn-taking: Sharing the use of a toy or equipment for a specific period of time

     - Sharing: Host child cuts a banana in half, with mother's help, and gives a portion to his or her guest

With these objectives in mind, you can plan a visit that will be both enjoyable and beneficial to the children. However, if you expect that you will have time to sit and chat with a playmate's mother after turning the children loose with a pile of toys, the goals that you may have for teaching your child how to make friends and how to play constructively are likely to fail.

Planning for Playtime with a Playmate

For each play period, plan to spend a total of 45 to 60 minutes, divided into 15-minute segments of three different activities. Table 19.1 will help you to plan and participate in the play activities.

Activity 1: 15 minutes of quiet parallel play. Water play or play dough make good choices.

Water play. Provide two fairly large dishpans, half-filled with lukewarm water. Set the pans sides by side or across from each other on a bench or a low table that is waist high to the standing children. Provide aprons made out of plastic bags for the children as well as plastic, metal, or wooden objects to float in the water such as measuring cups, spoons, floating toys, and so on. After a few minutes of play, you can enhance the activity by adding food coloring, gentle liquid soap, or bubble bath to the water.

Dough play. Provide small rolling pins, (short lengths of doweling that are 2 inches in diameter work well), cookie cutters, buttons, old beads, colored toothpicks, or birthday candles for decorating their "cakes" and "cookies." Seat the children at a low table. If this is a new experience for the children, model with your own piece of play dough. Demonstrate how it can be rolled out, shaped, and decorated. Remind the children before the 15 minutes are up that it is time to clean up and put the toys away. Show and tell them what to do, and allow them to gather the toys, and wipe off the table.

Table 19.1
Strategies for Peer Interaction to Increase Communicative Interaction and Cooperative Play Among Children

A. Planning and set-up

  1. Choose activities that the children like. They will stay long enough to become involved.
  2. Choose activities that get children to group together to share the materials or to share a defined area of space (e.g., the water table, a circle on the floor, the doll corner).
  3. Choose activities that create the need to interact and to cooperate.
      a. To ask for, pass, share, trade
      b. To show each other
      c. To help (seesaw, rocking boat)
      d. To cooperate in role-playing (doctor–patient)
  4. Arrange materials and activities in such a way as to bring children together in groups. Put out fewer materials to have children trade or share. Put things in baskets that are easy to pass. Set up activities within prescribed areas.

B. Parent participation

  1. Redirect child's nondirected or parent-directed utterances to another child.
  2. Prompt or suggest one child to contact another.
      a. To ask
      b. To tell
      c. To show
      d. To invite
      e. To share or trade
      f. To praise
      g. To defend
  3. Model ways of interacting for child to notice or imitate (e.g., parent assumes role of doctor, parent notices and comments on child's haircut).
  4. Translate or interpret for children talking to each other. Encourage them to use each other's names and to look at each other when talking.
  5. Help children to respond to their peers. See that child who initiates is reinforced.

Note. Adapted from the Communication Program, the Experimental Education Unit of the College of Education and the Child Development and Mental Retardation Center, renamed the Center on Human Development and Disabilities, University of Washington, Seattle, WA 98195.

Photo 19.2. Time for dough play and sharing.

Activity 2: 15 minutes of active cooperative play. Indoors, this could be music time that might involve holding hands and dancing in a circle, marching with flags or scarves, stamping, jumping in place, or clapping and singing to music. If possible, provide rhythm toys such as bells, pairs of narrow doweling sticks to tap together, and large coffee cans with lids that can be substituted for drums. If there is only one set of bells or one drum, use this opportunity to teach turn-taking and sharing. Cooperative play occurs, for example, when the children dance holding hands, or when they sit on the floor and hold hands as they face each other, rocking back and forth to the song "Row, Row, Row Your Boat."

Weather permitting, you can plan 15 minutes of active cooperative and turn-taking play outside. Balls, swings, rockers, and trikes provide opportunities for turn-taking, sharing, parallel, and cooperative play. Teach the children to say "my turn." This is the first step toward the final component of the socialization process: negotiation and compromise.

Activity 3: The final 15 to 25 minutes should be allotted for toileting, hand-washing, and snacks: milk, juice, cookies, or crackers. This is the time for your child to practice passing out napkins and crackers, and verbalizing and gesturing for juice or milk. If the playmate is already talking, encourage the child to engage in the skills to provide a model for your child.

Children need to learn that sharing food with a friend is a social time for conversation. To reinforce this concept, join the children at the snack table and keep them actively involved. One way to do this is to prepare a grab bag. Place several small, familiar objects such as a tiny ball, a toy car, a spoon, or a mitten into a paper bag. Allow the children to take turns feeling inside the bag and identifying an object by touch, if they can, and then pulling the object out and naming it. After they take their turns, it is your turn to tell them what each object is. This activity promotes turn-taking, verbalization, and identification of objects by touch. If the playmate is very verbal, make sure that your child is given equal opportunities to speak up or express his or her own thoughts. At another time, you can bring a large picture book to the snack table and invite the children to talk about what they see.

When the children are finished with the snack, they should help clear and wipe off the table. Then it is time for the friend to go home. Remind your child to see the playmate to the door and to say good-bye.

During the first few visits, it is important to supervise the children closely. Join them in their activities and demonstrate how materials and equipment should be used, focusing on turn-taking and sharing. Provide opportunities for both parallel and cooperative play. When it becomes apparent that the playmate and your child have learned to enjoy each other's company and have learned how to play together, you can begin withdrawing your supervision. Nevertheless, you must continue to provide structured quiet, parallel play and snack time. During the active 15 minutes, you can begin allowing the children more freedom, encouraging them to initiate more self-directed play. If disputes arise, help them to resolve the problems through turn-taking and sharing, and by suggesting alternative solutions. Since your objective is social interaction between playmates, you should discourage solitary play. If you discover that, left on their own, the children consistently drift apart to play by themselves, it may be necessary to intervene by finding ways to bring them together in a related activity. You may also discover that two youngsters are incompatible, although this is not likely to happen if their levels of development are fairly equal and if the activities that you pro- vide are sufficiently engrossing to keep the children happily occupied.

Your ultimate goal is, of course, to assure that your child has the companionship of playmates during early childhood, and friends and a social life in high school and beyond. Therefore, even if your child attends preschool, it is still important to invite playmates into your home. Later, when friendships are established, your child should be able to visit his or her friends in their homes. Too often a child with special needs has little or no peer group contact outside of school. Even then, unless the teachers make a point of encouraging friendships, the child with DS may remain isolated. By finding playmates for your toddler, you are not only teaching your child important social skills, but you may also be laying the foundation for lifetime friendships.

20. Understanding and Managing Problem Behaviors

Like everyone else, children with DS do not always behave appropriately. While some misbehaviors may cause only mild irritation, others can be extremely disruptive and create havoc at home and in school. Before parents can deal with such occurrences effectively, however, it is necessary to understand why the behaviors are occurring. To be able to do this, parents must comprehend the dynamics, the causes, or motivations underlying the undesirable conduct.

Understanding Behavior

Basically there are two types of behavior: operant and respondent.

Operant behaviors. These are voluntary and refer to behaviors that act on the environment and are goal oriented. An operant behavior is performed either to achieve a desired result or to avoid an unwanted consequence. Pressing a light switch is an operant behavior that results in a lighted lamp, which in turn satisfies the need or goal for more brightness. At the same time, this action avoids the consequence of remaining in darkness.

Hitting or grabbing another child's toy are also operant behaviors. The goal may be to hurt, to possess the toy, or to receive attention from an adult. Contrary to what may be believed, scolding or punishing a child does not guarantee that the bad behavior will stop. If this were true-if punishment were indeed a deterrent to misdeeds-then criminals would never again commit crimes after serving their jail sentences. Imprisonment may be considered to be a punishment, yet in far too many instances, it fails to deter inmates from committing future crimes.

This means that the crimes of the felon and the misbehaviors of the child are governed by impulses, influences, needs, and desires, the gratification of which is stronger than the adverse effect of what is believed to be punishment. Thus, any behavior, whether socially acceptable or not, which results in attaining a goal, for which the desire is stronger than the pain of punishment, will continue.

Respondent behaviors. These behaviors, on the other hand, are involuntary. These are the emotional reactions to pain, joy, sorrow, fear, anger, or depression. Tears, laughter, even aggressiveness can, on occasion, be a respondent behavior. Sometimes it can be difficult to distinguish between operant and respondent behaviors. This was the case with Adam.

Adam was a handsome, sturdy boy with DS, who at 2-and-a-half years of age had already been expelled from two nursery schools and labeled incorrigible. Finally, his desperate parents brought him to the Down Syndrome Model Preschool at the University of Washington, even though it meant a round-trip drive of over 70 miles.

Adam's mother confessed that he bit. So far no one had been able to anticipate or control his behavior. Generally a smiling, congenial child, Adam would suddenly, with no apparent provocation, sink his teeth into the arm, cheek, or neck of the nearest child.

My staff and I agreed to accept Adam into the program with the intention of observing and preventing the biting incidents. This meant constant vigilance, and I volunteered to shadow Adam until we could figure out what was motivating these attacks. Day after day I followed Adam about the room, as closely, yet as unobtrusively, as possible. Whenever it appeared that he was dangerously near another child and turned as if to bite, I immediately placed my hand under his chin, clamping his mouth shut. Adam never protested. As soon as it appeared that the impulse to sink his teeth into the flesh of a class- mate had passed, I removed my hand, and Adam would resume his play as if nothing had happened. In this manner 2 weeks passed without incident, and then it was time for Christmas break.

When classes resumed after the first day of the new year, Adam's mother reported that the boy had been very ill with a high fever over the holidays. A doctor diagnosed a severe ear infection, the result of a chronic condition that must have given Adam a great deal of pain. By the time Adam returned to school, he was quite well again, and surprisingly and coincidentally, even without further intervention, never bit anyone again. We could only conclude that the biting had occurred as an involuntary, respondent reaction to sudden spasms of pain in his ear.

The ABC of Behavior

Every behavior, whether operant or respondent, is a three-step process. There is the antecedent event (A), the behavior (B), and the consequence (C) of the behavior. One of three things occurs as the result of every operant

The consequence, the result of the behavior can be reinforcing (e.g., positive, the goal is attained), neutral (e.g., nothing happens), or aversive (e.g., something bad or unpleasant happens as a result of the behavior).

The following is an example:

A. The room is dark: antecedent event.

B. The light switch is pressed: behavior.

C. (1) The light comes on: positive consequence. Positive consequences increase the probability that the behavior will be repeated.

C. (2) The light fails to come on: neutral consequence, nothing happens. A neutral consequence increases the probability that the behavior will not be repeated. If the light bulb or lamp is defective, it is unlikely that you will continue pressing that particular light switch.

C. (3) Pressing the light switch results in an electrical shock: aversive consequence. An aversive consequence (e.g., punishment) increases the probability that the behavior will stop, but not necessarily permanently. A defective light switch that produces an electric shock will not stop a person from turning on other light switches.

In Adam's case the antecedent event was a sudden stabbing pain in his ear. This prompted the act of clamping down with his teeth. The consequence of that action appeared to relieve the discomfort. When

Adam's earache was cured, the antecedent event no longer occurred and, as a result, neither did Adam's biting.

Tom and Gary were two boys with DS. They attended a regular public school and both boys, 9-year-old Tom and 11-year-old Gary, were so disruptive in their respective classrooms that I was asked to help their teachers deal with the boys' unmanageable behaviors. Oddly enough, although the boys attended different classes, their behaviors were almost identical in that both boys refused to comply when it was time to leave the room. In each case, the antecedent event was the teacher's announcement that it was time for the children to line up at the door. Spurred by this antecedent event, Tom would hide under a table. The consequence of this action was that every day the teacher ended up forcibly dragging Tom to the door.

Although Gary did not throw himself on the floor, he also caused a disturbance by clinging to his chair or making the teacher chase him around the desks. Although the boys failed in their attempts to remain in the rooms, the consequences of their conduct brought other rewards: teacher and peer attention, which both boys apparently sought and enjoyed.

It is quite possible that in the beginning the boys reacted respondently (emotionally, involuntarily) to the antecedent event out of fear or misunderstanding of what they were required to do, or of what could happen if they left the room. Subsequently, as a result of the teachers' rather violent reactions to their antics, which were no doubt exciting and entertaining to the whole class, the noncompliance became operant, deliberate behavior.

Realizing that in some instances it is difficult for children with DS to shift gears, to move from one activity to another without adequate preparation, it was obvious to me that Tom and Gary needed something concrete to motivate them to obey their teachers' verbal directions. With this in mind, I suggested that the teachers prepare visual cues by making cards on which they would print the activity that followed the children's leaving the class-room, be it lunch, physical education, or the bus that would take them home. For example, if the children were leaving to go to the gym, the teachers would hand the boys a card with the letters P. E. printed on it and say "P. E." Then, standing at the door and holding up a similar card, the teacher would make a specific announcement addressing either Tom or Gary by saying, "It's time to go to P. E., Tom (or Gary). Give me your P. E. card." At other times the cards might read BUS, LUNCH, or RECESS.

The boys' quick compliance once the teachers began dispensing the cards prior to telling them to get in line suggests two things. The visual cues helped Tom and Gary to understand what they were expected to do and pacified any emotional reactions that they might have experienced. In addition, it was fairly obvious that both boys were gratified by their teachers' exclusive attention, which they received in a more legitimate way when they were addressed directly and given the cards.

Universal Needs and Goals

It can be said that all operant behaviors, those of children as well as adults, are geared toward the attainment of a cluster of universal survival and self-realization goals. For children the two most powerful motivational forces are food and adult attention. Most children's behaviors, good and bad, are aimed at obtaining one or both of these goals. Other objectives that motivate adults and children include the following:

>Air to breathe
>Food
>Shelter
>Adult attention (children)
>Freedom to move
>Novelty
>Love, recognition, approval, status, and power
>Success
>Autonomy and independence

Food

For a baby, nourishment is the primary goal. At first, crying for food is a respondent, instinctive behavior. Later, as the baby matures, crying for food or asking for a treat become operant behaviors. A favorite food can, in fact, become a strong incentive for behavior. The anticipation of a yummy dessert, for example, can motivate a child to show good manners at the dinner table.

Adult Attention

The second strongest force governing a child's operant behavior is the desire for adult, especially parental, attention. If quiet, appropriate play does not result in the desired recognition, the child will try other tactics, usually some sort of misbehavior which cannot or will not be ignored.

Later, when the child enters school, teacher and peer attention will also influence the child's attention-getting behaviors.

Freedom to Move

The freedom to move is an intrinsic need that is related to physical development. A child that is required to sit at a desk before he is maturationally ready to endure long periods of inactivity, becomes restless, irascible, or inattentive. This restlessness, especially among children with DS, can easily transform itself into disruptive behaviors such as throwing objects, noncompliance, running about a classroom, or even running out of the classroom.

Rest

A child needs to move, but he or she also needs to rest. A tired child cries, fusses, whines, or becomes destructively overactive. Much of this behavior can be classified as respondent, involuntary responses to bodily fatigue, but these behaviors can also become learned strategies for gaining parental attention and relieving stress.

Novelty

New experiences play an essential role in a child's cognitive and emotional development. Children crave novelty as much as they may crave the need for movement. The child who is denied appropriate novel experiences, whether in schoolwork or simple daily activities, becomes bored. A chronically bored child may resort to mischief because the naughtiness provides novelty and excitement, as well as adult attention.

Success

No less than adults, children have a need to succeed. A young child measures his or her success in terms of parental attention and approval. Success builds self-esteem. Children who have self-esteem feel good about themselves. The)) are not afraid of failure and are willing to try harder to achieve an objective. Self-worth makes children confident. They feel lovable, and this makes it easier for these children to be friendly because they do not doubt that others will like them.

Above all, children with DS, as well as those with other disabilities, mus1 be given every opportunity to succeed. It is essential for their well-being, and for their social and general development. Life can be hard for these children. Poor health, and the inability to communicate fluently and compete physically and academically with normal peers, can make them feel like failures. Many behavior problems arise because a child is acting out his or her feelings of worthlessness. The negative attention that the child receives for the misbehaviors serves to confirm the child's low self-opinion, and that, in a perverse way, is the child's goal.

Modifying Undesirable Behaviors

I hope that it is clear by now that behaviors, both positive and negative, are motivated by a desired result. Behavior is also a form of communication. Parents confronted with a problem behavior, especially a chronic situation, car begin by asking themselves the following questions:

1. What is the behavior? Is the child aggressive, fidgety, noncompliant, messy, destructive? Define the behavior. Describe it, and write it down as clearly as possible.

2. What is the antecedent? What precipitates the behavior? Define, describe, and write it down.

3. What is the consequence of the behavior?

    - What do you do?

    - What do other family members do?

    - What does the behavior accomplish for the child? What need does it fulfill?

- What does the behavior communicate to you? Is it hunger, boredom, anger, jealousy, self-hate, overstimulation, or the inability to stop?

- How can you help your child fulfill his or her need in a more acceptable manner?

- Can you change the consequence of the behavior by changing your response to the behavior? What can you do differently? What would happen if you ignored the behavior (neutral consequence)?

- Can you change the antecedent that evokes the behavior?

- What positive behavior can you substitute for your child's undesirable actions?

If you understand the needs and emotions that are motivating your child to behave in a certain way, become aware of the circumstances surrounding the behavior, and determine the goals your child is attaining through the misbehavior, then you have the power to change your child's conduct by manipulating the antecedents and the consequences. Remember that while you are eliminating your child's bad behavior, you must also concentrate on teaching your child a better response in its place. Be sure to give consistent praise and encouragement while your child is learning to behave more appropriately. Help your child to feel worthy and successful.

Of course, the best way of dealing with behavior problems is by never allowing them to occur, or if they do happen, by never allowing them to become established habits. The ideal way to prevent some of the more common problem behaviors from developing is by teaching social and interactive skills at the time when they become evident in normal development. The 2-year-old who aggressively hugged younger children should have been stopped with a firm "No" the first time it happened, and then shown how to approach children without being physically overwhelming.

Chapter 21 will list some of the most frequent behavior problems, the ages at which they are likely to occur, possible reasons for their occurrence, and solutions.

21. Common Behavior Problems: Birth to 6 Years

Behavior problems can occur as a result of many causes, the most prominent of which is poor health.

Poor Health

Ear infections. As parents of a child with DS, you have undoubtedly encountered many frequently recurring health problems related to this condition. Since negative behavior may be the only way that a young child can communicate discomfort, parents must be alert to any sudden change in their child's usual way of behaving. Adam's biting was a case in point. Additionally, noncompliance, hyperactivity, restlessness, inattentiveness, or withdrawal are almost always caused by hearing problems. Moreover, children suffering from otitis media (inner ear infection) can feel dizzy and disoriented, making them suddenly reluctant to walk or participate in school activities.

Allergies. Allergic reactions frequently have a negative effect on behavior. Hives or skin rashes can make a child restless and uncooperative. Itching eyes and congested nasal passages make it equally difficult for a child to behave well at home or in school.

Vision. Uncorrected poor vision can adversely affect a child's physical development and behavior. Young children with poor vision may refuse to walk, to use climbing equipment, to step off a curb, or to step from a carpeted area to a bare floor or vice versa. Such behavior is often considered stubbornness. My experience has shown, however, that attention to the child's vision and the use of proper glasses almost miraculously remedy such non-compliant behaviors.

Seizures. About 25% of children with DS have been diagnosed as having some form of epilepsy, ranging from petit mal seizures, momentary black outs, to full-blown episodes of convulsive fits.

Since the latter condition is readily recognized and routinely treated, such severe seizures are less likely to affect the child's general behavior. The petit mal attacks, however, are often overlooked by both parents and teachers, and because in some cases a child may have as many as 200 episodes of blacking out a day, learning and development suffers, and the child may be unfairly accused of noncompliance and inattention.

Depression. There is a myth that individuals with DS are always happy and outgoing. However, like every other human being, they can experience joy, sorrow, disappointment, and even depression. Depression can be defined as a chronic feeling of sadness and sometimes total apathy, due to guilt or the inability to cope with one's problems. Depression can also be the result of frustration, conflict or, possibly, chemical imbalances in the brain (Kagan & Havermann, 1972).

Children with DS who have low self-esteem, who are frustrated by tasks beyond their ability, or who feel inferior to normal peers may become seriously depressed. This depression can result in aggression or other forms of misbehavior, including running away and engaging in dangerous behaviors such as riding a bicycle on a freeway against heavy traffic (Ayers, 1993).

Serious illness. Sometimes an unsuspected serious illness can abruptly change a child's behavior. One friendly, 4-year-old girl without DS suddenly became extremely aggressive toward her peers. She also had periods of rage during which she would wildly throw and destroy materials. Wisely, her mother took her to a doctor. Further neurological tests tragically revealed a brain tumor. Poor little Annette died within a few months.

None of this is written to unduly alarm parents. Nevertheless, as stated earlier, any disturbing change in a child's usual behavior, which remains unchanged by behavior management techniques, requires medical attention. In seeking professional advice, it is essential to find a physician who understands the implications of Down syndrome and who is knowledgeable and sensitive to the health needs that may occur. Unfortunately, there are doctors who are still too willing to dismiss any and every problem as some- thing inherent to the condition of Down syndrome and fail to give proper treatment.

Finally, although there are many health problems that can affect behavior, I must caution parents against falling into the trap of assuming that every misbehavior is a health-related manifestation. There can be many other reasons why a child behaves inappropriately. Fortunately, if one under- stands the cause and the dynamics of the behavior, a consistent application of management principles can usually remedy the situation.

Other Common Problems-Their Possible Causes and Solutions: 18 Months to 5 Years

Throwing Objects

Cause: Normal behavior until about 15 months of age. Child is learning how to release objects voluntarily. It becomes a problem if the child does not progress to the next stage: placing objects specifically.

Solution 1: Shape the child to place {release) objects into a container. Do this by moving the child's hand that is holding an object over the container. Say, "Drop." If the child does not comply, shape by gently pressing the child's wrist downward. The object will drop spontaneously. Praise the child. Fade shaping as the child begins to release on command.

Solution 2: Shape and teach the child to respond to the command, "Give." The child will learn to place objects in your hand on command.

Refusal To Eat Solid Food

Cause: Solid foods with different textures were not introduced when the child was developmentally ready.

Solution: Review section on feeding in Chapter 16. Refusal To Stand with Support

Cause: Delay in bringing child to standing position

Solutions: Allow child to experience pressure on the soles of the feet by bringing the child to a standing position by 6 months. With older children, massage the soles of the feet. Place weights {4 to 8 ounces) on the child's ankles and stand the child in front of a couch or low table with toys. Give back support. Keep the child standing for 3 to 5 minutes.

Screeching

Cause: Delay in training how to communicate

Solution: Shape gestures and model vocal sounds while offering the child a favorite food. Be sure the child is relaxed and not fussing. Tongue Thrust, or Protrusion

Cause: Hypotonia, poor neck control, or not chewing food

Solution: Review Chapter 16.

Refusal To Walk

Cause: Many young children with DS, after walking a short distance, will drop down to sit on the ground. When pulled up, they will lift their legs and hold them up by bending their knees. The child is probably tired, due to poor muscle tone, and you should delay in teaching walking skills.

Immediate solution: Lift the child, your arms around the child's waist, and continue holding the child in midair until the child lowers his or her legs. This will happen very quickly because it is difficult to keep the legs raised like that for any length of time. Once the feet are on the ground, praise the child and start walking.

If the child refuses to walk, but is still upright, walk behind the child, holding the child around the waist and pushing his or her feet forward with your own legs.

Long term solution: Practice walking short distances. For example, walk 10 steps, counting each step out loud. Praise and give a treat after each set of 10 steps. The treat can be a Cheerio, a raisin, or a bit of cracker. Gradually extend the number of steps that must be taken before dispensing the treat. Continue practicing over a period of days until the child will walk the necessary distance without stopping. Fade out the treat when the goal is reached.

Refusal To Sit on Toilet

Causes: Delay in toilet training, or the seat is unstable or uncomfortable

> *Solution:* Place the child on the toilet. Entertain the child with a toy or a treat. Juice is a good choice. Praise and remove the child as soon as he or she stops fussing. Do not expect the child to urinate at this time. The goal is f01 the child to remain seated quietly for 3 to 5 minutes, with an adult in attendance. Praise, and give sips of juice while the child is on the toilet.
>
> If the child stiffens, arching the back as you try to place him or her on the seat, lift the child, even if the child is stiff, and wait the child out. The child will not be able to maintain the arched back and straightened legs more than a few seconds. As soon as the child's muscles begin to sag, plop the child on the seat, and before he or she can start fussing or jump off, praise the child and give a sip of juice. This approach has worked well for me with children whose parents were unable to place or keep them seated on a toilet.

Hair Pulling, Biting, and Hitting

Causes: Lack of proper social and play skills, inability to interact with children, inappropriate adult attention, behavior not stopped the first time i1 occurred, or a health problem

> *Solutions:* Examine the ABC of the behavior. Intervene before the behavior occurs. If the behavior is ongoing, keep a record of the number of times it happens each day for 3 to 5 days, or until there are three consecutive days of fairly stable data. Begin behavior management based on the ABC. If the behavior does not begin to diminish after a week of consistent management, review the antecedents and your procedures (consequence). Concentrate on teaching social skills. Remember to rule out health problems.

Teeth Grinding

Causes: Earache or dental problem

Solution: See an audiologist, a dentist, or both.

Refusal To Step Off a Curb

Causes: Vision problem, poor motor control, or otitis media (ear infection)

Solution: Seek appropriate medical advice. Practice walking up and down stairs. Practice stepping off curbs by shaping, and placing a sheet of white paper onto which the child can step as he or she gets off the curb. Gradually reduce the size of the paper until it disappears and is no longer needed as a visual cue.

Running Away from the Home or Out of the Classroom

Causes: Impulsive behavior, boredom, immaturity, depression, desire for adult attention, and desire for excitement (may think behavior is a game)

Solution 1: Make home, yard, and schoolroom escape-proof for the child. If the child is running in order to create excitement and get adult attention, an escape-proof environment eliminates the ability to run out. It also enables the adult to relax and focus on managing the other reasons that may be motivating the running behavior. An ID bracelet adds to the child's security and safety in case he does escape.

Solution 2: Teach walking and safety rules.

Solution 3: Avoid playing chasing games during toddlerhood or until the child is old enough to know when it is appropriate to run and when it is not.

Spitting

Causes: Imitation of an observed behavior, or attention-getting device

Solution 1: Stay calm. Direct the child to the bathroom to spit in the toilet. Tell the child, "Spitting is private. You do it in the bathroom."

Demonstrate, and have the child imitate you. Praise the response. Repeat the exercise at odd times during the day, for several days.

Solution 2: If a child spits at you, another person, or another child in anger, be firm. Say, "No." If it happens again, bring the child into the bath- room and repeat the procedures in Solution 1. Outdoors, hand the child a tis- sue, and make the child use it for spitting.

Solution 3: If spitting is indeed an angry response, teach your child to express his or her anger verbally or with body language (e.g., by stamping his or her foot). Make it clear that spitting anywhere other than into a tissue or into the toilet is not acceptable.

Swearing

Causes: Imitation of an observed behavior, or an attention-getting device

Solution 1: Remain calm and ignore the behavior.

Solution 2: Substitute non-offensive words and phrases such as "fiddle-faddle" and "bah, humbug." Children like funny-sounding words.

Solution 3: If a child swears in anger or frustration, teach the child how to express anger (e.g., "I'm mad!").

Solution 4: Send the child to his or her room and tell the child, "You may swear in your room, but not in public."

Roughhousing

Cause: This is generally a learned behavior as a result of parents' and siblings' playful wrestling with a child with DS. Difficulties arise because children with DS easily become overstimulated, and then are unable to stop. Also, as a result of learning how to wrestle at home, children with DS often try to continue doing it on the playground or in the classroom by attacking and knocking down other children inappropriately, thinking it is a game.

> *Solution:* Do not roughhouse with your child. If you do, make it a structured situation with a definite time limit (use a timer). Never begin rough-housing without a formal invitation. Say, "Let's wrestle." Teach your child to do the same, and to accept a yes or no reply.

Masturbation

Causes: Genital irritation, late toilet training (children in diapers past 3 years of age), uncomfortable clothing, or simply a natural behavior common among children

> *Solution 1:* Stay calm, and eliminate the possible physical cause or irritation, if any.
>
> *Solution 2:* Tell the child that masturbation is a private behavior, limited to the bedroom or bathroom.
>
> *Solution 3:* Provide sex education. Children who become anxious about their bodies after noting the difference between themselves and a child of the opposite sex can become obsessed with handling their own genitals.
>
> *Solution 4:* Keep the child busy and active, distract the child, or change the antecedent. For example, Shannon, a little girl with DS who still wore diapers at age 3, learned to masturbate by lying face down on the floor and rocking back and forth, rubbing herself against the floor. Apparently it was the pressure of the diapers against her genitals that elicited that behavior. Since lying on her stomach was the antecedent for Shannon's masturbation, she was never allowed to assume this position in class. Naturally, the next step was to confer with her parents and begin toilet training.

Tantrums

Causes: Fatigue, frustration, learned behavior as a way to get adult attention and one's own way, inability to communicate needs and desires

> *Solution 1:* Apply ABC principles of behavior management.

Solution 2: Develop better verbal and social skills. Problems that might arise in school will be addressed in the next chapter.

22. Inclusion in Early Childhood Education

The passage of the Education for All Handicapped Children Act (P.L. 94-142) in 1975, renamed the Individuals with Disabilities Education Act (IDEA) of 1990, brought major changes in public educational policies. This law entitles everyone with a disability from age 3 to age 21 to a free and appropriate education. No longer isolated, categorized, and segregated by the public school system, children with disabilities are to be placed in school settings that are the same or similar to those enjoyed by their nondisabled peers. In an attempt to comply with these goals, disabled children were initially mainstreamed, or integrated into classrooms serving typically developing youngsters. Before entering these programs, however, the child with disabilities had to be deemed "ready."

Inclusion, the latest approach to the education of children with special needs, is a more structured and comprehensive program than previous endeavors, and readiness is no longer required. Furthermore, inclusion is based on a specific philosophical approach with clearly defined educational and developmental goals (Allen & Schwartz, 1996).

Inclusion: Goals and Philosophy

1. Total participation and belonging by a child with special needs as a member of his or her typically developing peer group
2. Support based on the individual needs of the disabled children
    a. Curriculum and materials adaptation
    b. Specific and appropriate instructional strategies
    c. Speech and physical therapy within the school setting

  d. Additional staff and specialized training for regular teachers
3. Recognition of the personal beliefs and values of the family. Program must be geared to meet the child's individual needs and parental priorities.
4. Individualized Education Plan (IEP). Based on initial assessments, parents and teacher set short- and long-term educational goals for children participating in the inclusion program. Ongoing data and evaluations measure progress.
5. Cooperation and coordination between the sending programs (early intervention or developmental programs for children with disabilities from birth until age 3), and receiving program (the public school system) prepare the child for a smooth transition by using the following strategies.
  a. Parent/teacher conferences
  b. Visits to the classroom
  c. Identification of necessary support systems to meet each child's specific requirements
6. Specific demonstrable outcome objectives for each inclusive program
  a. Developmental changes among the participants
  b. Peer group acceptance and support of children with disabilities as participating members of their classes
  c. Opportunities for children with disabilities to contribute and reciprocate in peer relationships

Photo 22.1. Grady (second from left) attends an inclusive preschool.

Parent Involvement

Parents play a major role as equal partners in the process of inclusion. It is, therefore, important to recognize that parents, like their children, have their own individual needs, attitudes, and concerns, which can affect their involvement in their child's education. This section lists some of the most frequently encountered parental perspectives, attitudes, and feelings when children with special needs enter inclusive public school settings.

Parental Perspectives and Attitudes

Parents of children with disabilities may hold certain attitudes or have unique perspectives regarding inclusion.

1. Parents may prefer segregation.
2. Parents may have doubts about inclusion but see it as the better of two evils.
3. Parents may prefer inclusion in one setting but not in another.
4. Parents may want inclusion.

Parental Feelings

Parents also have strong feelings about inclusion for their child with disabilities, including those in the following list.

1. Parents may be anxious for their child and themselves.
2. Parents may be anxious about how parents of typically developing children will feel about their disabled child.
3. Parents may feel pressured to conform and to accept a situation, even if they have misgivings, in order not to "rock the boat" or complain.
4. Parents may feel excited, pleased, and proud, viewing inclusion as a positive experience for their child.

Administration and Teacher Involvement

It should be recognized that school administrators, staff, and teachers may also have prejudices, reservations, and feelings about inclusion, both positive and negative, similar to those experienced by parents.

Teacher Perspectives and Attitudes

Like parents, teachers hold certain perspectives and attitudes about inclusion, including the following:

1. Teachers may not want inclusion.
2. Teachers may acknowledge the value of inclusion, but do not want to be involved.
3. Teachers may want and support inclusion.

Teacher and Staff Feelings

Teachers and staff at the school can also have strong feelings about inclusion, which may include the following:

1. Teachers may be fearful, sensing their lack of knowledge about disabilities and uncertainty about the amount of support that they will receive.
2. Teachers may feel anxious about dealing with an unfamiliar situation.

3. Teachers may feel pressured and resentful of the extra work, training, and meetings that inclusion involves.
4. Teachers may feel challenged, enthusiastic, or eager to learn new skills.

Whatever perspectives and feelings that parents and teaching staff may bring to the process of inclusion, the best way to resolve any difficulties or misgivings that may arise is to acknowledge the existence of individual concerns, personalities, and attitudes. An honest acknowledgement of one's feelings and a frank discussion between parents and teaching staff can promote a better understanding of the goals and rationale for inclusion, and ways of resolving differences.

Nevertheless, in the best-run programs problems may arise, especially as children move into kindergarten and beyond. Difficulties may occur, for example, when a teacher lacks experience in working with children who have special needs and who may require a more individualized and sensitive approach to their instruction.

Parents who are concerned about their child's progress or behavior in school might benefit from turning their attention to the following section on teaching and learning problems that frequently occur in classrooms.

Problems in School: Age 5 and Beyond

Poor Instruction Techniques

Most behavior problems are the result of poor instructional techniques. If your child is inattentive or misbehaves, visit the classroom and confer with the teacher if you suspect or notice any of the following deficiencies in your child's school program:

- Overtraining: failure to move on to new tasks after previous ones have been mastered
- Drilling: endless repetitions of the same response. More than three responses to the same question is one too many.
- Allowing too many failures due to the teacher's failure to anticipate and prepare for the next sequential step in the

program, lack of prerequisite skills, or unrealistic expectations

- Failure to program for success: failure to show the child how to respond correctly
- Assigning meaningless tasks and allowing poor work habits to develop: teacher fails to recognize and praise achievement thus minimizing the importance of good work habits
- Failure to recognize individual needs, interests, and abilities
- Failure to teach play and peer-interaction skills
- Too much emphasis on the negative and little or no praise for appropriate behaviors and work well done

The following illustrates how any one of these poor techniques can affect a child's performance and attitude toward school.

One day I visited a kindergarten class where a girl with DS was learning to write the first letter of her name, Kathy. The teacher gave Kathy a sheet of paper and told her to write the letter.

Kathy set promptly to work and within a few minutes filled half a page with perfectly shaped letters. It was obvious that the girl already knew how to write K, and was ready for other work. Apparently satisfied with what she had already written, Kathy laid down her pencil. Without even glancing at Kathy's neatly written assignment, the teacher ordered her to keep on filling the page. The child complied, but she was bored by now, and letter by letter her writing deteriorated until she ended up filling the rest of the page with illegible scribbles.

When the teacher finally looked at Kathy's paper, she was annoyed. "When are you going to learn to write properly?" she snapped, handing

Kathy another sheet of paper. "Now go back to your seat and do it right!"

Kathy returned to her desk, tore up the paper, and folded her arms. She was through with school for the day.

Distressed by what I had witnessed, I tried to talk to the teacher after school, but as I was merely visiting, and not at the school in the official role of consultant, there was not much that I could say. When I suggested that Kathy was bored and ready to write other letters, the teacher dismissed my remarks, calling Kathy stubborn and uncooperative.

Parental Advocacy and Achievement

Unfortunately, similar situations continue to occur in many classrooms, especially among inexperienced teachers who have had little preparation in teaching children with special needs, and who probably resent having these children in their regular classrooms.

Photo 22.2. At age 7, Aaron reads at a third-grade level.

One solution would be for parents to monitor their child's school progress by reviewing the child's daily school-work. Parents must also insist on specific and realistic criteria for progression to new material. These demands should be included in the Individualized Education Plan (IEP) contract. Parents have a moral and legal right to ensure that their children receive the education that they deserve. From the day that your special child is born you must become his or her advocate, even though it might involve confronting professionals, doctors, teachers, and society itself. Great strides have been made toward better health care, education, and acceptance of children and adults with disabilities. None of this would have taken place without the advocacy of dedicated parents.

Photo 22.3. Eighteen-year-old Maria Isabel waltzes with her brother at her "coming out party." Maria Isabel lives in Guatemala.

In conclusion, social and behavioral competence, like every other aspect of a child's development, are so irrevocably interrelated that if you attend to one area, it follows that the other will also be affected. Thus, if you have helped your child achieve the basic components of socialization, if you have monitored your child's health and have actively participated in planning your child's school program, making sure that high, but realistic education objectives are fulfilled, you can expect that your child with DS will be a well-functioning, delightful child with few if any behavior problems.

All of this may seem to be a huge burden for any parent to undertake, but the future rewards, based on the success stories of our former preschool students who are now leading happy, productive, and extremely competent lives, should be well worth your expenditure of time during your child's early years. Moreover, the joy and satisfaction of seeing your child fulfill previously undetected potentials can be far greater than you ever imagined.

23. Appendix A: Records of Development

Name: _____

Date of Birth: _____

Table A.1

Record of Physical Development: The First 3 Months

Objective	Emerging Skills/Date	Mastered Skills/Date
1. Child is able to lift chin slightly when lying in the prone position (face down).		
2. Child is able to push with both feet against your hands.		
3. Child is able to hold head erect for a few seconds.		
4. Child is able to lift head well up when lying prone.		
5. Child is able to kick feet vigorously.		
6. Child is able to move the arms and legs in the bath.		
7. Child is able to lift head slightly when in the dorsal (on the back) position.		
8. Child is able to roll from side to back.		
9. Child is able to scoot forward on the stomach.		

Name: _____

Date of Birth: _____

Table A.2

Record of Physical Development: 3 to 6 Months

Objective	Emerging Skills/Date	Mastered Skills/Date
1. Child must be able to lift head 45 degrees when prone.		
2. Child must be able to lift head 90 degrees when prone.		
3. Child must be able to support weight on elbows when prone and lift chest and head.		
4. Child must be able to support weight on extended arms when prone, lifting head and upper torso.		
5. Child must be able to hold head erect without support when held upright against your shoulder.		
6. Child must be able to hold head erect and turn it freely when held upright against your shoulder.		
7. Child must be able to sit, head up, with adult support.		
8. Child must be able to independently complete an adult-assisted roll from back to stomach.		
9. Child must be able to maintain a propped sitting position for 5 minutes.		
10. Child must be able to maintain a weight-bearing stance (with support) for 1 minute.		

Name: _____

Date of Birth: _____

Table A.3

Record of Physical Development: 6 to 12 Months

Objective	Emerging Skills/Date	Mastered Skills/Date
1. Child must be able to sit in an upright position with a steady head and straight back, with minimum adult help.		
2. Child must be able to sit self-supported, hands resting on knees, for at least 3 minutes.		
3. Child must be able to exhibit balance and righting reactions (protective extensions).		
4. Child must be able to sit independently, head up, back straight, hands free to play with toys.		
5. Child must be able to sit safely and independently on a small stool, knees bent, feet resting firmly on the floor.		
6. Child must be able to pull to a standing position from a stool-sitting position.		
7. Child must be able to creep, that is, propel self forward or backward over a flat surface "commando" style.		
8. Child must be able to hold a crawl position for at least 3 minutes.		
9. Child must be able to come to sitting from a prone (lying down) position.		

Name: _____

Date of Birth: _____

Table A.4

Record of Physical Development: 12 to 24 Months

Objective	Emerging Skills/Date	Mastered Skills/Date
1. Child must be able to shift from a sitting position to a crawling position and back to sitting.		
2. Child must be able to creep, crawl, scoot, or roll across the floor.		
3. Child must be able to stand on knees with straight legs and back for at least 10 seconds.		
4. Child must be able to pull self up from sitting or kneeling to a standing position.		
5. Child must be able to stand self-supported.		
6. Child must be able to lower self from a standing position to a sitting or kneeling position without falling.		
7. Child must be able to shift weight and raise one foot when standing with support.		
8. Child must be able to cruise: walk sideways around a playpen or around a room holding onto furniture.		
9. Child must be able to take forward steps with adult support.		
10. Child must be able to stand without support for at least 30 seconds.		
11. Having achieved these prerequisite skills, the child is able to walk independently.		

Name: _____

Date of Birth: _____

Table A.6

Record of Fine Motor/Cognitive and Social Development: 5 to 12 Months

Objective	Emerging Skills/Date	Skills Mastered/Date
1. Transfers objects from hand to hand		
2. Reaches for and obtains objects consistently		
3. Picks up two objects—one with each hand		
4. Bangs two blocks or objects together		
5. Touches pictures in books		
6. Picks up objects using pincer grasp		
7. Responds to: a. Own name b. "Look" c. "No"		
8. Holds arms out to be picked up (in response)		
9. Resists giving up held toy		
10. Works for toy out of reach		
11. Plays peek-a-boo		
12. Plays pat-a-cake		
13. Says "dada" or "mama" nonspecifically		
14. Imitates speech sounds: a. *ah* b. *oo* c. *ee* d. *dada* e. *mama* f. *baba*		
15. Says "dada" or "mama" specifically		
16. Shows objects to others and vocalizes		
17. Feeds self finger foods		

24. Appendix B What Should a Parent Look for in a Classroom?

What is my child being taught?

		Yes	No
1. Individual Objectives for Child			
a. Are these written?		___	___
b. Are there at least five short-term objectives?		___	___
c. Are there long-term objectives related to these short-term objectives?		___	___
d. Are there social objectives as well as academic?		___	___
e. Are the objectives in terms that I can measure (no education jargon)?		___	___
f. Are there individual objectives in language, self-help, and motor?		___	___
2. Is there an overall curriculum for the classroom?		___	___
a. Is this curriculum task analyzed?		___	___
b. Are the individual objectives for my child task analyzed?		___	___

Does the teacher know how well my child is doing?

1. Is the teacher keeping track of my child's progress in each objective? ___ ___
   a. Objective _____ ___ ___
   b. Objective _____ ___ ___
   c. Objective _____ ___ ___
   d. Objective _____ ___ ___
   e. Objective _____ ___ ___
   f. Objective _____ ___ ___
   g. Objective _____ ___ ___
   h. Objective _____ ___ ___

Does the teacher know how well my child is doing? *Continued*

		Yes	No
2. Is the teacher keeping track of progress:			
a. Daily?		____	____
b. Weekly?		____	____
If less frequently, how often? _____			
3. Does my child have to perform the task three times or less before he or she moves on to the next step in the teaching sequence? (If more than three, why?) _____		____	____
4. If my child has spent a week in a program (objective) without progressing, has the teacher changed either the reinforcer, the cue, or the task?		____	____

Is my child's time being used efficiently?

1. Is my child receiving at least 10 minutes instruction daily in each objective? ____ ____
   a. Individual instruction? ____ ____
   b. Group instruction? ____ ____
2. Is each activity of the day related to an objective? ____ ____
   a. Which are not? _____
   _____
   b. Is at least 75% of my child's day related to instructional objectives? ____ ____
3. Is the teacher using volunteers or peer teaching to assist in increasing the amount of instructional time? ____ ____

Am I, as a parent, involved in my child's program?

1. Did I help choose the instructional objectives for my child? ____ ____
2. Have I spent at least half a day in my child's classroom every 3 months? ____ ____
3. Am I volunteering in my child's classroom? ____ ____
   a. When I volunteer, am I instructing children? ____ ____
4. Has the teacher contacted me and asked me to conduct home programs with my child? ____ ____
5. Have I conducted the programs when asked? ____ ____
6. Has the teacher contacted me (telephone, note, conference) at least once monthly? ____ ____
7. Have I monitored the quality of my child's program? ____ ____

25. Appendix C National Resources List for Down Syndrome

The ARC (National)
2501 Avenue J
Arlington, TX 76006
817/640-0204

National Down Syndrome Congress
1605 Chantilly Drive, Suite 250
Atlanta, GA 30324
800/232-NDSC; 404/633-1555 (GA)
E-mail: ndsc@charitiesusa.com
Web site: http://www.carol.net/~ndsc/

National Down Syndrome Society
666 Broadway
New York, NY 10012
800/221-4602; 212/460-9330

Siblings for Significant Change
105 East 22nd Street
New York, NY 10010
212/420-0776

Siblings Information Network, CUAP
991 Main Street
East Hartford, CT 06108
203/282-7050

National Association for Down Syndrome
P.O. Box 4542
Oakbrook, IL 60522
630/325-9112
Web site: http://www.nads.org

Trisomy 21 of Northern New York
428 S. Meadow Street
Watertown, NY 13601
316/788-9613
E-mail: Rdleona@banet.net

26. Glossary

Dimethyl sulfoxide (DMSO) is an industrial solvent produced during the process of making paper out of trees. It is used medically because it has the ability to reduce inflammations in tissues. A version of DMSO, approved by the United States Food and Drug Administration, is used for treating a bladder condition called interstitial cystitis. In Down syndrome, the rationale for using DMSO is based on the belief that it supposedly can carry amino acids and other nutrients into the brain to affect cerebral metabolism. To date, there have been no well-documented studies or data to justify the treatment of children with Down syndrome with DMSO.

Facilitated communication is a technique in which another person physically assists someone who is unable to sign, write, or speak, to type messages in order to communicate. This is achieved by holding the subject's arm or hand over a keyboard to produce words by striking letters and spelling out messages. For someone who is severely brain damaged or paralyzed, facilitated communication may be the only way such an individual can communicate.

Like patterning, however, facilitated communication is neither appropriate nor necessary for children with Down syndrome. Although shaping-physically guiding a child's response such as pointing, stacking blocks, signing, crawling, or rolling over- is helpful in showing a young child how to perform a task, shaping is but a brief, initial step in the educational process. Shaping is discontinued as soon as a child learns what is expected and is able to initiate and perform the required developmental tasks independently. It must be understood that children with Down syndrome are inherently far too capable to have to rely on a system as rigid and artificial as facilitated communication.

5-Hydroxytryptophan (5-HTP) is an aromatic amino acid naturally produced in the body. Commercially, it is extracted from the seeds of the African plant, *Griffonia simplicifolia*. Because 5-HTP has the ability to increase the production of serotonin in the brain, it is used in treating a variety of conditions including depression, fibromyalgia, insomnia, binge eating, and chronic headaches. Unless a child with DS suffers from one of those specific conditions, there is no scientific basis for administering 5-HTP.

Glumatic acid is an amino acid that widely occurs in proteins. Research has shown that children with DS do not benefit from the administration of this chemical.

Megavitamins/minerals refers to the administration of vitamins and minerals far exceeding the normal daily dose recommended by physicians and nutritionists. Excessive amounts of vitamins and minerals do not benefit children with DS because megadoses can cause toxic effects, resulting in serious illnesses.

Patterning is a method of physical therapy originated primarily for the purpose of stimulating movement patterns among children who are severely or profoundly dis- abled. The program entails a passive manipulation of a child's body in repetitive motions for hours at a time, 5 days a week.

Although physical therapy is an important and necessary aspect of early intervention for children with Down syndrome, patterning is neither appropriate nor necessary for the physical development of these children. Physiologically and neurologically, children with DS are able to function normally without this time-consuming regime, which is likely to conflict with the children's natural physical development and interfere with opportunities for cognitive, language, and social learning.

Pituitary extract is a synthetic pituitary hormone. The pituitary gland, which is located at the base of the brain, produces hormones that regulate physical growth, metabolism, and sexual development. Unless there is a medically proven deficiency ill the level of pituitary hormones, treatment with pituitary extracts will not benefit children with DS.

Serotonin, a "mood enhancer," is a crystalline protein found in the blood. It is associated with a wide range of physiological processes, especially in the brain and blood vessels. Individuals who are depressed, for example, are likely to have low levels of serotonin.

Siccacell/cell therapy began in 1930. This is a treatment that involves the injection of fetal cells taken from unborn sheep or cattle. Although practitioners advocating cell therapy claim great success in enhancing the development of children with DS serious researchers dispute these claims. According to their findings, "siccacell/cell therapy is completely ineffective" (Bardon, 1964). Other investigators (Black, Kato, & Walker, 1966; Freman & Ward, 1987) confirm these findings. In fact, a number of children have died as a result of these treatments.

27. References

Allen, K. E., & Martotz, L. (1994). *Developmental profiles* (2nd ed.). Albany, NY: Delmar.

Allen, K. E.,& Schwartz, I. S. (1996). *The exceptional child: Inclusion in early childhood* (3rd ed.). Albany, NY: Delmar.

Ayers, C. B. (1993, April/May). Tough choices. *Exceptional Parent.*

Bardon, L. (1964). Siccacell treatment among mongolism. *Lancet2*, 7353, 234-235.

Bayley, N. (1993). *Bayley Scales of Infant Development-Second Edition.* New York: Psychological Corp.

Bee, H. (1975). *The developing child.* New York: Harper & Row.

Bennett, F., McClelland, S., Kriegsmann, E., Andrus, L., & Sells. (1983). Vitamin and mineral supplementation in Down's syndrome. *Pediatrics*, 75(5), 707-714.

Black, D., Kato, J., & Walker, G. (1966). A study of improvement in mentally retarded children occurring from siccacell therapy. *American Journal of Mental Deficiency*, 70, 499-508.

Bornstein, H., & Saulnier, L. B. (1984). *Basic preschool signed English dictionary.* Washington, D.C.: Gallaudet College Press.

Brazelton, T. B. (1973). *Neonatal behavior assessment.* (Clinics in Developmental Medicine, No. 50). Philadelphia: Lippincott.

Brazelton, T. B. (1978, October). *Four stages of affective development as it relates to neonatal behavior.* Paper presented at the Charles R. Strother Seminar, Seattle, WA.

Brigance, A. H. (1991). *Brigance Diagnostic Inventory of Early Development-Revised.* Woburn, MA: Curriculum Associates.

Canning, C., & Pueschel, S. (1978). An overview of developmental expectations. In S. Pueschel, D. Canning, A. Murphy, & E. Zausmer (Eds.), *Down Syndrome: Growing and learning* (pp. 66-74). Franklin, WI: Sheed & Ward.

Chess, S., & Thomas, A. (1973). Temperament in the normal infant. In J. C. Westman (Ed.), *Individual differences in children.* New York: Wiley.

Coleman, M. (1988). Medical care of children and adults with Down syndrome. In V. Dmitriev & P. L. Oelwein (Eds.), *Advances in Down syndrome*. Seattle, WA: Special Child Publications.

Dennis, W. (1960). Causes of retardation among institutionalized children in Iran. *Journal of Genetic Psychology*, 96, 17-50.

Dmitriev, V. (1979). *Synchronous visual reinforcement of babbling in infants with Down syndrome.* Doctoral dissertation, University of Washington, Seattle.

Dmitriev, V. (1981). *The effects of early intervention on cognitive and behavioral development in children with Down syndrome.* Paper presented at the First International Conference on Down Syndrome, Mexico City, Mexico.

Dmitriev, V. (1988). Cognition and the acceleration and maintenance of developmental gains among children with Down syndrome: Longitudinal data. *Down syndrome: Papers and Abstracts for Professionals*, 11(1), 6-11.

Dmitriev, V. (1997). *Tears and triumphs: A look into the world of children with Down syndrome and other developmental delays.* Seattle, WA: Peanut Butter Publishing.

Doll, E. A. (1965). *Vineland Social Maturity Scale.* Circle Pines, MN: American Guidance Service.

Dunn, L. M., & Dunn, L. M. (1981). *Peabody Picture Vocabulary Test-Revised.* Circle Pines, MN: American Guidance Service.

Education for All Handicapped Children Act of 1975, 20 U.S.C. § 1400 et seq.

Ferguson, C. A. (1978). Learning to pronounce: The earliest stages of phonological development in the child. In F. D. Minifie & L. L. Lloyd (Eds.), *Communicative and cognitive abilities: Early behavioral assessment.* Baltimore: University Park Press.

Foley, T. P., Jr. (1995). Thyroid conditions and other endocrine concerns in children with Down• syndrome. In D. C. Van Dyke, P. Mathers, S. S. Eberly, & J. Williams (Eds.), *Medical and surgical care for children with Down syndrome: A guide for parents* (pp. 97-104). Bethesda, MD: Woodbine House.

Foxx, R. M., & Azrin, N. H. (1973). *Toilet training the retarded.* Champaign, IL: Research Press.

Frankenburg, W. K., Dodds, J., Archer, P., Shapiro, H., & Bresnick, B. (1989). *Denver II.* Denver: Denver Developmental Materials.

Freman, P., & Ward, J. (1987). *An evaluation of cell therapy in Down's syndrome.* Unpublished manuscript. North Ryde, Australia: Macquarie University.

Furuno, S. F., O'Reilly, K. A., Hodaka, C. M., Inasaka, T. T., Zeislost-Falbey, B. & Allman, T. A. (1988). *Hawaii Early Learning Profile* (HELP). Palo Alto, CA: VORT Corporation.

Gesell, A., & Amatruda, C. S. (1969). *Developmental diagnosis* (2nd ed.). New York: Harper & Row.

Guralnick, M. J. (1989). Social competence as a future direction for early intervention programmes. *Journal of Mental Deficiency Research,* 33, 275-281.

Guralnick, M. J. (1990). Social competence and early intervention. *Journal of Early Intervention,* 14, 1, 3-14.

Harrell, R., Capp, R. H., Davis, D. R., Peerless, J., & Ravitz, L. R. (1981). Can nutritional supplements help mentally retarded children? An exploratory study. *National Academy of Sciences, U.S.A.,* 78, 1, 574-578.

Harrison, P. L., Kaufman, A. S., Kaufman, N. L., Bruininks, R. H. Rynders, J., Ilmer, S., Sparrow, S. S., & Cicchetti, D. V. (1990). *AGS Early Screening Profiles.* Circle Pines, MN: American Guidance Service.

Kagan, J., & Havermann, E. (1972). *Psychology: An introduction* (2nd ed.). New York: Harcourt Brace Jovanovich.

Kavanagh, K. T. (1995). Ear, nose, and sinus conditions of children with Down syndrome. In C. Van Dyke et al. (Eds.), *Medical and surgical care for children with Down syndrome. A guide for parents* (pp. 155-164). Bethesda, MD: Woodbine House.

Komer, A. F. (1971). Individual differences at birth: Implication for early experience and later development. *American Journal of Orthopsychiatry,* 41, 608-619.

Meyer, D. J. (1995). *Uncommon fathers.* Bethesda, MD: Woodbine House.

Meyer, D. J., Vadasy, P. F., & Fewell, R. R. (1985). *Living with a brother or sister with special needs.* Seattle: University of Washington Press.

Model Preschool Down Syndrome Program. (1974). *Developmental Sequence Performance Inventory.* Unpublished manuscript, University of Washington, Seattle.

Oelwein, P.(1995). *Teaching reading to children with Down syndrome.* Bethesda, MD: Woodbine House.

Pueschel, S. M., Canning, C. D., Murphy,A., & Zausmer, E. (1978). *Down syndrome: Growing and learning.* Franklin, WI: Sheed & Ward.

Rynders, J. E., Spiker, D., & Horrobin, J. M. (1978). Underestimating the educability of Down's syndrome children: Examination of methodological problems in recent literature. *American Journal of Mental Deficiency,* 82, 5, 440-448.

Schmid, F.(1982). The Down syndrome: Treatment and care. *Cytobiologische Review,* 1, 28-41.

Smart, M. S., & Smart, R. C. (1973). I*nfants: Development and relationships.* New York: Macmillan.

Sparrow, S. S., Balla, D. A., & Cicchetti, D. V. (1998). *Vineland Social-Emotional Early Child- hood Scales.* Circle Pines, MN: American Guidance Service.

Uzgiris, I. C. (1973). Patterns of vocal and gestural imitations in infants. In L. J. Stone, H. T. Smith, & L. B. Murphy (Eds.), *The competent infant* (pp. 599-604). New York: Basic Books.

Van Dyke, D. C., Matheis, P., Eberly, S., & Williams, J. (Eds.). (1995). *Medical and surgical care for children with Down syndrome.* Bethesda, MD: Woodbine House.

Winders, P. C. (1997). *Gross motor skills in children with Down syndrome.* Bethesda, MD: Wood- bine House.

28. About The Author

Valentine (Val) Dmitriev held a doctor of philosophy degree in early childhood education/special education from the University of Washington. She worked in the field of early education with typically as well as with atypically developing children. A pioneer in infant learning and early intervention, she developed and coordinated the Down syndrome program described in Time to Begin.

Val Dmitriev was born in Shanghai, China, of Russian parents who fled their homeland at the height of the Bolshevik Revolution. From China, the family migrated to Canada. After a few years in Vancouver, B.C., they settled in the Seattle area.

At 19, she graduated with a B.A. from the University of Washington, and a year later married a fellow alumnus, Nick Dmitriev. In 1950, after the last of their three children had been born, Dr. Dmitriev went to work as a part-time nursery school teacher and family life instructor for the Seattle Public Schools Family Life Program.

During the years that followed, she developed a growing concern for developmentally disabled children. In the early 1960's, she entered graduate school to pursue her interest in special education and to join the academic staff of the UW Developmental Psychology Laboratory Preschool. In 1970, Dr. Dmitriev accepted a staff position at the Experimental Education Unit, also at the University of Washington. A year later the Down syndrome program was established.

Following an early retirement and the death of her husband, Dr. Dmitriev left the Seattle area to live in a quiet, waterfront community on Whidbey Island. She later married Richard F. O'Donovan, a retired Federal civil servant and a holder of a black belt in Karate. Until his death, she continued her career as an educator, consultant and author.

Valentine Dmitriev died June 4, 2015 in Hackettstown New Jersey where she moved to from Whidbey Island in 2005 to be near a son and daughter.

Made in the USA
Coppell, TX
17 April 2023